TOPSPIN

ALSO BY ELIOT BERRY

Tough Draw: The Path to Tennis Glory

Four Quarters Make a Season

A Poetry of Force and Darkness: The Fiction of John Hawkes

Ups and Downs
in Big-Time Tennis

TOPSPIN

Eliot Berry

A JOHN MACRAE BOOK

HENRY HOLT AND COMPANY

NEW YORK

Henry Holt and Company, Inc.
Publishers since 1866
115 West 18th Street
New York, New York 10011

Henry Holt® is a registered trademark of
Henry Holt and Company, Inc.

Published in Canada by Fitzhenry & Whiteside Ltd.,
195 Allstate Parkway, Markham, Ontario L3R 4T8.

Library of Congress Cataloging-in-Publication Data

Berry, Eliot.
Topspin: ups and downs in big-time tennis / Eliot Berry. — 1st ed.
    p. cm.
  "A John Macrae book."
  Includes index.
  1. Tennis—Tournaments.   2. Tennis players—Biography.   I. Title.
GV999.B466 1996   95-37235
796.342—dc20   CIP

ISBN 0-8050-3543-5

Henry Holt books are available for special promotions
and premiums. For details contact:
Director, Special Markets.

First Edition—1996

Designed by Brian Mulligan

Printed in the United States of America
All first editions are printed on acid-free paper. ∞

10   9   8   7   6   5   4   3   2   1

For

Gloria and Christopher Berry
with love

For Bill Harris,
one of Florida's greatest all-time players

For William Henry III,
theater critic, writer, tennis lover, great friend

CONTENTS

ACKNOWLEDGMENTS

Special thanks to:

Carl Brandt and Jack Macrae.

Rod Laver. Ken Rosewall. Brad Gilbert. Bob Brett. Dennis Van Der Meer.

Kevin O'Keefe, Greg Sharko, Jim McManus, and Joe Lynch of the ATP Tour in Ponte Vedra Beach, Florida.

Page Crosland, Bruce Levy, Jeanne Lucido, and Randy Walker of the USTA.

Greg Shark and Randy Walker, who were kind enough to fact-check the proofs.

David Benjamin, Nina Miller, and Tim Curry of the Intercollegiate Tennis Association.

Richard Berens at Wimbledon. Donna Fales at the Orange Bowl. Cliff and Butch Buchholz at the Lipton. Brian Roberts, Tom Gowen, and the Fernbergers in Philadelphia.

Greg Hamlin, Steve Tager, Raquel Jaramillo. John MacFarlane.

Albert LaFarge. Peter Balestrieri. Gail Henry.

Karen Piner and Ivan Blumberg.

My tennis mentors: John Nogrady, Elwood Cooke, Doris Hart, Eddie Moylan, Fred Botur, and Al Molloy. And that old wooden backboard with the honeysuckle and the bees behind it.

It takes all phases of courage to go through the years when defeat is your portion a large part of the time, and realize, amid all your discouragement, that you are steadily forging ahead toward your goal.

—BILL TILDEN

I am to this day profiting somewhat by that experience; for in that brief, sharp schooling, I got personally and familiarly acquainted with about all the different types of human nature.

—MARK TWAIN,
Life on the Mississippi

SERVE AND VOLLEY

A roar went up from the crowd. I can't remember whom I was watching on the U.S. Open stadium court at the time. I think Steffi Graf was dissecting a young woman's game in a first-round match. Suddenly there came another, even sharper noise from the nearby grandstand court, and the power and potential joy in that sound pulled me from my seat. I hurried across the walkway and slid into the press seats of the smaller, more intimate court. When I arrived, the two players were seated. The cause of the stir was not immediately clear.

I recognized one player immediately. Alexander Volkov was slumped low in a director's chair on one side of the net. Volkov's upper torso and hips were trim and his legs seemed to stretch halfway across the court. Everything about the Russian was left-handed, from the part in his short brush of light brown hair to the way he sat slumped low in the changeover chair. The twenty-seven-year-old tenth seed rose with a confident half smile and strode across the American hard court, smooth as a stretch of fresh tarmac. Volkov moved with short, almost disdainfully light steps and a tall but cocky lean. Volkov had wins over Stefan Edberg in a deep heat at the 1990 U.S. Open and over Pete Sampras five months earlier in 1993 at Indian Wells: Confident in his ability to win big matches, Alexander Volkov, about to return service, turned to face Stark and lightly, like a swordsman, tapped the top of his racket head to the ground.

The cause of the roar I had heard was now clear. The red-and-black numerals used to keep score had been flipped over. The American had broken Volkov's serve and led 2–1.

I did not know that much about Jonathan Stark. Twenty-two years old, a professional for only two years, Stark had broad shoulders, thinner legs, and blond all-American good looks made appealing by the slightly haunted look of determination about his eyes. He was tall, strong, and fresh as the springtime in his hometown of Medford, Oregon. And yet that look about his eyes, as he briefly weighed the two balls in his hand and picked the less fluffy one to serve first, suggested to me that Stark cared deeply about his task but had not yet realized his dreams.

Jonathan Stark was ranked fifty-second in the world; Alexander Volkov was fourteenth; and I was in second heaven. There was more than money on the line in this match—it was career. Volkov had been one of the top twenty-five ranked players in the world for four years in a row, and he looked like a seasoned pro, completely comfortable in his surroundings. Stark, wearing a red hairband and white shirt with purple about the shoulders, still seemed like the college star he had been at Stanford for two years after winning the 1989 U.S. Open junior title. His ranking had gone from 1,007 to 283 to 85. Now number 52 in the world, Stark's star was rising, albeit more slowly than those of his contemporaries Pete Sampras and Andre Agassi.

Stark looked across the net as the Russian bent over at his narrow waist in an easy, swaying serve returner's position. When Volkov was ready, Stark served a 119-mile-per-hour ace up the middle. He then delivered a 102-mph ace off the side of the court, fooling Volkov both with the ball's direction and the severity of its kick. Stark's second ball had the juice, and nearly the deception, of a John McEnroe second serve. At 40–love, Stark skidded a first serve off the corner of the service box with enough power on it to spin around the ducking lineperson's chair. Volkov had touched Stark's serve only once. Now down 3–1, the Russian smiled as if he had bitten a slice of lemon in a glass of vodka. Jonathan Stark had come to play.

I have always had a soft spot for serve-and-volley players. I greatly admire in others skills I do not possess myself. As a boy watching at Forest Hills, I got my biggest thrills from Roy Emerson, Rod Laver, John Newcombe, Chuck McKinley, Stan Smith and Arthur Ashe—the serve-and-volleyers. But when I tried to imitate them at Kalamazoo, I couldn't transform my Eastern clay-court game into that of other juniors such as Jeff Borowiak, Erik van Dillen, and Dick Stockton, who were then at the top of the juniors.

Stark, not Volkov, was the natural serve-and-volleyer, and that's why he caught my eye.

It takes a certain combination of bravery and athletic ability to serve-volley. Like Laver, John McEnroe had the instinct and did it beautifully. Ivan Lendl could not. Jack Kramer, Pancho Gonzalez, Edberg, and Boris Becker were naturals. Bobby Riggs could do it but worked the baseline more naturally, as does Andre Agassi. Sampras does it, but Courier can't. I always admired Chris Evert because she had great heart and wonderful control from deep in the court. But I *loved* watching Margaret Smith, Billie Jean King, Martina Navratilova, and my own personal favorite, Maria Bueno, because they put themselves in harm's way at the net. Serve-and-volley tennis was an instinct perfected into an art form, but the new rackets, which sent the balls back so much harder than the wooden rackets ever could, were putting enormous pressure on the server. Young players like Stark and Sampras still loved the prospect of taking the risk anyway—the way Edberg had so effortlessly for so many years—but they were the modern exceptions.

Andre Agassi, of course, was something else. Agassi's style represented as dramatic a change in the way men's tennis was played as Suzanne Lenglen's acrobatic style had been seventy years before in women's tennis. But Agassi was an innovator, an explosion, a whirling dervish reflex man, a ball basher. Not tall enough to serve down into the court, Agassi slugged it out with the short turns of a boxer with a great hook, the knock-out punch his father, a boxer himself, never had. The speed and the angle of Andre's blows were unusual.

Stark, who smiled as brightly and as easily as Agassi did, was more like Sampras in playing style, for he had the tremendous downward torque a tall man gets, especially serving with the new rackets. But Stark was also a product of his era. Like Agassi, he had a two-handed backhand he liked to rip.

In this match, Stark was making Volkov look like last year's model. But it was touch, not just power, that I loved to find in a new player,

and Stark had that, too. He rode a Volkov second serve up to net behind a solid two-handed backhand return of serve, and when Volkov,
who has great hands, volleyed back at him, Stark, sensing that Volkov
was leaning too far forward, played a lob volley up over the six-foot-
two-inch Volkov's head for a winner. The reflexes and creativity of
that lob volley made me roar with the crowd. Stark had broken Volkov
again.

Stark, up 4–1, was ready to serve again. But Volkov, settling his ruf-
fled, Kaliningrad persona into a comfortable returning position, let
the younger player wait just a fraction of a second beyond the time
that it was comfortable to have to wait to serve.

Stark bounced the ball, and there was another roar. It happened
that fast: the perfect, forward toss, legs thrusting upward, and the
outward flash of the racket head like a tomahawk up into the neon
lights and night sky. Ace.

Once lucky, twice good, they say. But this was Stark's sixth ace in
three service games. The kid was major league. He had a weapon.
Stark's service motion was free, like a bending willow. The sound of
the ball leaving his racket was almost silent, and the ball gathered
speed and weight through the air like a Nolan Ryan fastball. Each
time the ball exploded off the hard court there was a thud against the
canvas backstop.

But Volkov was not a fluke. He was a proven maestro. The Russian's determination, bordering on arrogance, was both elegant and
distinctly theatrical. Each time the young American's serve blew by
him, Volkov merely dropped his racket hand as if, just for that moment, his racket had felt too heavy to swing. In fact, Volkov had been
frozen twice, aced wide off the deuce court, then aced up the middle
where his lefty backhand might have been. Volkov's deadpan expression, a mixture of feigned boredom and acceptance, was worth the
price of admission. It was unyielding. Down 5–1, Volkov's cool disdain began to melt. Stark broke his serve again, with two fully ripped
backhand passing shots. Stark played with such tenacity that a look of
consternation appeared on the face of his higher-ranking opponent.
The Russian's eyebrows arched. He stopped suddenly and glared
across the net, but Stark had turned his back. A gorgeous display of
power tennis followed. Stark was incredible. The balls Volkov did re-

turn, Stark invariably put away with solid volleys. The five-thousand-plus spectators roared in approval and happy disbelief. The scoreboard clock showed that the first set had taken exactly twenty minutes for Stark to win 6–1.

Bobby Riggs, clad in long white pants and a bright yellow V-neck sweater, came in to watch. The 1939 Wimbledon singles champion settled into the first-row box of a friend and looked back at the crowd, basking in the warmth of recognition.

After Riggs, a great comeback artist, sat down, Volkov's play picked up. His hand suddenly seemed to move so effortlessly through the ball that Stark began to look slightly mechanical, as if so attached to his two-handed backhand he could not pry it loose from his hip. Volkov got hot like a Russian sailor on ship leave. He was everywhere and incredibly smooth.

Between games I walked down to the box where Bobby Riggs sat directly behind the court and eavesdropped, pretending to look for a friend nearby. I slipped in behind Riggs and stayed for three games. Known for his wild bets on and off the courts—playing for money, with chairs placed all over his side of the court, or with two dogs on leashes, or while wearing flippers—in real competition, he was rather conservative in style. Essentially Riggs was a salesman. He showed you a situation you didn't really want to buy, but nine times out of ten you wound up buying it, going for it when you really wanted no part of it until, too late, you realized you had been had. And there was Riggs on the other side of the net, smiling at your miss like a door-to-door salesman eager to sell you another one. Bobby Riggs sold bad situations on court, and almost all his contemporaries had bought them. There was something of Riggs in Volkov.

Volkov knew how to hold the ball on his racket incredibly late, and once Stark committed his body, Volkov would change the angle of his hand and put it behind Stark, like taking candy from a baby. Riggs loved it, and he spoke with his hands, miming the last-second turn of the hand with which Volkov fooled Stark again and again, both on his serve and off the ground. Volkov's service motion was leisurely, mesmerizing, and very difficult to read.

"I like his motion," Riggs, the aging cherub, said to his neighbor. "If you try to read his body, he's got you going the wrong way."

I grinned. Bobby Riggs liked the Russian's deception. Tennis was an international game. And still, Stark stayed with Volkov step for step, and when the young West Coast star aced Volkov at 118 mph, Bobby Riggs broke into another kind of grin that seemed to say, "I used to prefer oil to a hammer but, you know, [Don] Budge and Jack Kramer both had hammers."

At 3–4, serving at ad-out, Stark aced Volkov off the side of the line, and the ball was called wide by the ducking linesman. The crowd booed—and with good reason. Stark stood at midcourt for half a second, pondering what to say. He said nothing and went back to serve. Incredibly, Stark recocked his serve and aced Volkov with the second ball up the middle with a spinning twist that leaped off the line. Another lineman's arm extended, and Stark's second serve was called out. I had never seen a second true ace in the same point reversed into a double fault. It was terrible line calling. Game Volkov. Jimmy Connors would have sworn, or worse. The Russian, smiling lightly, was up 5–3 instead of being back at 4–3, deuce. Stark started to yell at the chair umpire but turned his back and waved instead in disgust as the crowd continued to boo. Stark kept his cool, but Volkov had just gotten even in a flash, 6–3. Bobby Riggs crossed his legs, put his chin on one hand, and leaned forward without talking.

The sight of Riggs in deep concentration reminded me of what another great competitor from his generation, Pancho Segura, had said about tennis: "People don't get it. They think tennis is a rich man's game. . . . [But] you get out on the court, and it doesn't matter who your Dad is or how much money you have or whether you went to Harvard. [On court] it's you and me, baby, right here, right now."

Volkov was as hard to read as an exotic speckled fish. He hit the ball flat or slightly undercut on about 60 percent of his shots, and they skidded on the green grandstand court—except when he rolled them over, delivering them like a crepe. The Russian was not naturally fast, but his game had been adapted perfectly to compensate for his shortcomings. Volkov's hand-eye coordination was so extraordinary that instead of being forced to volley up because he was a foot late getting to the net, he would willingly commit the cardinal sin of first volleys. Oddly, the Russian liked getting caught in no man's land. Halfway up to net, Volkov let the ball bounce and played the ball with a half volley so gentle that, no matter the speed of the ball coming in, Volkov seemed to wipe over the top of it, changing its direction at the last moment.

Stark's strength was more linear and purely American. He came right at Volkov, and the smooth Russian found the consistent pressure distasteful. By reputation sunny and outgoing off the court, Stark did have a touch of Edberg in him: He was aggressive without appearing to be so. Stark's volleys were crisp, deep, and brave. Volkov, cooler and less direct than the American, could not have been more different in style and personality, and yet their games fit together like pieces in a puzzle. No one in the packed crowd thought of leaving then, and others, hearing reports of the battle, hurried over to the court to try to get in.

Volkov, down 3–1 in the third set, broke Stark's serve, and the American got another very tough call on a first serve at 3–all. Stark's anger boiled ferociously for just the moment it takes to stop the whistling of a kettle. The more experienced Volkov used the moment like a salve and broke the young American disdainfully. "Go, Jonathan!" a voice in the New York crowd shouted. Volkov smiled strangely. At 5–4, 15–all, Volkov, a "pro's pro," served an ace off Stark's forehand side. Volkov held his serve. Largely outplayed, Volkov was up two sets to one.

I looked over at Stark. He had the talent, but did he have the heart? Did he have the joy, the cleverness, the fight inside himself to come roaring back against a player as smooth as a pickpocket? There was much I liked about Stark. He was not likely to surpass Sampras or Agassi, but he could make a real mark for himself. Even when he was down, Stark kept attacking. He pushed himself and thumped the ball fearlessly. He *wanted* it—and that's what I love in a player.

The fourth set was a thing of beauty. The points were very short when Stark hit a volley and long when Volkov had control of the point. Each rally was a microcosm of the larger battle. The wills of the angular Russian and the broad-shouldered American were fully engaged. It might have hurt physically, but they were so fit and so deep into the effort that they felt themselves buoyed, as if in a dream.

At 2–all in the fourth set, down two sets to one, Jonathan Stark came alive. He ripped a flat forehand winner from the baseline;

then, on a serve and volley, he hit a delicate drop shot with his third volley. Volkov raced up and got it, shoveling the ball right at Stark's chest, but Stark, anticipating the move, got out of the way and drilled the ball down into the empty green court as the sometimes fickle crowd stood as one and cheered. The American boy could play.

Volkov made no faces. He was so outwardly calm and nonchalant he was like a Russian cowboy, cool, disturbed, yet as seemingly disinterested as the actor, Steve McQueen in *Le Mans*. Like all great and near-great players, Volkov had the innate ability to absorb his opponent. It was a kind of vampirism; while seeming to accept whatever his opponent was dishing out, he was quietly waiting for the opportunity to strike at weakness. The Russian was good at sleight of hand. Suddenly Volkov would steal a point with a flat second serve or a drop shot from a sitting forehand when he hadn't played one all match. Volkov's reflexes were as amazing as Stark's power. When Stark hit a lob volley over Volkov's right side, Volkov, his back to the net, flicked a high backhand overhead while nearly horizontal in the air. The shot surprised Stark, but he struck the return down hard into the opposite service corner, only to see Volkov's long arm reach out and bunt it up Stark's line for a winner. They were like two perfectly matched prizefighters.

Stark broke Volkov's deceptively fast serve and went up 4–2 in the fourth set, but Volkov broke back immediately. Stark suddenly grabbed at the ball of his netted volley as if to launch it high into the night sky. But the moon was there, cradled gently amid the stars, spreading a soft light over the top of the old World's Fair globe, where only three days before, a man had perched for ten hours in the ninety-degree heat until the police managed to pull him down from the top of the world. Winning meant controlling a kind of madness. Stark stayed calm and dropped the ball back to the ballboy.

Volkov, a European master of alternating tempo, still could not control the pace of Stark's serve or volley. So he tried to manipulate the tempo in other ways. If Stark wanted to play fast, the Russian bounced the ball three extra times between serves. If Stark wanted a breather, Volkov stepped right up and served a quick one. Down 4–3, Volkov waited for everyone in the overflowing crowd to find a seat. Then, without even a look at Stark's return position, Volkov served an ace. "Alexi's a beauty," I thought, "a real pro." Volkov served another ace on game point, 40–30. It was 4–all, fourth set. Stark had miles to go.

Stark held his serve at love. Under such pressure, *that* was definitely the work of a professional. Jonathan Stark was emerging. He was shedding the collegiate cocoon.

Volkov went down on serve 0–30 and was two points from losing the fourth set. So he frowned, then served two aces without blinking. At 30–all, Stark attacked. There ensued a great side-to-side exchange at the net. At the last possible moment, Volkov stretched down low and hit a sweeping topspin backhand cross-court volley winner which he frosted moments later with his third ace, each hit at a different angle from the same toss and motion. Though considerably stiffer than McEnroe's, Volkov's left-handed service motion was almost as tough to read. The score was now 5–all.

Neither player planned to go into a tiebreaker. Each intended to strangle the other right then and there. Stark hit two aces that made the linespeople duck. Volkov's forehand return of serve, when he could touch Stark's serve, was like smoothing over a stick of butter with a silver spoon. Volkov passed Stark with a forehand that was so quiet the ball seemed to have only half the pace that was really on it. At 30–all, Stark took a deep breath before his second serve. To serve and volley, or to stay back? Stark served and raced forward to the net, where he carved a backhand volley low to Volkov's forehand. The Russian, almost smiling with anticipation, mishit the topspin drive slightly, and Stark, leaping wildly as if about to scream, bounced the overhead off the court ten rows up into the stands and pumped his fist.

Volkov's repertoire was endless. Nearing the two-million-dollar mark in career earnings, he was an original. No one, with the possible exception of Petr Korda, played as unexpectedly as Volkov. Down 30–40, he popped a lob volley over Stark and snuck into the net behind it. Stark blasted the ball deep and high above the grandstand lights, and Volkov, his left hand cocked, took it in the air and hit a winning overhead up the forehand line. Even Stark applauded. But Stark served an ace, punched a high backhand volley winner and was suddenly up 6–5 in the fourth set.

Annoyed with his young American opponent, Volkov began directing human traffic in the New York stands. He pointed with his racket. He was a bit like Ilie Nastase but not verbal, just totally dominant. Volkov held his serve with another ace in a game in which Stark appeared to get nervous. Now Stark reluctantly found himself in a tiebreaker with Alexander Volkov.

Stark's first serve was called out. The crowd hooted and Stark protested sharply but succinctly, not long enough to break his concentration but long enough to let the chair umpire know he wanted the next call to go his way. Stark ripped a kick second serve to Volkov's backhand, and after a first volley that made Volkov stretch to his laces, Stark thudded a backhand volley behind Volkov, only one foot inside the baseline. The score was 1–0, Stark. Volkov out-rallied the American from the baseline to even the score but then served a double fault, 1–2. Stark attacked the net, but Volkov, standing his ground, played a forehand topspin lob on the diagonal that had so much juice on it that the ball looked wet as it spun over Stark's outstretched arm and bounded crazily away, 2–all.

Stark hit another great volley winner, but when the umpire overruled on Stark's unreturnable next serve, the point was replayed and Volkov won it. Instead of 4–2 for Stark, the score was 3–all. Wisely, Stark said nothing, and Volkov, as if guilty, hit a jumping-off-the-ground forehand a foot long. They reached 5–all in the tiebreaker. There was a dark silence. Volkov was just two points from winning the match; Stark two points from defeat or evening the match.

Volkov came up to the net on a short approach shot but managed to hit a desperation backhand volley winner. 6–5. It was match point for Volkov. You could almost hear the players breathing. Stark put his first serve in play, and Volkov netted it, 6–all. Now Volkov showed a momentary nervousness and netted another forehand return of serve to fall behind. 7–6. Stark blasted a forehand into open court. It was long, 7–all. Stark was tight; his elbow had lockjaw. Suddenly, like boxers taking whacks at each other, both players found themselves at the net trying to punch volleys past each other. At the last second, Volkov popped a lob volley over Stark's head. Stark ran back after it like a maniac. The ball was called out. Jonathan Stark, up 8–7 in the breaker, hit a huge serve into Volkov's backhand corner, and Volkov, bending like a prince, blocked the return low, hard, and just wide. The tiebreaker and the fourth set were Stark's, 7–6 (9–7).

"Hey, Bobby," shouted someone in the crowd. "Could you have beaten them with a wooden racket?"

Riggs, who wasn't hearing so well, just stood and waved to the crowd, beaming as if recognition was still a magic elixir.

Back down on the court, Volkov banged his first serve out by twenty feet, the Russian's first concession to visible anger in the match. Then Volkov kicked the second ball in and flattened a smooth backhand volley winner up the line. But something appeared to be wrong with Volkov's shoulder. Was it nerves or a real injury? Volkov winced, rolled his arm in a circle, and kept hitting his first serves out by five or six feet. It got me wondering. He looked exhausted—the skin around his eyes was neon pink, while the rest of his face was clammy white—yet he kept winning points and games.

Stark still looked fresh. And he seemed to want the victory more than Volkov did. Stark was on the way up the mountain, and he now had the chance to beat a player ranked nearly forty places ahead of him. For a moment Stark looked like a right-handed McEnroe. He stood sideways to the court, rocked back, served an ace, then trotted forward. It was like a piano note hit just right.

But Volkov was a cool customer. He'd been raised in a barter economy. Quickly his serve began to fall back inside the service box as if he had just been whacking it long for a game to make Stark think something had happened to his arm. Volkov loved playing mind games. When Stark peered over the net after hitting a ball that fell out by six inches, Volkov gave him the Moscow version of a Bronx cheer, dropping his racket to the ground and putting both hands down over the mark like a linesman—except the spot where Volkov placed his hands was a foot behind the baseline. The Russian's smile was an unfriendly wince. Volkov went up 3–2 in the fifth set.

Now each point was a battle, with Stark's power and fifth set desire facing Volkov's drop-dead attitude and take-everything-on-the-rise smoothness. Volkov's serve kept penetrating low and deep into the box so that Stark's two-handed backhand had to shovel the ball up. Volkov was unusual. His half volleys from no-man's-land kept turning into winners. No one but Agassi and Volkov played half-volleys so consistently for winners. But Stark had the American answer in his repertoire—an ace—and Volkov winced.

The score was 4–3 for Volkov when it happened. Stark, serving again and playing beautifully, hit a misconceived drop shot that caught the top of the net and fell back at him. Suddenly Stark was down break point, ad-out. He had the choice again. Serve and volley, or stay back. Volkov had been staying back. Stark was brave, and coming in was what had brought him to where he was. He hit a huge serve to Volkov's backhand, but the ball came back at the very end of a reflex save that somehow leaped like a nerve's synapse across the net. Stark's hand was there to put away the volley, but at the very last moment Volkov's reflex backhand hit the top of the net with such topspin that the ball leaped right up and over Stark's shoulder. The crowd moaned, and Volkov shrugged. He would cut your heart out with a paint scraper.

Stark was broken but not beaten. Volkov's serve was twisting and sliding now but was not impossible to break. It lacked pure speed. Like a soldier attacking a citadel, Stark attacked Volkov's serve with everything he had. At 15–all, Volkov hit a second serve. I can still see that flattened lefty kick gathering speed after the bounce and Stark circling around it to nail it with his forehand. He absolutely creamed it. But the ball Stark hit sailed past Volkov and landed out by ten feet. The crowd gasped. Volkov jerked his head in the direction of the ball boy, and his left hand quickly played with the balls to find the hardest, least fluffy one. Volkov boomed a service winner into the forehand side. At double match point, Volkov was attacked again off a second serve, but he came in behind it and angled Stark's hard backhand topspin reply with a sure, undercut left-handed backhand volley that slunk away as if the match had always been his. The fifth set, the match, was over. Volkov had beaten Stark 1–6, 6–3, 6–4, 6–7, 6–3.

The audience fell silent for just a moment and then rose in the fresh night air and gave the two players a three-minute standing ovation. Stark and Volkov had played for over four hours. It was after midnight now.

The animated crowd moved toward the exits. I contemplated going home, too, but instead I rushed back inside to the players' lounge. It was too late for formal interviews in the press rooms, but I wanted to

talk to Volkov, and I *had* to talk to Stark. The difference between winning and losing was sometimes so slim. The losing player almost
always learned more and was more emotional. The young American
had shown me much that I really liked: the ability to fight, the big
serve-and-volley weapon, the Sampras-like single-volley winner, good
touch around the court, drop shots, topspin lob winners, a nearly full
but still imperfect repertoire. Jonathan Stark had many but not all of
the skills required of a top-ten player. But I wondered, how far would
he get?

The players' lounge was nearly deserted at half past twelve. A couple
of early round doubles matches were just finishing and one of the
stringers was still at work. Otherwise, the low seats where the competitors waited nervously during the day, watching TV and talking before they were called out of the holding pen to go play, were vacant.
Workmen pushed huge new gray plastic garbage cans over to the
pasta-and-fruit area. As I sat waiting for Volkov, I became aware of an
exotic-looking young woman with thick red lips who kept swinging
her long, crossed legs as she sat and waited, too. It was Volkov's wife
of two months, Yaroslava. She looked like a young Bianca Jagger,
though six inches taller and Russian, a wild black-haired flower.

According to the players, Volkov, who was twenty-seven and from
Kaliningrad near the Baltic Sea and the Polish border, had been dat-
ing Yaroslava for five years. She was eighteen now and in America. On
this evening, Yaroslava was wearing skin-tight jeans and red stiletto
heels. Her navel was bare beneath her tight halter top, and a thin
gold chain hung loosely around her long waist. When she stood to
greet Volkov as he came in with his racket bags, she was an inch taller
than her man. Her full red lips and jet-black eyes seemed to soften as
she saw him. Yaroslava cocked her head to one side, looked into his
pale, tired face, and smiled as she pulled Volkov down on top of her
on the big leather easy-chair, wrapping one long leg around his rear.
Volkov feigned falling into her arms, and then he did.

"Do you still want Volkov?" the older South American woman still
at the player desk asked me.

"Definitely," I said. "I do."

Volkov said something in Russian to his wife, kissed her lightly, and came over for his interview. His eyes were small, sharp, and close together under a pale, low forehead and sharply angled blondish brown pompadour.

"Alexi, what was happening in that first set when Stark blew you away? Was it just a warm-up for you?"

Volkov brushed back his wet hair. "You know," he said, "if you're playing against somebody who serves, like, 125 miles per hour, then *looks* like warm-up. But he destroyed me because he served so well." Volkov nodded his pointed head, his dark eyes darting as if remembering a difficult battlefield scene. "Also, he returned quite well, too."

"But it didn't seem to ruffle you. You just shook it off."

"It was five-set match, you know." He nodded in agreement. "I felt that in five sets, anything can happen. I thought, 'If he gonna play like that, so good, he's got to lose concentration sometime.' So I had to hold my own serve, and maybe I would get chance."

"What gave you the feeling in the second set that you were back into it?"

"Well, he came down just a little bit." Volkov put his fingers together, an inch apart. "And then I began to return him a little bit. Things changed in second, third sets."

"Mental things?"

"Ya. Mental things. I think he was getting little bit tired, and he lost self-concentration. Because to serve like that more than one set—it's very difficult. Only top players can do that, and not very often."

"Is there a weakness in Stark's game that you would say he needs to improve?"

Volkov sighed as if he had been lucky to solve Stark on the night. "I don't know. If he is going to be consistent and play like first set or the tiebreaker in fourth set, he will be very good player. But everybody has to lose sometime the concentration."

For a young player on the tour, just outside the top fifty, that word *concentration* could mean everything from training harder to making your own luck. I thanked Alexander Volkov. He picked up his huge red tennis bag and walked out into the night, shoulder to shoulder, hip to hip, with Yaroslava. They were both so tall and slender they seemed to be light-haired and dark-haired twins in love.

I called up to the locker room to ask for Stark, but the attendant was not encouraging.

"Stark just came in, and he doesn't much feel like talking."

Unlike victories, which are generally forgotten fast, losses linger. But if you learn anything in tennis, you learn it from a loss. I did not want to be pushy. I almost backed down. I could probably have set up an interview for the next day. But I wanted the wound to be fresh. Athletes never have their emotions as close to the surface as when they have just lost. It would have meant a lot to win; Volkov, at number fourteen in the world, would have been a major scalp. Stark had wanted victory very badly, and it had taken him nearly four hours to not quite achieve it. "I'll be here," I said patiently. "Please send him down whenever he's ready."

I called four more times and began to despair that I'd ever see him.

"It's very private when they lose one like that," said the woman at the player desk. "Sometimes it hurts them very much to have to talk afterward."

I winced and nodded but wouldn't leave. Suddenly there he was, tall, strong, blond, slightly rumpled in a dark blue T-shirt. Jonathan Stark looked young and defeated but not, I thought, tired. The loss hung all around him and was inside him still, but Stark had come to face the music and he had come alone, without an entourage. No agent or coach, no *parent*, accompanied him. I liked that. He was taking his responsibility and his beating as a professional athlete should. It was a quarter of one in the morning. Stark did not necessarily want to talk to me, but I am glad he did.

"When you looked at the draw and saw that you had drawn a guy like Volkov in the first round, what went through your mind?"

"Volkov's a pretty top-ranked guy," Stark said, nodding. "But really in today's tennis you have to be pretty well focused to play anyone. Like I drew [Goran] Ivanisevic in the first round of Wimbledon. Some people would say I got unlucky, that I got a tough draw to play him on grass. But you know, the best time to play some of these guys *is* the first round. I came close against Ivanisevic and against Volkov tonight." Stark cocked his head. "Hopefully, if I keep on working, the tides will turn a little bit."

"But when you know you have a very good chance of winning a match and it's against someone you want very much to beat, doesn't it make your heart quicken a little bit? Did you say, 'Ah! I've got a shot at him today!'?"

Stark smiled. "Yeah, I did. Any time you have a chance to play 'one of those guys,' especially in a Grand Slam, on a big court, yeah. It's exciting. We weren't stuck out on one of the side courts. The crowd today was huge and got into it. And it's fun. It really is fun. Yeah, your heart might quicken a bit." Stark laughed and brushed his hair to one side, grinning. I seemed to have struck in Stark the sides of the match that were a pleasure for him, including the first steps walking onto the court as the crowd roared its greeting. "Go Stark!" and the inevitable added weight on his shoulders, "Go, U.S.A.!" Stark was still smiling. He had found the joy of the match. The fun of competing at the highest—or nearly the highest—level was there for him, contained deep within him like natural water in a cave. When that inner reservoir of joy becomes depleted, it is time to quit the game.

Boris Becker had almost quit. Several players every year reach the point where they suddenly realize their reservoir is dry. And then they quickly exit the tennis highway. Rarely can the original supply of joy be replenished. But Stark still had his. I smiled; when a player has that source, that joy, that sense of how much fun the game of tennis really is and what a challenge it is to do battle with another person, when the mountain is all uphill but seems, psychologically, as if it is downhill, then everything from practice to losses in important matches can be absorbed and learned from. Without it, tennis is hell. Beyond the pillars of ability and technique, winning and losing are really questions of balance, passion, and state of mind. How much of either, wins or losses, can you take before you go off? Different players lose the joy at different times. Martina Navratilova seemed to have it at thirty-six but not at thirty-seven. Jimmy Connors at thirty-nine still had it. But Borg had lost it at twenty-six and McEnroe at twenty-nine, though Mac played three more years. Jonathan Stark was twenty-two. His heart was young.

"You blew Volkov away in the first set," I said. "It was 6–1 in twenty minutes. When you play a set like that, do you get a little nervous? Do you wonder, 'Now what's going to happen? Can I keep this up?' "

Stark shook his head. "No. You're just happy. You've got a 1–0 lead. You just did exactly what you wanted to do. You're excited." He laughed, feeling better already. "You're fired up. Bring on the second set. If you think like, jeez, he's going to start playing better, this is going to be a grind for me, that's not the right attitude. But three out of five sets is a marathon of sorts. There can be a lot of momentum swings. This guy is not number fourteen in the world for nothing. I started serving really well, but he started a little slowly. And that can happen. My game plan throughout was to attack him and be aggressive, but he made me hit a few more volleys in the second set and he got back into the match. I would have to expect that. Unless I can just ace him every time, which I did for a while."

"In the second set you got a couple of bad calls. You aced him off the side of the court and it was called a *fault*, and you aced him up the middle with the second serve and that was also called a *fault*. I thought those serves were in. Did it upset you as much as it seemed to?"

"Well, I got a couple of tough calls, but I was already down," Stark said, unwilling to blame the linespeople for missing the calls. "I thought they were both in, and it did mean a service break by calling it a double fault, but I had gotten down love–40 in the first place. And that was my own fault. That's the way it goes in pro tennis. You can't dwell on it. What Volkov did better was to start to serve smarter. I had been attacking his second serve. He started to put in a lot more first serves, and he began to put a little more speed and less kick on the second ball. He made it skid through so I couldn't attack it as easily. Basically, he adjusted well."

"Volkov's so smooth in the hand. That lefty service motion of his is very tough to read."

"He's unbelievably hard to read," agreed Stark. "What made it that tough was how he was jamming me on the serve, spinning it right into me, then another time he'd give me the big flat one wide from basically the same motion. A lot of times he'd hit a big first serve, and

I'd hit a great chip down at his feet. But Volkov takes that ball at the service line instead of at his feet better than anyone. I think he hits the half volley better than his volley. Not many players can do that."

"Volkov's volley is weaker than his half volley?"

"I think so," said Stark. "His hands are so good. Like Petr Korda's. He doesn't really close in on the net tight enough to be a great volleyer. You almost want to hit the return through the court more so he has to try to volley in the air, because when Volkov picks the ball up off the court on the half bounce he can be a magician."

"You played some beautiful drop volleys," I said. "And you played them not just to win the point outright, but so he'd have to run up and you could cut off the angle of his return with another volley. You did that great."

"Yeah. Thanks," Stark said happily, modestly. "My game plan going into the match was that Volkov is quite tall and thin and moves really well side to side. But he doesn't move as well up and back. So that's why I tried those shots against him."

"Did you feel like he kept you off balance a bit? Like when he hit those lob volleys. God, that's a tough shot to pull off, and you are six foot two. He hit three or four lob volleys when you both were at net."

"I might have gotten a little too predictable." Stark winced, thinking about it. "I'd hit a good shot and think I really stuck it, but then he would be right there. He seemed to be reading me easier than I was reading him. His half volleys were amazing that way. He was able to hold the half volley, wait for me to commit my body in one direction, and then he'd just bump the ball into the open court. I take my hat off to him. Those shots were just too good."

"In his last service game, the last game of the match, it seemed as if you were trying to apply pressure on every single point, and in a sense, by doing so, you might have been applying the pressure right back on yourself."

"Well," said Stark, sounding defensive for the first time. "With my type of game, I'm going to have to force the issue."

I wondered if his game, his need to "force the issue," was a reflection of the way he was going to be as a person off the court as well. There always seemed to be a relationship between the exteriors of a person's game and his or her interior. Stark had a big, power game.

Yet his voice with me was mild, as if he, too, was seeking to understand what had transpired.

"In the fifth set," he continued quietly, "I had a few second serves
I just had to attack. But at 15–all in his last service game, I made a
bad mistake. I didn't really want to hit the ball at Mach-10 force, but
I did. I barely missed it, but it was out. That was a dumb decision."

"The moment you did that, I said, 'Oh! He doesn't want to do that.'
Because then Volkov got one first serve in there, and it was double
match point. Like that." I snapped my finger.

I knew he should not have gone for a forehand that big at 15–all,
but Stark had been attacking so well that it did not seem like a "bailout" at all. He had hit it with full intent. And though I knew better,
I loved the fact that he had gone after the crucial point rather than
playing it defensively, because that was the way Agassi, Courier, and
Sampras would have played the same ball. It was the new tennis.
Stark was not afraid to go for it, but suddenly I seemed to have
touched the sore point, the vein of the loss, and it began to bleed in
front of me. He looked down now for the first time in our talk.

"If you make that shot, you're a *genius*," Stark said in a voice that
ridiculed himself. "If you miss it . . . *damn*! It's something I've *got* to
learn. You just *can't* give a guy like that a free point. You can still be
aggressive, but you've got to make him come up with the good shot.
You cannot make an unforced error. I seem too . . ." Stark's voice suddenly lost all its sunshine and fell away into total confession. "I seem
to just give away too many free points." He sighed. "I don't know why
I do it."

"In certain situations."

"In the whole match," Stark blurted. "I had him but I let him get
right back into the damn match. I have to get more consistent. Instead of having to crack that forehand, I should just push it up the
line, come into net, and say, 'Hey, try to pass me.' And if he passes
me, then that's too good. And if he can pass me for five straight sets,
then he did it, and I take my hat off to him." Stark's face clouded.
"That's [the] kind of approach you have to take in pro tennis. Instead, I let the whole thing slip away."

"What is the difference between being what you were, a top college
player, and making the top ten or fifteen?"

"There's an enormous difference," said Stark. "A lot of these guys that I'm playing, like Ivanisevic at Wimbledon and Volkov today and Sampras last week, you know, they're pretty used to it. The big thing is to be able to attack and be consistent at the same time. I'd like to be able to say that I feel really comfortable in that situation, playing those guys, but I honestly think it is going to take me some time. When you go five sets against them, you've got to be happy in one way, but it's still a loss. It's frustrating when you really want to win. It would be nice to pull one off. Being an optimist, I think that the more I play in those situations, the next time I won't make an unforced error on a big point like I did with Volkov. I'm sorry. I'm rambling."

"Go ahead." At just after one in the morning, I could see that Stark wanted to let the feelings all pour out so the loss would not be there in the morning. The ache is always worse the morning after. All I could do was lend a sympathetic ear.

"See, these guys aren't going to give you the match." Stark ridiculed himself again. "In junior and college tennis, sometimes the players will actually give you a match just because of who you are or what your record is. They'd kind of collapse for you. In the pros, you might occasionally see an opponent give a top guy a match. Or they'll say a top guy gets lucky. But it's not luck at all. The top guys just seem to come up with the big shot when they need to. It's partly because they're not giving free points away in crunch time. They're not making a lot of unforced errors. They've got their swing and the court size in sync long before they ever have to go for the big shot. And that's the difference between them and me," said Stark. "I *almost* have it. That's just not good enough."

To hear Stark speak of "an opponent" in tennis put the levels of the game in a new perspective for me. There were the champions in the top five places, the very top "contenders" filling out the top ten in the world; a second tier at eleven to twenty; and upset makers stashed another sixty or seventy deep. Stark was ranked number fifty-two, and his ranking could slide or rise thirty points in either direction, depending on the surface. A major move into the top twenty would not be a fluke but would also not be easy. A rise for him into the top ten would be distinctly tough, a goal he had to try to pursue but not talk much about, unless he got there. Still, I liked what I had seen of Jonathan Stark. Five sets with Ivanisevic at Wimbledon, five sets with Volkov at the U.S. Open, and he had almost beaten Pete Sampras in three sets at Indianapolis. "Jonathan Stark has the kind of talent and heart to definitely be world top ten," said Rick Macci, coach of Tommy Ho, Venus Williams, and Jennifer Capriati in her happy days. But could the young guy from Medford, Oregon, make it big on the pro tennis circuit, or would he end on the tire heap of the merely talented players, those good enough to hurt a star or entertain a crowd, but never good enough to lift the trophy?

"In trying to break through to the next level," I asked him, "is it a question of playing and playing and playing and just getting into those situations more, like that 15–all forehand return of serve, or are there things you can do in practice and off the court?"

Stark nodded. "I tell you, there is nothing like playing a match. You can simulate it in practice as much as you want, but there is *nothing* remotely like being out there and going through it." Stark nodded. His manner was more relaxed again.

"You'll get your breakthrough," I said. "You're beating people you should be beating."

"Yeah," said Stark, nodding more confidently again, "I am."

"And that's a damn tough thing to do, too," I said. "Because you've got about four hundred people shooting at you, too." The computer ranked a little more than a thousand players. Players as deep as number two hundred on the computer were capable of upsetting players in the top fifty. Jonathan Stark was considered a major scalp for all those ranked behind him. It was a tough road. "As Satchel Paige used to say, 'Don't look back; they may be gaining on you.' That's pro tennis, isn't it?"

Stark laughed. "It is. This is my second year on the tour, almost exactly. I turned pro in Indianapolis two years ago. I've had some good results. I've also had tendinitis in my knees and a stress fracture in each foot, but if I can get strong, like really strong, I'm going to break through."

"Your speed around court is okay, but it's not great." I whistled like a jet plane. "That was Michael Chang going by."

"You're right. My legs are too weak," said Stark. "I think some of their speed comes with confidence. Being strong and trusting your shots. I think for me to get where I want to be, which is at the top, I have to be a real physical presence, kind of like Boris is. I practiced with Boris last week, and he is so strong. And Edberg, too. Strong in the legs."

"If you were a young player trying to decide if you should leave college and come out on the tour, what is the point at which you know you are ready to leave college?"

"You just know," said Stark, brightening. "I really knew. College is important for your growth as a person, but as far as leaving it, you can just tell. I knew after my second year that I was just bursting to go. I saw these guys playing on TV, and I just *had* to go after them."

"And Dick Gould, your coach at Stanford, was understanding?"

"Yes. . . . Look at the guys who've gone through his program, the McEnroes, Mayottes, Mayers, and others. Coach Gould has had a lot of experience with that. So he sat me down, and we went over it carefully together, the pros and the cons. He said, 'Obviously I'd love for you to stay, but go for it.' "

"Do you see it like a season, or is it a continuum?"

"It's not really a season anymore when you're a pro. There is a season, but there's not much time off."

"Pace is part of this whole thing," I said. "How you control your time."

Stark nodded. "And I'm still working on that, being relatively new. We played, like, twenty-five total matches in college, and here you can do that in a month. The difference between college tennis and pro tennis is like the difference between college basketball and the pros. At first, it's mind-boggling."

"What were the cons you saw in leaving college?"

"In my mind there weren't any cons. I was just ready," said Stark.

"To go test yourself."

"Yeah." Stark smiled and nodded.

"What were you studying?"

"Economics. But I hated it. I wanted to go make some money."

Stark had made $240,471 through August. Volkov had made $381,920, but after beating Stark he reached the semifinals of that U.S. Open and finished the year with $568,300 and $1,901,000 in career earnings. Good money in Russia. Good money anywhere. For that kind of money, it was not going to be easy.

"You don't wish you had stayed in college more than just two years and had gone on to do an MBA?"

"No," said the twenty-two-year-old Stark. "Believe me. I'm happy doing this."

I believed him. I smiled at Stark, and we shook hands as the porters began to roll large trash bins through the players' lounge. Stark got up a bit stiffly, lifted his big Nike bag onto his shoulder, and walked out alone. I sat there for a moment longer, thinking about his possibilities. In two years on tour, Stark had improved his ranking from number 1,007 to 52 prior to his loss to Volkov. The air was more rarefied once inside the top fifty, and it seemed to me that he was about to get inside that circle, despite the loss to Alexander Volkov. He was angry with himself, but I no longer looked at Stark's match with Volkov as a loss. I looked on it as a beginning.

THE ORANGE BOWL:

GIRLS AND BOYS TOGETHER

They were so good so young. They were the best junior tennis players in the world, two or three from each country, from Spain to the United States, Brazil to Romania, Egypt to England. In the 1950s and 1960s, the tournament was top-heavy with American influence—Billy Lenore; Dick Stockton; Harold Solomon; Peaches Bartkowitz, who won four years in a row; and Chris Evert, who won it twice—but by the 1990s the draw, like the world, had changed. Fourteen-year-olds were playing in the sixteen-and-unders and sixteen-year-olds were consistently playing in the eighteens. Overreaching had become as basic as the game itself. Like chess champions and gymnasts, the tennis prodigies of the world were outperforming their own age groups as if their professional lives depended on it.

The American girls' team—Janet Lee, Amanda Basica, Nicole London, Stephanie Nickitas, Cristina Moros, Stephy Halsell, Meilen Tu, and Karin Miller—and the American boys' team, which included Scott Humphries, Paul Goldstein, and Justin Gimelstob, were all dressed in the red, white, and blue U.S. National Team colors. The young players from around the world eyed the Americans with a strange combination of deference and envy. Several of the young Americans were picked off in the early rounds by three promising players: an unknown Polish girl named Malec; by the number one boy's seed, Marcelo Rios, a short, slender, long-haired topspin artist from Chile already known as "the South American Agassi"; and by the tall Russian girl, Nino Louarsabishvily, whose smile was as wide and easy as her last name was difficult to pronounce on the first three tries. The Americans were no longer as dominant internationally, but before the junior season was over, they had produced the boys' junior champion at Wimbledon and the girls' junior champion at the U.S. Open. Not all the best American players made the two U.S. teams, and I confess a fascination with one who did not make the team.

The first day of the Orange Bowl was like a dream for me. I had always wanted to play in the Orange Bowl as a kid, but I wasn't good enough to get a spot in the draw. Each year around Christmastime, I read the newspaper box scores to see how players like Stan Smith and Bill Harris, Thomas Koch and Ismail El Shafei were faring. While I was freezing up north in New York City, I imagined the tennis Orange Bowl played in a huge football stadium, watched by thousands. I had played some of the players who got to escape to the Florida winter sunshine, and I thought I could tell from the box scores how each point had been played. Dick Stockton's father was reported to have gotten into a fistfight one winter with Eddie Dibbs's father over a disputed line call when the boys were in the twelve-and-unders and prone to follow that old junior tennis adage, "When in doubt, call 'em out." I didn't know what to expect from the girls.

The girls' eighteen-and-under singles tournament began on the third day of the Orange Bowl, and I climbed aboard the 8:30 A.M. bus out to Flamingo Park. The bus driver nearly caused a couple of defaults. The bus pulled out at 8:25, snorting carbon monoxide back at the Omni Hotel as a string of French juniors with overloaded tennis bags raced after it. The driver looked into the rearview mirror under the sign Tips Are Appreciated and popped open the door for the French. The bus lurched, the driver slid a twelve-track cassette of *Greatest Soul Love Songs* into its chamber, and we were off.

Long-legged teenage boys and girls sat next to each other on the bus only when two free seats were not available. Otherwise, they pretended the other sex was not there. As we glided past palm trees on the way to the courts, the old soul love ballad "Me and Mrs. Jones" came on, and the entire bus fell back into a nervous kind of reverie, each player dressed and ready to play. Bare thighs brushed inadvertently to the sway of the large bus taking corners in the narrow highway lanes as Billy Paul sang in a strong but plaintive voice, "Me an . . . Mrs. Jones . . . We got a thing . . . going on."

I felt such a spirit of excitement on that bus, new worlds imagined but not yet seen, eighteen-and-under dreams. On arrival at the courts, the girls flicked their hair to one side, and the boys, stoic like young soldiers going off to boot camp, marched off the bus holding their large bags out in front of them. We were greeted by palm trees with brown leaves, a little dog leaping in the air after a Frisbee, and a team of Romanian boys playing three-on-three soccer against tall Italian boys who loped rather than ran in order to maintain their cool.

Despite my expectations throughout the years, the tennis Orange Bowl was nowhere near as big as the Miami football stadium. In fact, Flamingo Park was a public park surrounded on one side by a public elementary school and on the other three sides by modest one-family homes in a predominantly Spanish-speaking neighborhood of Miami Beach that was not quite what it used to be. I liked the place. The lockers were new but too narrow for most of the bags, and the three toilets were in great demand by nervous players of all nationalities. Over the years many of the great players of the world had competed here as juniors, and in a tennis world sometimes gone money-mad, I thought Flamingo Park was still the perfect spot for the most precocious tennis juniors in the world to meet and play.

America's Cristina Moros, chunky yet incredibly deft in her volleying hand, was down 5–4, 0–40 in her first-round match before she started to turn it on. Her father was a short, talented tennis pro who had moved to the United States from Venezuela, and her mother was a quiet woman with high cheekbones and a nice overbite smile who sat nervously in the stands with Stephanie Nickitas's mother. Bronze as an American Indian, Cristina Moros had silky smooth black hair, a touch like Rosie Casals's, and a moodiness that disappeared only when she attacked the ball and came in to the net. She saved two set points against Kristina Brandi from Florida, but Brandi's solid two-handed backhand skipped off the sideline on the third set point, and all Moros could do was scrape the ball into the net. Brandi, a talented qualifier, went up 4–0 in the second set as if a vacuum had been created in her opponent by the loss of the first set. Moros, who was on the U.S. National team, seemed to have the greater long-range potential, especially as a doubles player, but she had miles to go to become a real player. The Brandi girl was in far better control of her talent, and she won.

Dennis Van Der Meer, whose bright white tennis-camp traveling vans were in the parking lot along with the customized vans from the Palmer Tennis Academy and the Nick Bollettieri and Rick Macci tennis camps, was seated near me talking to Kristina Brandi's father, when I heard Van Der Meer say something that caught my ear.

"The player with the more simple game wins," said Van Der Meer. "Cristina Moros understands the game, but she needs more pattern to her play."

Van Der Meer had hit the nail right on the head. Moros played as if she wanted to get to stardom in a limousine, but first she had to learn that a point, especially a clay-court point, was made up of many twisting side streets, not just wide-open American highways. Moros's mother gave her a hug when she came off court, but Cristina shook her head in disgust and walked off to be alone.

"So," Van Der Meer said enthusiastically to Mr. Brandi, "what are your plans for your daughter? Pro tennis or college?"

My ears pricked up again. It was the million-dollar question. I thought Kristina Brandi was a very solid singles player but not quite pro material yet.

"Well," said Mr. Brandi, a parent with both eyes open, "she's only sixteen. But if she does well on her SATs, she might go to college."

"I'm of the old school," said Van Der Meer, nodding. "Unless you are extremely talented, go to college for at least a year."

It was a new approach to college. Agents and college coaches seemed to be everywhere around the courts, working somewhat different sides of the same fence. It was adult hunger, a talent feeding frenzy. While college was not the solution for everybody, I thought that college teams full of one- and two-year foreign and American players were making a mockery of what college really should be all about, a place to learn, not a place to incubate as an athlete.

"But also think of pro tennis," Van Der Meer was saying to Kristina Brandi's father. "She's a good player. And at some point she may want to get some power on her serve." A little hook for business never hurt. Van Der Meer was sympathetic and cheerful, as well.

Making the choice between pro and college tennis is never easy. In the back of their minds, all the junior players, despite their denials, secretly hope to break through and play professional tennis before crowds that seem to be sitting straight up in the clouds while down below Sampras, Agassi, and Graf move about on the court.

Parents may think they are grooming the next Graf or Agassi, but there is a perverse unpredictability to life. One rule generally holds true: The girls and boys who first seem destined for greatness at thirteen and fourteen, usually hit a wall by age seventeen or eighteen. I did. That wall is partly the limits of talent, partly the fear of losing. Tennis is hard on the juniors and hard on the parents, too. The parents pay for the lessons, provide the transportation to the tournaments, and then sit, white-knuckled or outwardly calm, wishing nothing but the best for their children, rooting shamelessly for their own genes exploding right in front of their eyes on the court. In the intensity of parental care, nothing in junior tennis has changed in twenty-five years. In other ways, nothing is the same.

The next morning Dennis Van Der Meer, dressed in white shorts and a windbreaker, was having a large coffee and a glazed donut at one of the wooden tables in the food court beside the draw sheets. I introduced myself, and he nodded for me to sit down.

Dennis Van Der Meer was a tall man in his midfifties with marcelled blond hair and a firm chin that softened at the jowls when he turned his head. The former South African Davis Cup player had movie star good looks and thirty years' experience fixing forehands and handling competitive egos. He shouted something to one of his pupils that made her laugh just as she opened the gate to go play her match, and I could see her opponent's shoulders tighten at the sound of the laughter.

"Well," said Van Der Meer in his clipped South African accent that made *well* sound like *will*, "my girl has a good chance. But I wouldn't bet on it." It was eight in the morning. Van Der Meer took a long sip of black coffee and smiled. He seemed to like the uncertainty, even the craziness, of the junior tennis world. There was a perpetual newness to it.

"How has tennis changed in just the past five years?"

"Face it," Van Der Meer said, "ninety percent of the people over forty in this country are playing dinosaur tennis."

I smiled. I knew he was right, but I liked to think of Rod Laver, Stan Smith, and Ken Rosewall as more than early palaeosaurs. They had hit the ball so beautifully, even if it was with the wood rackets.

"The analogy I use is Ping-Pong," Van Der Meer continued quickly. "All the Ping-Pong rackets used to be made of sandpaper. The best players were either strictly defensive or attacking players, and the best defense in Ping-Pong used to be to stand five or six yards behind the table while the aggressive player just banged away."

"That sounds like Rafael Osuna returning serve against Frank Froehling in the final at Forest Hills in 1963." Osuna had been as quick as Andre Agassi and smoother, but he could never generate with a wooden racket and slice backhand the amazing power Agassi generated with his boxer-like turns on the ball. Osuna had overcome Froehling's power with reflexes and gentle cunning. Agassi overcame power with reflexes and an unrelenting, suffocating power of his own.

"That's right," said Van Der Meer. "Osuna-Froehling. Well, in Ping-Pong, the fundamental relationship with the server up and the returner sometimes standing as deep behind the table as Osuna was behind the baseline that day against Froehling all changed with the advent of the dimpled, sponge-rubber paddles. The new equipment has had the same effect in tennis. The baseliner is no longer defending but attacking. And the big server has had to learn how to play from the baseline because the returns are coming back so fast you just can't come up to net on every second serve the way they did on grass in the 1960s—not with an Andre Agassi or Jimmy Connors returning serve with a composite racket. Connors hit the returns at their feet, but Agassi just blows them by you. But the change in tennis is only partly due to racket technology. Something subtler and more dramatic took place along with it." Van Der Meer now sounded like an excited teacher. "You see, tennis remained the same game for a very long time because the techniques used to teach hitting the ball did not change all that much from the time of Bill Tilden to the time of Gonzalez or Emerson. The weight of the wooden rackets and the minimal speed you could generate with them made the old-style tennis very much a game of linear motion. Tennis pros at clubs were always saying, 'Turn sideways, now step in and follow through,' because you had to step forward to generate power with a wooden racket.

"*That* is what Agassi more than anyone has changed," said Van Der Meer dramatically. "Once the players got the bigger, lighter rackets, they discovered they could make contact anywhere on the frame and still generate incredible power. We lost some control of the ball, which is why some old wood racket players like Sampras still prefer a frame that is closer in size to the old Kramer rackets. But in order for most players to get control with power, they needed a faster racket head. It didn't work at first. Jimmy Connors was the only player who could control that trampoline racket of his. Connors could do it because he got so low to the ball and his stroke was like a long line right through the ball. But in the 1990s, the strokes themselves have changed completely." Van Der Meer smiled at the audacity of it.

"Borg and McEnroe weren't revolutionaries," I said, thinking of the famous 18–16 fourth-set tiebreaker at Wimbledon that was one of the last great matches of the wooden racket era. "They were just great individuals, as stubborn as Tilden and Laver."

Van Der Meer nodded and smiled. "The revolutionaries are here now," he said, pointing to the junior boys who held the rackets with "western" grips so pronounced they seemed nearly backward to me. They were doing nearly the very opposite of what my contemporaries and I had been taught. The difference in technique was dramatic.

"Beyond the new racket frames, we've discovered that there is a lot more racket head speed in an upward motion than in a straight line," said Van Der Meer softly. "The next dimension, which has really come on in the past five years and has been perfected by Andre Agassi, is that the players not only go upwards with the racket head—because topspin like Vilas's and Sabatini's eventually slows the ball down—but now, like Agassi, they have started to go up and across the body through the ball. And *that*, starting with Agassi and Michael Chang, is what is so different and has given the young players an even faster stroke. They don't have to be sideways or step in the way we used to teach it. They can still murder the ball standing open-faced as long as they turn on the ball quickly with their shoulders. It's up and across, and that is really a boxing technique."

I nodded. That was part of it. Agassi and Chang generated incredible racket head speed that way.

"As you hit the ball faster and faster on the ground—and they all are, especially the women," said Van Der Meer, "tactics have had to change even in baseline play. Both Andre Agassi and Jim Courier made the court shorter. They take the ball as early as Borg, and they stand *inside* the baseline. That's what we used to call no-man's-land when I was growing up, but that's where the best tennis is being played right now. *In front of the baseline.* For that matter, that's where John McEnroe liked to play from before he lost his reflexes. But I think the real innovator, the real revolutionary, was Monica Seles. She understood that because she was hitting the ball from so much closer to the net that she also had a better margin of error. And that, I believe, is the future of this game for the next ten years. You see it already in the next half generation, in Andrei Medvedev. The best players always took the ball on the rise," he said with a smile. "These players take it before it is out of bed."

I laughed out loud. I love the way people who have dedicated themselves to something their entire life can talk about it. I was not convinced Andrei Medvedev or Michael Chang would have beaten Roy Emerson on any surface, even clay, but Emerson, like Edberg after him, would have had to have been playing very well to beat Chang consistently.

"What difference do you see between top junior girls and the young women who go on to be solid tour professionals?"

Van Der Meer did not hesitate. "The junior girls who go on to make it as pros are the ones who continue to hit out on the ball when they are under pressure in their junior matches. It's almost that simple—and it applies to the boys, too. It's interesting how they go. Kids are constantly adding new experiences to their tennis games, but the ones my coaches and I discount immediately are the ones who play aggressively at first but when they start to lose or make errors, revert to a defensive mode."

"The kid who gets conservative . . ."

"Defensive or conservative," said the South African ex-patriot, smiling, "it's just no good in tennis. Finally, the only people we know who make it as professionals are those players who can make a high percentage of aggressive shots. Aggressiveness is what we as coaches like to see first of all. We look for a young player who may be losing but who keeps on hitting out on the ball while trying to reduce errors. That's ideal to start with. It's much easier to bring balls back into the court than it is to teach a child the instinct to hit out with menace under pressure. If a girl is going to become a pro player, it's like a mountain climb. She has to go through consistency and establish a base there. You can never skip that stage. It must be done. But if you don't make the transition from consistency to the next level where you hit out on everything, you aren't going to make it as a professional."

"What about what Fred Stolle says about the return of serve today? He says the players are taking such full swings on the return of serve that they don't manage to put the ball onto the court nearly as much as they used to in big situations."

Van Der Meer smiled. "Fred was a great player, and I agree they've ruined doubles with all the banging. But what's different now is that both players are making more errors on the return of serve. The new attitude on return of serve, even for a fellow like Agassi who has by far the best return of serve in the game, is this: If you're making errors and I'm making errors, but I'm also hitting winners, then eventually you are going to lose. So, like Agassi, most players are going all-out for winners on the returns."

"No more chip returns on big points? Laver, Emerson, even McEnroe used to do it. Aren't there some points when you just have to put the ball in play?"

Van Der Meer shook his head. "I'm not saying a chip return is always a bad idea, but generally it just won't do anymore because the rackets are so light they're much easier to handle up close to net than the heavier wood rackets were. Now they can make you pay more for a bad short ball. No. You must go for winners on the returns of serve."

I was not 100 percent convinced. Goran Ivanisevic was the type of player who kept walloping his returns of serve even if he had hit ten in a row out. Was that the bravery Van Der Meer had been alluding to, or was it really a bailout, a kind of fear disguised as power? McEnroe, Connors, and Sampras always managed to put the ball in play against a big server.

"What is the difference between Mary Pierce, Anke Huber, Amanda Coetzer, and some of the top junior players here who may not make it in the pros?"

"Speed," said Van Der Meer quickly. "All the girls you mentioned can run. The second ingredient is the hand. You need good hands that can alternate between touch shots and a more powerful stroke."

"Doesn't the hand just come naturally? Can you teach good touch?"

Van Der Meer shrugged and revealed a businessman's smile. "I'd say the hand can be 'naturally developed.' You can work on the base. You can show the kids how to use their hands in different situations. How to be articulate with their hands."

"But we've missed the third ingredient," I said, "the one that made players like Chris Evert and Billie Jean King so tough to beat. It's the heart."

"Yes," said Van Der Meer. "What separates them all—all other things considered—is their heart. It's the most important of all and the hardest thing to teach. How much do they *really* want to win?" Van Der Meer laughed out loud, nervously. "I tell you, I watch them off the court in the rain delays or on a bus or in a motel room playing cards. You watch one kid, and he or she is always in there saying, 'Give me the deck. I want to deal the cards.' She's aggressive just playing a silly game of cards or backgammon. But in a match, watch her. When there is an important point, like a return of serve in a tiebreak, she doesn't want her partner to receive. She'll insist, like Martina always did, on taking that return of serve herself. People ignore doubles now, but I still watch doubles. I watch it in part because it tells me about their instincts as singles players. And as soon as I see one player leaving the ball for his partner over and over again, I say, 'ah-ah.' Because what you want is the player who says with his swing, 'It's *my* ball. I *want* the pressure; it's my ball!' " Van Der Meer smiled broadly.

"When I go to Rome," continued Van Der Meer, sounding a bit like Hannibal, "I always make a point of visiting the Coliseum. I wonder if in the days when they set the fellow in there to fight, and after he won they told him he was free to go because he had won, if he didn't turn around and say, *'But I don't want to be free. I want to go back in there and do it again!'* That's the way Martina Navratilova and Chris Evert were, the way Connors and McEnroe were too. Now *that's* the kind of kid I like to find and coach!" We both laughed at Van Der Meer's Coliseum description, knowing that the real stars grew by the decade, not by the bushel. I thanked him and turned toward the courts to check out the rising and falling junior talent.

Contenders in any sport don't grow on trees. I was not certain I could find a future women's champion among this crop of junior girls, but I hoped to find a good junior player about to go on to the pro tour or to college, and watch how that choice might play out for her. I was not looking for the absolute best junior girl player; I was looking for an outsider with a chance. The beauty and frustration of junior tennis is that teenagers are living and playing in the midst of an enormous period of change. In a sense I felt like just another astonished parent, rolling with the emerging emotions.

I scanned the courts. The level of play was very high. The boys were just murdering the ball off the ground, but I saw no complete packages ready for immediate unwrapping. Scott Humphries and Paul Goldstein played very well, but both were struggling a bit on clay. Marcelo Rios, the "South American Agassi," had a wonderful game on clay but did not win the Orange Bowl. Anna Kournikova looked to be about three years away from making it, but at twelve she was already precocious like a ballerina, and when she lost to a French girl in the semifinals of the fourteen-and-unders she turned away from her opponent as if the French girl was beneath knowing. Venus Williams was not playing the Orange Bowl, but her father had come down to scout future opponents for his daughter.

Gradually, as my eyes settled into the ebb and flow of the battles, I began to recognize the telltale signs of victory and defeat. The huge serves of some of the tallest boys began to be returned with regularity, and deficiencies showed up in another part of their game in much the same way that John McEnroe took apart David Wheaton at the 1990 U.S. Open by first dismantling Wheaton's biggest weapon, his serve.

Among the junior girls, I saw a great forehand here, a volleyer there, a girl tall but a half step slow, a girl fast but perhaps a trifle small. I checked out the American team with interest. Would Karin Miller, a player with great court sense and heart, grow above five feet, four inches? Probably not. Could Cristina Moros become faster and more consistent? I particularly liked Stephanie Nickitas because she was so wild and out of control, and yet she was beautifully coordinated and kept coming forward to serve and volley. Would Nickitas have the self-control and the heart? I thought she might.

Meilen Tu, the slender Chinese-American with the quick smile and steely eyes, lost in the first round of the Orange Bowl in straight sets to what is referred to in the junior world as a "nobody." Many nobodies become champions. Fourteen-year-old Stephanie Halsell, who would win the sixteen-and-unders at the Orange Bowl, kept losing first sets and winning matches, but she, too, was shorter than five feet, six inches. She was like a little Chris Evert, very smart and all business about the court, but would Halsell grow in all the necessary ways? Would these young girls keep their desire to play the game or lose it the way Jennifer Capriati had? Would any top girls consider college as a real alternative? There were some big names in women's junior tennis that remained largely unknown to me and to the larger pro tennis world.

One such name was Ania Bleszynski.

I first heard of Bleszynski quite by accident. I was standing up in the small press room behind the stadium court with Donna Fales, the former U.S. top-ten player in the 1960s who ran the Orange Bowl with great love and firmness, when a weary photographer, draped in cameras like a pack animal, trudged up the steep concrete stairs and nearly had a meltdown in front of us. Fales, whose blond hair was still cut in that distinctive pageboy style that used to sway out under her tennis visor when she played in a Fred Perry shirt and white shorts that seemed long by today's standards, was called away to deal with an emergency regarding the plumbing in the boys' bathroom. I was left with Art Seitz, the enormous freelance photographer from Florida, who was weary from trying to make a living.

"I tell you," he said, sighing soberly at midday, "sometimes I feel like I'm the only person out there trying to be creative."

"My feelings exactly!" I said, laughing, but he did not appear to hear me.

"Last week I was over in Tampa to shoot little Kournikova," the photographer continued. "I got little Kournikova to pose with her mother and this Russian teddy bear I bought at a flower store in Palm Beach. I shot two rolls of film and got one beautiful shot of the two of them with the bear. I couldn't sell the picture to *Tennis*, and the *Miami Herald* takes their own pictures, and the AP told me they didn't want to run my picture because Kournikova trains at Bollettieri's camp, and they don't want to give Nick any more free publicity. So I wound up giving Kournikova's mother all my bear pictures for free. Today I was shooting the girls' eighteens. I tried to tell the other photographers that there is a girl here named Ania Bleszynski. She's six foot one. She's got a face like Grace Kelly's, and she really blasts her serve. They didn't want to take her picture. She's American, but everybody thought she was Polish, so they ran off to take pictures of Janet Lee, for Christ sake."

I was chuckling. In fairness to the *Miami Herald*, Janet Lee was then the highest ranked American junior internationally, the number six junior in the world. But I checked my draw sheet, and this Ania Bleszynski from California, whoever she was, had beaten Janet Lee 6–4, 6–2.

I made a point of finding Ania Bleszynski. I guessed which one she was. She looked like a cross between Grace Kelly and Christine Truman, although that is a bit of a stretch because the big, shy English player of twenty-five years ago had been about six inches taller and heavier than Grace Kelly. I spotted the young Polish-American girl sipping from a green squeeze bottle of Gatorade at a wood table with Julie Scott, her doubles partner from Texas. They were the long and the short of it, but I watched them together in the doubles, and they could play, especially Bleszynski.

That night back at the Omni Hotel, a twelve-story concrete palace with three subterranean floors of movie theaters, pizza parlors, and take-out restaurants, I talked to the girls on the U.S. girls' team on a couch down in the lobby. The girls were all so different, nice in different ways, yet only Nicole London expressed any interest at all in college, books, or much of anything outside tennis. It gave me pause. The agents were looking for future champions. My search was not quite the same. As I talked to the girls, I thought back to what Dennis Van Der Meer had said that morning.

"What is still attractive for me as a coach is the parent who comes to me and says, 'I've got this sixteen-year-old girl who says she can't make it as a pro because she's over the hill at sixteen.' I tell that girl she is *not* over the hill." Van Der Meer paused. "In fact, there are instances when she may be. But the fact that Jennifer Capriati's life in tennis has not fulfilled its final promise and that she has had some big problems already has kids saying, 'Maybe I'll start a bit later.' I insist to all parents and girls who want to turn professional one day that sixteen or eighteen years old is *not* too late for a girl to bloom into an outstanding women's professional player. This baby boom in women's tennis is a sham!" Van Der Meer had said, slamming the wooden table softly. "You see, we know historically just how long most tennis careers will be—and I am talking about all tournament tennis. It's normally—"

"Ten years?" I asked, thinking of Stefan Edberg.

"No. Not even ten years. It's usually more like seven years, from tennis cradle to tennis grave. If you're a superstar, it may last a little longer."

Amanda Basica, fifteen years old and already five feet eight inches tall with classic sunny California good looks and smile, sat down opposite me in the lobby of the Omni Hotel. One of the top young players in the United States, Basica had been seeded twelfth in the girls' eighteens, but in the first round she lost in three sets to Poland's very talented but virtually unknown Katarzyna Malec. I had watched the whole match. An essential part of Basica's personality, like her tennis game, was still unformed. While watching Basica compete, I had sensed that her game had about an equal chance of turning out like steel or Jell-o. There *was* a middle ground, and she might find it. Right now she was struggling, mostly with herself. She was in ninth grade.

Amanda Basica, whose sister Amber was also a top junior player, laughed nervously and shook her pretty head. "In the U.S. tournaments you might have two or three easy rounds. Internationally every round is tough. All the girls are so good and very competitive. What do I like about playing tennis? I like the competing. Each match is like meeting someone for the first or second time, but you're both trying to win. Each person I play is so different. You have to be able to adapt your own style of play to their style."

"What about the match you lost yesterday?"

Basica's head and voice dropped. "She was just a good player. She had heavy topspin off both sides. I wasn't used to it. Most American girls don't play like that. The European girls use more topspin. Basically it was tiring. Mentally tiring."

I liked the fact that Basica acknowledged her opponent's talent, but she seemed tired.

"Do you like school?"

"Not really." Basica laughed and pulled nervously at her smooth blond hair. "I'm much more interested in tennis. But I do want to learn French."

A month later, Amanda Basica dropped out of high school to go to Australia with the U.S. National Team. Then she gained about twelve pounds and grew another inch. She had long, classic flat hard ground strokes that her team's coach, Lynne Rolley, told me "we would never try to change." Would Amanda Basica ultimately be tough enough to emerge from the juniors and make it on the women's pro tour? It was a coin toss.

Stephanie Nickitas, a particular favorite of mine, would be the next player to come down to the lobby and talk to me. That morning I had sat, incognito, directly behind Nickitas's mother and the mother of her doubles partner, Cristina Moros, with whom she had won the girls' junior doubles event at the U.S. National Championships the year before. The mothers, huddled together for survival, were trying to follow Nickitas's match, which took place three courts over from the gallery. The American teen played a short Argentine girl with a wicked left-handed serve that consistently pulled Nickitas wide into the alley to try to return it. I could see the faces of the players begin to show the strain, but the mothers were also telling barometers of the action.

"Oh, God!" said Irene Nickitas, sensing the end was near for her talented daughter against the more physically mature Argentine. "Stephanie's abandoned her game plan. . . . Gee, I hope the other girl has another double fault in her bag."

The other girl *did* have another double fault in her bag, and the two girls went into a third set. The two American mothers were seated next to a sports psychologist, Ann Thomas, who seemed to have a suggestion for every lost point. By the time young Nickitas had her serve broken in the third set, Irene Nickitas looked ready to be fitted for a straitjacket, and I had the impression that Ann Thomas had one in the trunk of her car for just such occasions. As the third set got close, the line calls between the girls on the far court began to get sticky.

"That Argentinean girl called that shot out!" Irene Nickitas said incredulously as her daughter appeared to have gotten hooked again on a passing shot up the line.

"No. It was out," the mother of Christina Moros had said softly, not bothered by "mother vision" when her own daughter was not playing.

"Circle the mark," the Florida octogenarian in the umpire's chair had called out bravely, clutching his floppy white Australian sun hat, as he dropped slowly to the court to dispatch justice. He bent over the sideline as if examining a fossil, dramatically extended an arm to call the ball "out," and climbed back atop his chair. Nickitas eventually lost the match, but it had been a very close third set.

At sixteen, Nickitas was as aggressive and happy *on* court as she appeared uncertain offcourt. Wild but talented and unafraid to come to the net in pressure situations, Stephanie Nickitas had worn a bright-colored headband in her match, but as she spoke to me, she let her thick brown hair fall over her face as if she were trying to hide in it.

"When did your tennis career start to take off?"

Stephanie looked up as if to remember. "Well, when I was fourteen, I had mono. I started back again last year when I was fifteen. I had a pretty good year. I've been playing tennis since I was about four or five. I don't remember how I started. My parents didn't belong to a country club. My grandmother says I used to watch her and a friend. I don't know, really. I was just always playing. My dad worked for Seagram's for twenty-seven years and retired a few years ago. He runs his own business now. My mom runs her own business, too. She's a general contractor."

I nodded. At the match, Irene Nickitas had looked very competitive. I could see her putting in plenty of contractor's bids, and winning many of them. "What is fun for you in tennis?" I asked her daughter.

"I like the traveling. If you don't like it, it's going to be really hard to stay competitive. My biggest strength? My style is aggressive. A lot of girls you see are just baseliners." The word came out of her mouth with some derision. "They're afraid to even go in front of the service line, you know? I don't mind coming up to net at all. Even on clay I like to serve and volley."

"Have you played any pro events yet?"

Her voice and confidence dropped, but she maintained a firmness in her answers. "We've played some WTA [Women's Tennis Association] challengers. It's been all right. I played a couple this year. My WTA ranking is like nine hundred in singles and about five hundred in doubles."

"What is the difference you see between the girls who are already up in the women's rankings and yourself?"

Stephanie shrugged dismissively. "I don't see a lot of difference. Some of those girls played college tennis for a year or two. They've been out on the tour. It's experience."

"You want to be a pro?"

"Oh, yes. But people ask if I want to turn pro or go to college. It's hard to make that decision. I don't think anyone should try to answer that one too early. I'm just a junior in high school, and I don't graduate for another two years. I'm not ruling out either, college or pro tennis. Do I like school?" She shook her head. "No. Not so much."

She smiled. She was telling the truth. They were all out there battling so hard to let their games come through their personalities and win. Stephanie Nickitas got up, shook my hand, and walked to the elevators, letting her brown hair hide her face. It was hard to tell if she had freckles or a little acne. Now her bouncy gait showed an almost boundless enthusiasm that nearly masked her shyness.

Nickitas's doubles partner, Cristina Moros, was slightly heavy and handsomely Incan. Her father, Julio, played Davis Cup for Venezuela before coming to Florida to work for several years under Nick Bollettieri. He had recently split off from Bollettieri to try to start his own tennis camp. Cristina Moros had been playing tennis tournaments since she was seven years old, and she was almost seventeen. She spoke with appealing modesty and a surprising fear of the professional world her talent and life seemed to be propelling her toward as naturally as a flower floats downstream.

"My dad. He was the national champion in Venezuela. That's about as far as he got in tennis. What's my biggest strength as a player? Probably my quickness."

I nodded, stunned. Moros has very fast hands, but she was a bit chunky to ever be considered a great "mover."

"My hands at net are good," she added.

"You've got beautiful hands. Great touch on the volley." In fact Cristina Moros's hands were so naturally deft on the racket that, almost like Maria Bueno, she had the kind of touch that simply can never be taught.

Moros's face warmed considerably to the compliment. She had a broad, white-toothed smile. "Thanks." She looked me in the eye and nodded. "There is such a big change from juniors to the pros," admitted Cristina. "I played in a couple of challengers this year, and it was *so* different."

"How was it different?"

"Basically, everybody is unsocial," said Cristina. "If you're an up-and-coming junior player, forget it. The pro girls don't even take the time to say even hi or anything."

"Every new face is a potential rival," I said. "Friendship *is* secondary on tour. You're knocking on their livelihood. It's very different. Do you think you can stand up to the pro life?"

"Yes. I think I can."

"You don't think it would hurt you too much?" I asked in conclusion.

"No," Cristina Moros said. "I think I can do it."

And I believed her. She was going to be a successful pro, at least in doubles.

Meilen Tu, who had lost in the first round, had a far more assertive voice, bell clear and totally unafraid. She sounded even more confident than Michael Chang.

"My strength is that I am very competitive," said Meilen Tu, smiling as if her life depended on it. "Also, my forehand is excellent. My weakness is probably my movement. I'm not naturally fast. But we are working on that. Right now I want to go to college, because college tennis is very competitive and it gets people ready to go out on the tour. But I don't go to school anymore. I do home study. It is the exact same curriculum as they have at school, except I can do it faster and learn everything at home. I have tutors," said Meilen Tu, whose father had made a lot of money through real estate investment in California. "And they come whenever I want them. But most of the stuff you can learn on your own. If I have problems, I just go in and see my teachers."

Modesty was not going to be Meilen's long suit, but it had not been young Jimmy Connors's either. I didn't agree with her about the merits of home study, but Meilen Tu was articulate, bright, and unflappable. She made life sound quite easy, though later I learned that her California high school had asked Tu to leave school because she was skipping classes for a week or two at a time with such regularity that it upset the other girls in school. Clearly I was in prodigy, child-star territory. Was it any surprise that so many child movie stars, who also generally relied on home study in the formative years, had such a difficult time adjusting to life after stardom when they had passed up school? And yet, when I spoke to Gerry Smith, the former CEO of the women's tour during Capriati's rise, I was in for a big surprise. Not only did Smith disagree with my assessment that it was wrong to pull young girls out of school early, but he told me that his daughters had also been taken out of school in favor of home study. Smith had thought it was a great idea. I thought it was nearly criminal.

"I love tennis *a lot*," Meilen Tu said in her perky, California-valley-girl talk. "I love playing tournaments. I like the feeling of being maybe six—all in the third-set tiebreaker. You come out and lose. Or you come out and win. But it *happens*. It just happens, and it's fun."

"How do you deal with an opponent?" I asked.

"When I get on a court," said the fifteen-year-old Tu, "I check them over in the warm-up. If they run around their backhand, I know their forehand is stronger, so first I try to pull them wide out to the forehand side for a while. That makes the backhand opening get even wider. I play their strength to get to their weakness. Then they cannot cover up their weakness. I can also tell if they are impatient girls. I can tell just by looking at them, by how they walk between points. If they're walking, like, really quickly?" she said it as a question. "It's like they are girls who want to have their way right away and are going to get impatient if they don't get their way? I can't explain it, but I see it."

Meilen Tu was clearly smart as well as talented. She knew how to compete—and how to get under an opponent's skin—and she had impressive verbal skills for a girl her age.

"Everything just adds up," said Tu. "If a girl walks too quickly and wants to play too fast, then I play them slow and steady. But in a tight situation, I hit out. I don't wait any more for the other girl to make a mistake. I tried that, but I learned the hard way that it does not work. You cannot sit back and hope someone is going to miss for you. Because it will *not* happen. It might work in the early rounds, but not later, and tennis is a habit, so I now say, 'If you're going to lose, Meilen, lose doing the right things. Don't be afraid.' If you get a short ball, hit it to put it away."

"What's your ranking?"

"Nationally I'm probably four or five in the eighteens. And world, I'm ranked number thirty-five. But I'm improving." She smiled.

"Your goal in the next year or two is to become a professional?"

"Definitely," said Meilen Tu. And I believed her. "I have a plan and long-term goals, and a lot of people have been helping me. I changed my forehand backswing with Carol Watson and Lynne Rolley, and it took me six months to get control of it. The other girls on the U.S. [National] Team?" Meilen Tu shrugged. "They're pretty nice, I guess, but you always get a little tension. Mostly I like them, but the European girls are stronger than we Americans are now. They have something inside them that we Americans girls don't have. I can't say exactly what it is. It's a different kind of instinct. How do you say it? They are just more *strict* with themselves. More disciplined. They work very hard. I admire that a lot in the European girls. I'm working to be more like that myself," said Meilen Tu, and she nodded brightly.

.   .   .

Nicole London was the oldest and the last American girl on the U.S. National Team left in the draw of the Orange Bowl. One other American girl, who was not on the team—Ania Bleszynski—was to be her round-of-sixteen opponent. London had been very good at a very young age and still had a beautiful all-round game that lacked, if anything, a special weapon. Everything about Nicole London seemed different from the other girls. She was only eighteen, but she seemed much older. Now slender, brown haired, articulate, and outwardly very self-assured, at age fourteen Nicole London won the famous Petites As tournament in Tours, France, where fourteen-year-olds played in front of a stadium crowd of eight thousand people. She had also won the Easter Bowl fourteens in 1989 and sixteens in 1990. And yet, she now seemed as if she had seen it all and was going to end her competitive career in the next year or so while attending college at the University of Southern California. London had been the best in her age group when Jennifer Capriati turned pro. She played extremely smart tennis, yet I sensed she had almost had enough of the game. She wanted one last big showing, and only Ania Bleszynski stood between her and this goal.

"Why did you decide to go to college?"

"Probably because I never wanted tennis to take up my whole life," said London. "I have other interests. I love tennis, but it has just taken so much dedication that I just don't know if I'm ready for more of that. I like going out with my friends on weekends. Also, I don't know if I am really ready for the tour. So I want to go to college. The tour is very hard. It doesn't really fit my personality that much right now."

"What is your personality like?"

"Well, it's just not all tennis. I work very hard on the court, but I like to think about other things, too. I like being around people. I don't think I would like it just being out on tour by myself. When you have other people around, you can have dinner at night and have friends. That's better than being alone or just being in a hotel with your mom. It can be very solitary. Now Lindsay Davenport," said London, who had won the U.S. junior doubles with Davenport in 1992, "we were pretty good friends, and Lindsay tells me she really loves it so far. Of course, she is doing very well right now. But she doesn't have a lot of other things she likes to do yet, so her personality fits the tour better. I hate the traveling because you never get to settle down into one place. But I know another girl who didn't go to college and who is not doing well at all on the tour, but she's just not into college—she hates studying—and she just wants to travel and be around the other girls on the tour. She was a top junior player. She's been a pro three years and she's ranked somewhere in the three hundreds but she doesn't care. She likes it anyway."

Nicole London was a perfectionist, and I sensed that if she could not break into the top hundred women in the world within a year, she would look at a pro tennis career as a failure. I asked her, "Can you tell, watching the other top international girls here at the Orange Bowl, which ones are going to make it as pros?"

"Pretty much," she said. "You can tell the ones who are really competitive and the ones who maybe aren't. Some of them are competing for everything and try to run every single ball down for the whole match. The ones who aren't as competitive are the ones who just kind of play and stop running after balls when they are losing. Those girls won't be pros. They just aren't intense enough in a match."

"And you?" I had seen her play beautifully for two rounds, giving a clinic, 6–3, 6–0, to a girl from Ecuador that afternoon.

"I'm really competitive, but it's hard to see." London laughed as if it were her secret. "I try hard not to show it on court, but inside I am *very* competitive. Very!"

Tomorrow she would play Ania Bleszynski, who was also from California, and the winner would be the only American girl to reach the quarterfinals of the Orange Bowl.

The next morning, three days before Christmas, it was ninety-degrees in Miami. The plants and flowers were bright green and red. The air was clear and fresh but piercing hot. Everything living seemed to need watering. The dry green clay, watered heavily the night before, was nearly white. It was perfect tennis weather.

I felt the anxiety of the junior players, the serious faces, the forced laughter to cut the tension, the more gregarious aspect to the boys, the quieter, more reflective, but no less competitive mood of the girls waiting to do battle. The throngs of junior players had been thinned out by three days of winning and losing. It was easier to navigate around Flamingo Park, but the mood was a little sad. Tournaments get like that toward the end of the first week after the size of the draw is cut in half or less. A few of the losers in the early rounds stayed on to watch, but most had gone home to save on expenses. Two boys were seated directly behind Paul Goldstein's court, rooting him on. I thought they knew each other, but they were just meeting.

"I lost first round," the taller boy suddenly confessed quietly to the other young man. "How about you?"

"First round," the shorter, more muscular boy said sheepishly, adding, "of the qualifiers."

There was no shame in it. There were lots of players who would have loved the chance just to get into the qualifier at the Orange Bowl. These kids were putting themselves on the line, and if this was done quietly and with all effort possible, there was something attractive in it.

Waiting for the Nicole London–Ania Bleszynski match, I saw Anna Kournikova's mother braiding her twelve-year-old daughter's blond hair slowly, gently in the empty stands before Kournikova went out to play. On the next court I saw a short Argentine with a faint black mustache, baggy tennis shorts, and a plain white T-shirt with the sleeves rolled up slightly on the sides. The jet-black hair was cut short a bit like Emilio Sanchez's but shorter on the sides. The forehand was powerful, the attitude aggressive and thickset. I had never seen anything quite like her in the juniors. She was short and powerful, like a dark bottom fish swimming among speckled surface species. Her sexuality seemed to have been set at birth. At night at the player banquet, she flirted with the girls far more outrageously than any of the boys dared to. Most but not all of the girls turned their backs on her, except when they had to go out and face her rough, very particular music. She was not going to be a champion, but she was going to be strong enough to make it out on the pro tour.

Business pressures were already a factor for the best players. The night before, I had a beer at the hotel bar and found myself next to a portly Swiss man in his late fifties who was wearing a Fila shirt and had an air of nervous prosperity about him. After we exchanged a few pleasantries about tennis, he pulled a business card out of his pocket.

"I am here with the two girls from Madagascar," he explained.

"You're their coach?"

"No. I am their financial adviser—their guardian."

The last time I had heard the term *guardian* applied to children was in Charles Dickens's *Bleak House*.

"When the girls were young," he continued, "I became aware of the two of them on a trip from Switzerland to Madagascar. I arranged for them to come live with me. I have housed them and trained them ever since. It's been nearly six years. Dally Randriantefy, the better player, was seeded seventh here, but Dally got upset today by this Montolio [the eventual Orange Bowl junior winner] from Spain in three sets. Dally is still in the doubles. We're a little disappointed with the singles result, because if we had won here we would have turned pro. Now we may wait a few more months until after the U.S. Open." The Swiss man shrugged, disappointed yet determined to continue as their sponsor-guardian.

It was different from the junior days I had experienced, when "big money" was the fifty dollars a sixteen-year-old Jeff Borowiak had hustled with great skill and cool from grown black men in a pool hall in St. Louis. Today, tennis "investors" were signing young kids almost faster than the pro agents or college coaches could get to them. It kept the kids artificially young and out of touch with life. The investors seemed to like the human gamble. The children almost felt like chips in their hands. For supporting the young players, the investors locked in a percentage of all future pro earnings. It made investors feel benevolent; it gave me the creeps.

Tennis was still a game—not a business—to some of us. The coach of the English girls' team came out to watch the Ania Bleszynski–Nicole London match with a large vanilla ice cream cone covered in bright colored M&Ms. The small gallery was packed. Ania Bleszynski followed the more experienced Nicole London out onto the front court. There were coaches and agents in the crowd of about sixty. A Miami Beach mother caught her short son staring at the tall, attractive Bleszynski.

"Listen," said the mother matter-of-factly with a New York accent. "she's the right size for somebody, but maybe not for you."

London and Bleszynski locked onto each other's personalities from the first ball hit in the warm-up, and the two California girls did not let up. It should not have surprised me that they did not seem to like each other. Nicole London wore a short tennis skirt, and everything about her was neat and dead-center on the ball. Ania Bleszynski seemed youthfully awkward, large where she wanted to be fast, but graceful in spite of the height she was still growing into.

The two girls played beautifully. It was primarily a baseline battle, but the pace they generated on the ball was as heavy and dead-center on the racket frame as anything I had seen all week. London won points with a flair of disdain, a little flick of her racket head at the end of the stroke. But Bleszynski kept hitting aces and unreturnable second serves. They did not say a word to each other for two whole sets, and on the changeovers they stared at the ground or off into the sky. When London served at 4–all in the first set, Bleszynski attacked her serve and came to the net behind deep returns of serve until finally London sailed a low, hard forehand, just long. I looked at Bleszynski, tall and statuesque in her tennis visor on the baseline. Could she hold her serve while up 5–4? On the first point Ania Bleszynski came up to the net behind her serve and put a low volley away. She smashed an overhead away on another point and began to lift her backhand with such power and strength that the lighter, smaller London began to lean backward as she hit. The scores, which in no way were a measure of how close and tension-filled the match had been, were 6–4, 6–2 for Ania Bleszynski. She broke into a shy smile after they shook hands, gathered up her rackets and her water jug, and came off the court, walking in front of the suddenly fragile and slumped-over Nicole London, who at eighteen was a year older than the girl she had just lost to.

London was headed to USC. I was not sure where Ania Bleszynski was heading, but I wanted to find out. She was the only American girl left in the quarterfinals of the Orange Bowl.

I called Louise Gengler, the Princeton women's coach and ITA official, one of the fine women's coaches in the game. I had grown up knowing the Genglers, a tennis-playing family, especially Marjorie Gengler, a top junior player who had married Stan Smith.

"Louise," I said, "who is this Ania Bleszynski? I never really heard of her before."

"Oh, she's good," said Gengler. "She's one of the top three or four juniors in the country, and she's still improving. I tried to recruit her for a while here at Princeton, but we were never really in the running. I think it came down to Stanford and Harvard. She's unbelievably smart. She was born in Poland, I think, but she came over here when her parents escaped. She's definitely a player."

Ania Bleszynski—seventeen, slightly taller than me, wearing blue jeans and a man's plain green T-shirt, coppery-blond hair held off the side of her face with a gold barrette—came down to the hotel lobby to talk to me looking older and more self-assured than she really was. Her face had the freshness of an open field in Poland on a slightly raw morning. She had arrived in the United States at age three, and now she spoke English like a native American. She had an appealing blend of American and European outlooks on the world. She was a fighter with a difference.

"Your parents left Poland in 1977. That was still not an easy time to leave."

Bleszynski shrugged. Her voice was sunny California-American, her brown eyes serious, intelligent. "I guess it wasn't an easy time, but they never talk to me about it. I know we moved to Germany first, for work." She smiled, struggling to describe what she could hardly remember, the movement, the changes, all the hopes and fears of the repeated, sudden starting-overs. A tennis court was a place that did not move.

"What kind of work do your parents do?"

"They are both physicists," said Ania Bleszynski shyly. "They work at Rockwell International. On design of wings." She paused. "Different kinds of planes. And radar cross sections. Things like that. I'm not actually sure." She laughed again, loudly, nervously, "It's all math. A *lot* of math."

"What about yourself at school? What are you interested in?"

"Well, I'm interested in things like that, too. Math, physics, and biology. I took calculus last year, and I'm in linear algebra right now."

I have an English and history major's horror of the world of numbers. "And you like the algebra?"

"It's my favorite subject," confided Ania Bleszynski.

Hearing Bleszynski speak so enthusiastically about schoolwork, I thought of Anna Kournikova. The two girls had contrasting approaches to becoming a tennis player: to develop early with little care for education, like Kournikova, or to develop a little later but with the depth that education can give, like Bleszynski.

There was something loyal and dedicated about Ania Bleszynski that I liked from the first time I spotted her playing doubles. Despite her size and ranking, she played doubles with her best friend, the five-foot-four-inch Texan Julie Scott. Scott was a very good regional player, but a player who had lost in the first round at the Orange Bowl 6–1, 6–0. Bleszynski had kept the plucky Texas girl as her partner, and they had won a few rounds in doubles together.

"Math and science are definitely my interests over English and history," she continued.

"Aside from the fact that your parents are rocket scientists, what appeals to you about math and science?"

Ania laughed. "Probably that they are a lot more logical. It's kind of figuring things out, whereas English is a lot of writing, and sometimes I really have to do up those English essays to suit the teacher, to give the teachers back what they want. That doesn't happen in science and math." She smiled. "I guess it's just natural in me. I prefer going home and having to do math problems rather than having to do an essay."

"Was the English language tough for you in the beginning?"

"That could have been part of it," Ania Bleszynski admitted. She had an intelligence that made her seem just a bit unsure of herself despite her considerable accomplishments. "At home we speak Polish or English, so at first I was behind the rest of my class. I have also taken Latin for six years. It's made French pretty easy for me." She said it matter-of-factly, not boastfully. "I like languages a lot. It's not practical to major in them, but I do want to learn them."

"Is reading English—"

"Difficult? No. I love reading." Ania Bleszynski said it again, and it was the first time I had heard anyone say it all week. "I love reading."

"What do you like to read?"

"I guess my favorite authors are, like, Thomas Hardy and Jane Austen, Charles Dickens and Jules Verne."

I grinned. "I taught Jane Austen once."

"I have this book at home, I think it's called *Mansfield Park.*"

"That's the one!" I said. "That is a *great* book."

"I haven't read it yet. I still have to finish this other one by her."

"Well, there is a famous stone bench in *Mansfield Park*," I said, "and a large gardened park that they call a 'wilderness,' and the book is really about why Fanny Price decides to stay on that bench even though it means possibly being alone and struggling rather than going outside the boundaries of that garden into the artificial wilderness. She does not go out through the gate, but most of the others do. And you have to decide for yourself if she does the right thing or not. It's always easier to go out through the gate with the others."

Ania Bleszynski nodded slowly. "I read *Persuasion*," she said. "And I loved that book."

She was bright and I sensed she was equally enthusiastic about becoming a real player. "Why aren't you on the American junior girls' team?"

She rolled her head in a big circle and sighed. "Well, my first year in the sixteens, I thought I would be. I was ranked fourth in the nation, ahead of two people on the national team, and that year I really thought I might have my chance." Her voice had an edge of disappointment to it. Now she had defeated Nicole London and had reached the quarterfinals of the Orange Bowl. "I guess they have their way of picking the U.S. team. I played up into the eighteens my second year of sixteens, and I was ranked thirteen or fourteen in the nation as a fifteen-year-old. I just didn't have the wins necessary to be chosen that year."

"But this year you've beaten Janet Lee, who is ranked number one in the country and was seeded fourth here."

She nodded. "I played Janet in a women's open tournament a

month ago. It was called 'Top Gun.' I beat Janet there, too. My game kind of fits hers well." She shifted nervously, not wanting to dwell any longer on why she had not been chosen.

"Are you going to play in some pro events soon, or do you just intend to go to college first?"

Ania Bleszynski smiled and shook her head. "I was accepted to Stanford, but I'm entered in two ten-thousand-dollar satellites in Texas in January. I'm going to be missing school, which is going to be really difficult. It was kind of a choice there between school and tennis. But I decided I wanted to play. I'm going to see how I do. Hopefully I'll do well. After that, I don't really know all the pro tournaments yet, and it's really hard for me to get into them by myself. I don't have the ITF ranking yet, and I don't have a chance to go to all these places yet to play. I need to get some computer points."

"Don't sell yourself short. How did you do with the number-one seed here, Nino Louarsabishvily? Ever play her?"

"I played her on grass last year. She beat me 6–4, 7–6. She's strong and very precise with her ground strokes. But it was close." Ania shrugged. "The thing is that it's expensive to travel. My parents aren't so crazy about it because they pay when I travel and they pay for my lessons. My only international experience has been at the Canadian and U.S. Opens and at the grass courts."

I liked her. Ania Bleszynski was not a gym rat.

"Could the Stanford coach, Frank Brennan, or Lynne Rolley help you get into a few pro events?"

"I don't think Frank really wants us to get too involved in pro tournaments. He wants . . ."

"To keep you around campus?'

Ania shrugged. "Yeah. When I talked to him about a week ago, he said that when you turn pro you just start worrying too much about your ranking. He's more for just having you play your college tennis. If I do it . . . I mean, I just have to do it on my own."

"But have you spoken to Lynne Rolley?"

Ania Bleszynski shook her head. "I've tried a couple of times. At Orange Bowl two years ago, I asked her about getting on the team because it was hard for my parents to come with me. And expensive for them even just to send me alone. They take care of all the U.S. players at the U.S. Open and put us up in the hotel and give us meals. But that's one tournament a year, and it would be great to get on the U.S. team because they have everything, including coaching, paid for."

"How much do your tennis lessons cost?"

"Well, Robert Lansdorp taught Tracy Austin. He is seventy-five an hour. And Kathy Bryan, who was Kathy Blake when she played on the tour, charges fifty an hour. She's great, too."

I whistled. Tennis was not nearly as expensive as golf, but it was expensive to learn. It always had been and always would be. She went to two top teaching pros on alternate weeks.

"My parents make a lot of sacrifices for my lessons," said Ania.

"Who travels with you?"

"I travel by myself."

"You're six feet, one inch tall. Maybe a little taller?"

"Maybe a little shorter," she said quickly. She was a bit self-conscious about her height, except when she got a little mad on court, and then she poured it on. "[My height has] meant I have to work even harder on moving. Last year was really frustrating because I grew, like, four inches. I used to be able to get to certain balls that I couldn't get to after I grew. But this year I'm starting to get to them again. I'm doing wind sprints at school. My father is tall. He played basketball for one year back in Poland, and my mother ran track at her high school. They run together in the afternoons, but between school and their work, we have pretty busy schedules."

"I saw your doubles partner with you here. Julie Scott."

"Yeah, yeah!" said Ania Bleszynski, brightening as if leading a cheer. "We're *great* buddies. When we're at the same tournament, we always stay together. She's more than just a doubles partner. We're really friends." She paused. "Julie is really spunky. She's got two hands off both sides. She's great to play with, but she just left this afternoon, so now I'm feeling a little down."

"Oh, no, no," I said. "You're going to do great tomorrow. You play that Brazilian girl, Miriam D'Agostini, right?"

"Right," she said, nodding. A determined look came into her brown eyes.

"What time do you play?"

"Nine A.M.," said Ania Bleszynski. It was now nine at night.

The Miami sun was bright over old Flamingo Park the next morning at 8:30. A torrential burst of rain had rolled up from the Florida Keys late the night before. There were no puddles on the court and all the court sweepers had to do that morning was pull the big brooms behind them in soothingly slow concentric circles until a man came out to sweep the lines and make the whole surface seem rectilinear again. The courts had been dry and thirsty, but now they were dark and a little soft from the rainstorm. The slower surface would probably favor the Brazilian, but I had not seen her play.

Ania Bleszynski and Miriam D'Agostini were already warming up when I took my seat in the old wooden stands. Nicole London had been seeded thirteenth; D'Agostini was seeded tenth. She was very short with good foot speed and a solid South American topspin game off both sides. The Brazilian was at home on the clay court, but when they spun for serve at the net she kept staring up at Ania Bleszynski, who towered over her by seven inches. If Ania could get through this match, she would be into the semifinals of the Orange Bowl, and I was sure Lynne Rolley would reconsider and offer her a position on the U.S. National Team.

Warm-ups are often deceptive. D'Agostini, wearing a light blue sweatshirt over her tennis whites, was bouncing on the baseline, looking happy and relaxed and generally quite pleased with herself. Ania, on the other hand, looked incredibly tight as if she knew the importance of the match. Her big-girl ground strokes seemed locked at the elbow, and a number of them made the net sway. She began to relax as she hit her volleys, but D'Agostini began to frown, unhappy that her opponent's volleys were not all hit right back to her in the warm-up. The girls were a bit like bees getting to know the shared space.

Suddenly I heard a loud, snapping sound—Ania's serve hitting the net cord. She hit her serve with such fine timing and power that the ball leaped back to no-man's-land on the fly. Her next practice serve boomed past D'Agostini and made the wire backstop jingle. Ania Bleszynski had a high service toss and the good easy wrist action and timing that could deliver bullets over and over again. Nervous as she was, Ania Bleszynski had a weapon.

"Ania served really well against me yesterday," said Nicole London, sitting down next to me in the stands.

But this match against a clay-court specialist was going to be a lot tougher. The California girl tried to follow deep approach shots into the net, but the Brazilian turned her back to the court, flipped her racket head at the ball at the last moment, and passed the tall American nearly every time she came in. The points got longer and longer. Fifteen- and twenty-shot rallies ended with one girl left stretching for an unreachable ball. They drove each other mercilessly from side to side. D'Agostini was as steady as Arantxa Sanchez-Vicaro. Her little smile could take the wind out of another girl's sails. Ania started grunting with every shot she played, the way Seles did but not quite as loudly. She was nervous. The day before against Nicole London, she had hardly grunted at all.

Ania reached break point on D'Agostini's serve in the first game but tensed up trying to guide a backhand down the line, pirouetting in disgust and swiping the air when she missed the great chance to break serve right away. Bleszynski looked like the better player, but D'Agostini had a wide variety of shots and paces. Ania shook her head when she lost the deuce point from the middle of the baseline. At ad-in, D'Agostini hit a spongy but very deep serve and a quick drop shot from midcourt that Ania slid at but could not reach. The little Brazilian smiled at her taller, American opponent as the girls changed ends.

Ania Bleszynski wanted to beat Miriam D'Agostini so badly it was making her appear hesitant. It looked almost as if she was afraid her body language might inadvertently reveal to D'Agostini exactly how much she wanted to beat her. But Ania was not leaning into the ball with the same assurance she had the day before against Nicole London. D'Agostini was like a mosquito. She was quick, quick, quick, always hurrying the bigger American girl, trying to minimize the Californian's power by keeping her on the move. Ania both hesitated and rushed. Serving at ad-out, she played a chip backhand approach shot up the line into D'Agostini's forehand over the highest part of the net and was immediately passed. Her serve got broken in her first service game. D'Agostini smiled over at her mother, her sisters, and her coach. She was up 2–0, then 3–0. Then 4–0, when Ania, serve and volleying well for three points, missed an easy high forehand volley on break point.

Ania Bleszynski's face was becoming red. She was down 4–0 to the Brazilian. She already looked self-conscious, and then the number one men's seed, Marcelo Rios, his jet-black hair pouring down his back, pulled a chair right behind the fence and put his feet up to watch the two girls from up close. Their skirts rose each time they served. Ania took a deep breath, trying to compose herself, trying to figure out how the points could be so close and the score so one-sided. The court was clay, D'Agostini's birth surface. Ania was accustomed to California hard courts, but I thought she still had in her the Eastern European temperament that seemed to take to clay as the surface on which much suffering and much patience pay off. But the American's size worked against her, as it did when players like Sampras, Becker, and Edberg tried to win the French Open. On clay, power is almost always a runner-up to mobility. Even Andre Agassi has struggled with the surface. Suddenly, impossibly, the first set was gone, 6–0.

Ania Bleszynski sat down in the striped plastic chair beside the umpire's tall green wooden chair and lay a towel loosely over her legs. D'Agostini had a little hand cloth with which she seemed to be brushing aside the few flecks of sweat that, much to her displeasure and surprise, seemed to have appeared near her hair despite the one-sided score.

It was like watching a river rise, and Ania Bleszynski was not the river this day. Her serve went way off. She tried to hit it harder and harder and forgot to cover the top of it so almost all of her first serves went long. D'Agostini was driving her opponent's increasingly tentative second serves into the corners or playing drop shots off them, lobbing over the tall American girl's head if she reached the drop shot. It was not all one-sided. Over and over again Ania would open up huge gaps of space on the court by attacking D'Agostini to the corners, but each time she went to put the ball away, she netted it or struck it long at the moment of truth.

It was a fascinating match to watch. Ania Bleszynski had been so consistent and dominant against Nicole London just the day before. But this was a different-sized opponent, a wetter, slower court, and a more pressured situation. The men and women pros are the ones who can keep their worst days in closer relationship to their best days. The Brazilian girl was grinding it out, and in the process she was able to split open the hard-courter from California. A gap I had not anticipated in her was widening. She was not yet one player but two, one very strong, one still fearful of losing.

D'Agostini was killing her now, up 3–0 in the second set. You could not tell Ania to play more aggressively. She had tried attacking but seemingly at all the wrong times. Cristina Moros and Stephanie Nickitas came by and stood briefly at the rear corner of the court as if to offer their compatriot encouragement. But when Ania lost her serve again and went down 4–0 in the second set, Stephanie Nickitas smiled knowingly and the two girls on the American team went off together. In a flash, Ania was down 5–0. The margin was stunning in view of the very slim difference in ability between the two.

"She played *so* well yesterday," said Nicole London.

"And she's going to lose love and love today." I was stunned, too.

"Whatever she's trying is just not working," said London.

"Sometimes," I said, "if you have to try things, you're in big trouble."

And then the quarterfinal match was over. Little Miriam D'Agostini threw her racket several stories into the bright blue sky and ran to the net as if she wanted to hug and befriend Ania Bleszynski forever for being such a wonderful, losing opponent. It was a Sanchez-Vicario–style move. Ania trotted up to the net reluctantly. She was still seven inches taller than D'Agostini, but she had lost, 6–0, 6–0. The only American girl in the quarterfinals was no longer in the tournament.

Ania Bleszynski went back to her change-over chair and stayed there for a moment, then quickly got up. She picked up her big red-and-white water jug and racket bag with six rackets and walked slowly across the court while in the corner nearest the entry gate D'Agostini was jumping for joy, hugging her mother and sisters on the court. A tennis tournament can be like a game of dominoes. The Brazilian's joy would be short-lived because Angeles Montolio, the freckled Spaniard who practiced regularly with Arantxa Sanchez-Vicario but had no junior record, would beat the Brazilian soundly the next round and win the Orange Bowl in three sets over the talented Canadian from Bombay, Sonya Jeyaseelan. But on this day D'Agostini was all joy. When Ania Bleszynski came off the court, almost everyone had already left the stands. I stayed and called her over.

"Listen, Ania," I said. "You played beautifully yesterday. You just weren't in it today. You wanted it too much. I shouldn't have talked to you last night."

"That's OK," she said, her ponytail sticking out the back of her red visor, her face still red and wet from the effort.

Here was a girl bright as hell. A seventeen-year-old who had been offered a full academic scholarship to Stanford for the following year. Moreover, Ania Bleszynski had gone one round farther in the Orange Bowl than any other American girl. So what happened next took me completely by surprise. Ania Bleszynski's lower lip started to tremble. Then her chin. She held on to the side of the stands. Her eyes filled up, and the overflow ran down her cheeks. Her face cracked, and I could feel her heart break right open. She had wanted to win that match and get on the American team. Ania Bleszynski was crying.

I didn't know what to do. I wanted to give her a hug but was afraid it could be misconstrued. She started to weep. Losing at its worst is a total rupture, like trust shattered, love lost, cruelty experienced, hope torn down like a childhood dream. Losing at its best can be a road to better days. "You got blown away," I said. "But so did Sampras playing Jonas Svenson on clay in Munich in 1990. He lost 6–0, 6–1 on the the slow clay. So wait for D'Agostini, get her on a hard court, and turn up the pace."

She exhaled deeply and finally smiled. "Thanks," she said. "I just wanted to win that match so much." She blew air out through her mouth. Her face was a mess of tears. "I've got to go change my plane ticket."

On the bus back to the hotel, she stared straight ahead, sipping deeply from her water jug as if trying to keep herself so full of water she would not cry again.

"Was that your worst loss ever?" I asked.

She nodded.

"Good," I said cheerfully. "It can't get any worse. Remember what this feels like and *never* let it happen again."

Ania Bleszynski looked at me, and a big smile started to form—until she started to feel embarrassed again.

I knew she had the hand-eye skills. She could become a very good player, even a pro, if she so desired. I was not bothered by the scores. The South American girls seemed to grow into their bodies before most of the American and European girls did. Ania, I hoped, had stopped growing; the Brazilian had looked and moved as if she had not grown an inch in several years.

The South Americans and Spaniards had dominated in Miami on the Orange Bowl clay. Paul Goldstein and Scott Humphries had both lost early. But the young American juniors were all becoming more international as players and as people, and that was not a bad thing to become.

Two weeks after Ania Bleszynski played so well to reach the quarterfinals of the Orange Bowl, I called her to find out if she had recovered completely from the loss. Her parents' phone doubled as a fax machine and an answering machine. Ania picked up the phone at eight in the morning, California time. Her voice sounded upbeat and bright. The young seem to recover easily. She had gone for her biweekly lesson with Robert Lansdorp.

"And what did Lansdorp tell you about the loss to the Brazilian girl?" I asked.

The tall California star hesitated a second. Her voice was high. "He said, 'OK, Ania. You had a car wreck. Now climb out of it.' "

THE SHADOW LINE

It is the privilege of early youth to live in advance of its days in
all the beautiful continuity of hope which knows no pauses and
introspection. One goes on recognizing the landmarks of the
predecessors. . . . And the time, too, goes on—till one per-
ceives ahead a shadow-line warning one that the region of early
youth, too, must be left behind.

—Joseph Conrad, *The Shadow Line*

There is a magic to a champion's time, and the odd thing is that
champions rarely know when it is going to come or finish. The great
tennis figures—John McEnroe, Boris Becker, and Stefan Edberg qualify, as will the next half-generation of Pete Sampras and Andre
Agassi—have an aura about them that will continue to glow in our
imagination long after they are finished as players. Some champions,
like McEnroe and Bjorn Borg, do not realize what it is they have until
they no longer have it. McEnroe went down into the cocoon of his
talent a dozen times or more. Eleven times he emerged like a brilliant
orange-and-black butterfly. The twelfth time he came out a moth: his
time was done, and he knew it.

Age claimed Don Budge's skills just as Bobby Riggs was waiting in
the wings for him. Jack Kramer got injured early enough in his career
never to have to face the long, slow eroding process. Ken Rosewall,
who won the French Open in 1953 and 1968, could not get by
twenty-two-year-old Jimmy Connors in the 1974 Wimbledon final at
age thirty-nine. Every champion eventually meets his nemesis in a
younger player. The years themselves may be the toughest opponent
to beat back.

Pancho Gonzalez was probably the most remarkable player at stem-
ming the tide of time. At age forty-one in 1969, he defeated Charlie

Pasarell, the former U.S. number one amateur, saving seven match points on grass at Wimbledon en route to a 22–24, 1–6, 16–14, 6–3, 11–9, five-hour-and-twelve-minute victory. Now that's a well-cooked bird. Rod Laver at thirty-seven won three tour events, including the 1975 WCT Classic in Orlando over twenty-one-year-old Vitas Gerulaitas. Gardnar Mulloy reached the final of Forest Hills when he was thirty-eight. Martina Navratilova reached the 1994 Wimbledon final at age thirty-seven. Connors reached the U.S. Open semi-final in 1991 at thirty-nine, and he played with a joyous capacity that had the fans leaping to their feet up in the stands. And Bill Tilden, the ultimate boy in a man's body, was still playing the U.S. Pro Championships in Cleveland in his fifties.

These players all managed to keep something of the child alive inside them. True champions are insatiable questers. But their amazing gifts of body and heart rarely make personal relationships easier. Pancho Gonzales was married six times. Martina Navratilova struggled similarly with the distinction many athletes fail to make between love and attention. There has always been a difference between maturity on the court and off it, and age does not always change that aspect of the life-spirit.

Stefan Edberg was slightly different. Edberg always struck me as a young, Nordic Gary Cooper: shy, tough, good-looking, and able to get the job done nearly every time with seeming ease where others gave off lots of tension. John McEnroe had classic tennis skills marred by a Bruce Willis personality. For a long while that combination passed for charisma. Boris Becker had charisma, but he lost it when his personality became more insistent and his game turned too far inward as he lost his boyhood charm and powerful innocence through too much repetition. Andre Agassi now has that magic brightness around him like a light, but the Nevadan charisma is still a lot like flashing neon: great fun in small doses. Stefan Edberg's charisma, equally unthreatening, was always subtle, and it took me longer to recognize Edberg's greatness.

The first time Edberg won the U.S. Open in 1991, I thought it was a fluke—until the end when he played one of the most brilliant, one-sided finals of all time. Up against a dogged but not yet fully mature Jim Courier, Edberg swooped down on the net, volleying winners from incredible positions, and won the U.S. Open final 6–2, 6–4, 6–0. I have never seen anyone right-handed, not even Gonzalez, and only Laver and McEnroe among left-handers, close in on top of the net the way Edberg did behind his serve that day. Edberg made Courier—who was just five months away from becoming the number-one player in the world—look like a child playing against a man. The Swede moved like the late Alexander Godunov, the Russian ballet star. Even McEnroe in his prime did not cover the top of the net the way Stefan Edberg did that day. Each volley Edberg hit against Courier seemed to bite the court and glide away.

The next year in the 1992 U.S. Open Final, Stefan Edberg stopped a mildly ill Pete Sampras in Sampras's own highly artistic tracks 3–6, 6–4, 7–6, 6–2 with a perfect blend of speed, elasticity, power and balance.

The town of Västervik faces Finland and the cold winters that blow across the waters. Though isolated on the Swedish coast, the towns-people are gracious and polite, in much the same way Stefan Edberg was on court. The larger homes, which used to belong to the sea captains, sit high on the sharply sloping hill that looks down a narrow main street all the way to the water. A dust-red church with striking minarets occupies the highest point of land. In summer, the crowds arrive for the art festival. In the seven-month-long winter, the town is left to itself. The physical beauty of the town—the clear, quiet blue sky in summer evenings, the fjords which turn to solid ice during winter—is charming to the outsider but ultimately of no help to the resident. Many of the young shrugged when they spoke of the local economy and their future. Edberg's father, Bengt, was a police detective; his mother, Barbro, who taught him to play tennis, had raised her children and taught school. They divorced when Edberg was already a Wimbledon champion.

Like many small-town people with major talents, Stefan Edberg left home and rarely returned initially. But he remained a local hero. All the working people in town—the cabdriver, the hotel receptionist who told me where I could find a bargain on smoked salmon on open-fire-charred toast, the Mexican woman serving tacos in Västervik's all-night Mexican take-out restaurant down by the port—everybody remembered and liked Stefan Edberg. He was from modest roots, and he managed to remain so, a feat all the more remarkable when you consider that he had earned more then sixteen million dollars in career earnings—a movie star's wage. On the court, Edberg consistently exhibited that rare combination of skill, perfect movement, and gentle self-effacement that I had not seen since the days of Ken Rosewall, the great Australian.

Boris Becker could have married almost any woman in Germany; he chose instead to marry a beautiful, intelligent black woman and raise a multiracial child. It is hard to fight battles on and off the court at the same time. Less complicated or less imaginative than Becker, depending on one's point of view, Stefan Edberg saved his psychic energy. He married Annette Olsen, who came from the equally small town of Vaxjo, the next stop inland on the single-track train line through the soft, hanging pine trees. Becker chose to escape his past; Edberg chose to marry his.

Edberg's finest inner attribute as an athlete was his resilience. He never quit or tanked a match, as even Ivan Lendl did on occasion. Edberg's greatest victories often came on the heels of bitter disappointments. In 1990, he lost to Alexander Volkov in the first round of the U.S. Open; in 1991 and 1992 he won the tournament. He was crushed by Becker in the 1989 Wimbledon final; in 1990, down 3–1 in the fifth set to Becker, he came back to win it 6–4 and become the Wimbledon Champion for the second time. Many people thought that Becker's early Wimbledon victory was to be part of a long Boris Becker era, just as many felt John McEnroe would reign as champion for ten years when he beat Borg in 1980. But tennis time does not work that way. A generation of tennis players now lasts five to seven years, rarely ten. That Edberg had ranked in the top five in the world for nine straight years was no small feat.

The late Arthur Ashe, who won the U.S. Open in 1968 and Wimbledon over Jimmy Connors in 1975 when Ashe was thirty-two, used to admire Edberg greatly. They had the same quiet mien and grace under pressure. Like Edberg, Ashe used to be able to close down on the net for a volley with such ease that the movement looked effortless. But Stefan Edberg was even faster and firmer on the volley. Edberg's victories over Courier and Sampras in back-to-back U.S Open finals were incredible displays of grace that confirmed that movement, not power, is the real key to domination in sport.

Great players have a way of surviving a few more seasons once they've been at the top. Stefan Edberg had been faithful to his profession by keeping himself in terrific shape. But in tennis the pressures of time and travel have intensified over the years. In 1974, the average age of a player in the top ten was just over twenty-nine years old; by 1994, it was twenty-three. And Stefan Edberg was just turning twenty-eight.

Stefan Edberg's angular Swedish face was tanned buttery and handsome by the intense January summer sun in Australia. His legs looked incredibly sculpted though somewhat thicker than in previous years, as if he had spent a month on an exercise bicycle in his flat in London building up his legs for the new season. Edberg's hair was not as blond as it would be by the end of the American season. He walked slowly out onto center court at Flinders Park with his side-to-side gait, taking his time, moving with the familiar easy-natured grace that had brought him six grand-slam singles titles.

"I'd have to say that Todd Martin is the underdog by a wide margin," Fred Stolle said in the television booth to Cliff Drysdale. I agreed.

Todd Martin was on a high plateau of consistency, as yet unable to launch himself up into the very top rankings where talent and perseverance mix like rocket fuel. At six foot six, he was as tall as Jesse Willard but not as immobile as the old boxing great. Martin's head was enormous, and he had a long, narrow face under fiercely thick eyebrows. He was not a natural mover, but he had taught himself to cover the court and seemed to make up in wingspan what Edberg had in natural movement. Strong, earnest, and patient, Todd Martin had told me that the toughest thing for him about coming out on the pro tour after two years of college at Northwestern University was breaking up with the woman he had wanted to marry. She had given him an ultimatum back in Illinois. Stay in college and stay with her, or run away to join the circus, the pro tennis circuit. Todd Martin still seemed hurt when he talked about her. But despite his conservative looks and modest manner, he had left college for the uncertainty of the tennis tour.

Martin had risen very quickly at first, going from number 501 to 252 in just two weeks, but then he progressed more slowly than his American contemporaries, Pete Sampras, Andre Agassi, and Jim Courier. Todd Martin was poised to play the most important match of his career, and all the pressure was on him. He had lost four of five ATP tour finals the year before. He had to somehow overcome the fear of losing. As Bill Tilden wrote in his wonderful chapter "Match Play and Tennis Psychology" in *How to Play Better Tennis*, "Once more the specter of fear is haunting him. Many younger players take years trying to overcome this, and their progress is retarded. If they do not rise above it, they never become real players."

Martin, seeded ninth, looked edgy in the warm-up. Stefan Edberg, seeded fourth, was more relaxed; he won the first set of the Australian Open semifinal almost casually, 6–3. It was as if his younger American opponent had not yet understood or reached Edberg's level of play. Todd Martin tried to assert himself, but he seemed to defer to Edberg like a younger brother stuck in the admiration of an older brother. In tennis, those kinds of odd brotherly and sisterly relationships remain as hard to overcome as they do in actual families. Martin simply did not seem to possess the self-confidence or talent to do the job against this older opponent.

And yet there was no quit in the taller man. Todd Martin's long, oddly handsome face was flush-red from the sun, and he looked lean, willing, and healthy with all the hard work. There was something of Abraham Lincoln's build and determination in the Michigan player.

Suddenly, odd things began to happen to Edberg. It looked like the same car, but the air seemed to be going out of one of his tires. He suddenly seemed to have trouble changing directions. The pace went out of his serve, and Martin started to read its direction and hammer it back at will as if Edberg were somehow tipping off its location as he delivered it. I had never before seen Stefan Edberg look so awkward. The second set was still very close, but Martin took it 7–6, (9–7). Todd Martin stared down as he toweled off, wondering if it had been a fluke or the start of a victory. Edberg, who had squandered a great chance to go up by two sets, remained calm as a poker player, showing no disappointment at all.

That was the Edberg I knew and admired. I had seen him play and lose hard sets, then brush them off like a fly from his shoulder. And yet, midway through the third set, Edberg was puffing. I had never seen him do that before, not even in the fifth set against Becker at Wimbledon. Deep in the heat of the battle, Edberg no longer looked young or cherubic. After all those years of looking younger than he was, he suddenly looked his age or older. His eyes and mouth showed lines of pain and effort. Edberg's white shirt with plain checks straight across the shoulders seemed odd, as if designed for a younger player. Todd Martin wore all white and looked every inch a young giant.

Stefan Edberg squinted across the net at Martin. Whereas McEnroe and Connors would burst forth in displays of determination and angst, Edberg and Mats Wilander merely narrowed their eyes like cats and dug in deeper. To beat someone, it is usually necessary to beat that individual first at his or her own game before imposing one's own strengths. At 3–all in the third set, Edberg stopped serve and volleying, hung back, and outrallied Martin from the baseline. At 4–3, he came to the net, angled a volley, filled the possible cross-court with his body, leaving Martin just the opening up the line, which Edberg closed down as quickly as Martin, running the diagonal, blasted the ball up the line into the alley. The Swedes in the crowd, their chests painted blue and gold, cheered and waved their flags. Stefan Edberg led 5–3 in the third set.

Suddenly something happened. In retrospect, it was like watching two athletic lives in the process of change. There was a string of nine points, and Todd Martin won them all and went from 3–5 down to 5–all, 15–0. Six points had come on outright winners. By the time Edberg could regain his balance, they were in a tiebreaker. Again the Swede started fast. He went up 2–0, then 4–2 with a classic Edberg backhand volley, racket head high, punched on the run into the open court. They had played for two hours and thirty-three minutes in the Australian sun, and the match again seemed to be Edberg's. But Todd Martin exploded. He hit two unreturnable serves and two great returns of serve, led the tiebreaker 6–4, set point, and held on to take the third set by the identical score as the second set, 7–6 (9–7). This was more serious. What was wrong with Stefan Edberg? He had led the set 5–3 and served for it at 5–4 but lost his serve at love. Edberg, down two sets to one, shook his head and looked perplexed himself.

The fourth set was as good as a championship boxing match. Edberg was experienced, and his ability to come back from the brink of defeat was legend. He did not know much about losing close matches. It was his opponents who always seemed to snatch defeat from the jaws of victory. The year before, though Edberg got in only 64 percent of his first serves, he survived 334 break points or ad-out's. I once had seen Edberg overcome six match points to beat Jakob Hlasek at the Lipton. He knew how to play on the very edge. But now Todd Martin led the fourth set 5–3.

Edberg aced Martin wide on the forehand side, kicked the next serve up into Martin's chin, and drilled a low volley winner that he punctuated with three staccato little steps that left him looking down from on top of the net for a return that never came. It was Edberg's signature, post-winning-volley trot. The last point of Edberg's beautiful service game, held at love while down 3–5, was a backhand overhead smash into the open court. It was like a game of cards. Now it was Todd Martin's turn to bid and make the hand.

The younger player had to hold his serve to win the match. The year before, Martin had reached five winning once, ATP finals, a great accomplishment, but not if you want to become a champion. Martin lost to Courier in Memphis, Lendl in Tokyo, Amos Mansdorf in Washington D.C., and Michael Pernfors in Montreal, the last three of which were matches he was favored to win. There is no harder step in sport than winning the big one when you are expected to do it. I could almost see the faces of Courier, Mansdorf, Pernfors, Lendl, smiling at Martin from inside his head as he prepared to serve for the match against Stefan Edberg. And then I recalled Martin losing to Richard Krajicek at the U.S. Open in five hours and ten minutes by serving a double fault on match point. I winced as Stefan Edberg broke Todd Martin at 4–5, forcing a fourth-set tiebreaker.

A player with less fortitude than Martin might have crumbled right there, but it was Edberg who opened the tiebreaker strangely. He served a foot fault, a double fault, and then fell behind 0–4 and 1–5. Something beautiful inside Edberg was dying out there in the perfect Australian sun. And worst of all, he could not fathom it. Edberg had always been able to impose his serve-and-volley game and speed over less coordinated opponents like Martin, who in his worst moments moved like an oil derrick on wheels. But now Edberg shook his head. He was in big trouble, down 1–6 in the fourth-set tiebreaker. Things did not look good—even for Stefan Edberg.

Yet there is always hope in a tennis match. For a younger player, the last point is excruciatingly hard to win. For Todd Martin, it was like going west as a prospector and running into the Grand Canyon before there were bridges. Despite being up five match points, Todd Martin showed the signs of tension and fatigue in his body. The match was already four hours long, and now Martin began to lose match points. I was rooting for Edberg, but I felt terrible for Todd Martin. Now every bet he made was wrong. He missed a two-handed backhand return of serve by hitting it too hard. He lost the next match point by trying to carefully just redirect an Edberg serve up the line. The reply fell halfway up the net.

Edberg was cautious, respectful, but not fearful. He raised his head and looked over the net to consider the younger man. He could tell that his opponent was confused, and he nodded to Martin that he was ready for the next serve. Like a younger brother desperate to prove he can win, too, Martin belted a big serve, raced in behind it, and played a high forehand volley that made the ball crack the center of the net cord and fly crazily at a right angle out into the alley. As if afraid to disturb his opponent's misery, Stefan Edberg unobtrusively swept the errant ball along the ground to nearest ball boy. Todd Martin had lost three match points in a row.

Martin bounced the ball twice before serving. He had just one more serve in the tiebreaker. For one moment on the baseline Todd Martin looked up across the net at the player who had been his hero. And then, hanging on the precipice of victory or defeat, he reached back and served up the middle of the court. Stefan Edberg, as if shot in the back, spun after the ace in vain.

Todd Martin waved his clenched racket in triumph. Suddenly he had arrived, and he would never look back, never feel the same undermining degree of tension in a big match.

Stefan Edberg's mouth fell open in disbelief. Great players are always stunned when they lose. Winning has become second nature to them, like eating a good breakfast. Losing is mostly performed by others. This loss hurt. It seemed so avoidable. Edberg turned his head sideways and reluctantly came up to the net as if some referee had stopped the contest too quickly. Smiling, the Swede nodded and gently touched Todd Martin on the shoulder. As Todd Martin stood to accept the crowd's thunderous cheers, Stefan Edberg sat down, still not sure why he had lost. It was an unthinkable defeat. Todd Martin was a good player, but Edberg's face seemed to ask, "How could I ever have lost to someone that slow? What is wrong with me?"

Stefan Edberg leaned back in his chair for a moment and stared straight ahead as if he could see across the Yarra River. Only the greedy and the masterful expect to win every time. Edberg, like Rosewall, was masterful. The great ones from Gonzalez to Thomas Muster are stingy with a win. Going down to defeat has so many faces it is almost like watching sex. McEnroe would have screamed in pain. Jimmy Connors would have started to joke with someone in the crowd to try to upset Martin in the tiebreakers. Lendl might have defaulted in the fourth set and thus denied the loss. Boris Becker would have roared like a wounded bear and blamed himself too deeply. Stefan Edberg, red Wilson racket bags over both shoulders, left the court quietly, almost embarrassed, as if the Swedish policeman's son had been caught in a high-speed chase.

Upsets happen all the time. A great player can lose to a lesser player when the star is playing just 10 to 15 percent below his normal game and the opponent is really "on." But I was not so sure the loss to Todd Martin had been an upset. I thought perhaps it was due to the passage of time. But Edberg was a hero of mine. I comforted myself with the thought that on pure ability there were still only two players in the world I was convinced he had no chance of beating with any regularity.

Andre Agassi had always been a tough match for the Swede, because the Nevadan's great return of serve was a shade better than Edberg's serve itself. As a result, against Agassi as against no one else, Edberg was always a half step behind where he wanted to be. Pete Sampras had also passed Edberg. The Swede and the fluid Californian he had beaten in the past were like seamless stages from the same serve-and-volley rocket. Edberg rarely played Becker anymore—they were usually on opposite sides of the same draw. Courier passed Edberg temporarily and reached number one in the world rankings. But the Floridian, like a boxer without a knockout punch, had had to give too much to win each match; after several years of getting to the top, Courier was now so mentally and physically tired he was starting to slide back down the mountain. Michael Stich was extraordinarily talented but prone to fits of Germanic pique. Michael Chang was incredibly agile and always tenacious, but when Stefan Edberg was playing like he was capable of playing, he always had Chang's number. The shadowline I had seen in his match in Australia seemed to fade like a sunset on a watery horizon.

Bob Brett is a short, pale, sleekly blond Australian who has a well-deserved reputation as one of the best tennis coaches in the world. Brett was never a champion himself, but champions rarely make great coaches because they have done it all themselves and really want no more. Indeed, the finest coaches often turn out to be good ex-players still looking for perfection in themselves or in an alter ego. Bob Brett was from the old-fashioned Australian coaching tradition that believes a hard body makes a creative mind. I went to Bob Brett instead of Edberg's own coach of eleven years, Tony Pickard, to talk about Edberg because Pickard was deeply, impossibly loyal. Bob Brett had the necessary distance, having tried to attack Edberg first as Boris Becker's coach and now with the talented, temperamental Goran Ivanisevic.

"Longevity has been there for Stefan," began Brett. "He didn't have suspensions the way McEnroe did. John had so much interrupted time."

"But Stefan is twenty-eight now. Do you see a little of the aging process creeping in?"

"I saw it creeping in before," said Brett. "Stefan has started to fall apart a bit—mostly in his concentration."

"It's odd how the concentration seems to go almost before the legs," I said. "It's like they have been in big situations so many times and come out of them so many times that suddenly one day the well is dry."

"That's exactly what happens," said Brett, brightening. "All of a sudden you're a fraction from what you used to be. You're volleying up instead of down. Your first serve loses a little sting on it, and you try to overcompensate on your second ball. Those are the first signs of an aging player, but most people just think and say, 'Oh, well, Edberg's just not playing well.' In fact, he may still be playing as well as he possibly can. Then a year or two later, people see it and say, 'Yes. He's older.' But the process has been going on for some time. Competitive life is a short life, really." Brett nodded, and I thought he was now thinking of Ivanisevic. "A tennis career can be over before you know it unless you maximize it very consciously. And that's what Stefan has done better than almost anybody. He's been consistently brilliant." Brett smiled. "That's not easy."

"Does it happen often at the end of careers that the older player is still better than the other player but just can no longer *beat* the younger player?"

"Right," said Brett, nodding his head. "It comes down to a little bit of self-doubt, to being just a fraction slower, maybe not seeing the ball—hesitating—because they aren't seeing the ball quite the same way. That's the telltale sign, really, that hesitation on the volley, that split second of doubt, instead of just going with the ball."

"When you play a younger player, is there something you can do to try to compensate, to try to get through a match you think you should win?"

Brett smiled, having been through the wars himself. "Well, what happens is you end up gaining so much experience until you become too old to take advantage of it. You can even be hitting the ball better, but maybe you're not winning the points. Maybe you get into a 30–40 situation and you miss an easy volley, the type of thing you just can't afford to do. Maybe when Stefan was at the very top, he'd miss it and it would not matter. But maybe not. Now those kind of relatively routine but important points are causing Stefan to lose matches he used to win."

"It seemed to me," I said, "that Edberg actually played better than Sampras at Indian Wells. Sampras said as much after the match. Pete was a little off, except on one thing—his serve. Sampras was serving so well it got him through all Edberg's break points."

Brett smiled, as if thinking of young Becker's serve. "It's being able to really crack it." Brett paused in reflection. "You know, the temptation for a lot of people today is to talk disparagingly about the younger generation and say, 'It's not tennis anymore.' It *is* tennis. People just have to realize that when they were twenty, they were doing the same things to the older players back then."

"Pace kills," I said with a smile. "But how can a player like Edberg keep himself together and stay mentally refreshed?"

"The only way to do that is by being physically superior. You need to take breaks during the year when you go and just work on your physical condition. They *all* forget to do that. You need about a week of complete downtime and another ten days of hard physical work on court and off. That's seventeen days off the tour. Funnily enough, that's what really clears your mind and builds your confidence."

Brett's prescription was basic. So many fine athletes run afoul of themselves later in life because they forget the importance of staying physically fit. After all those years in which their bodies were tuned like fine engines, they ignore the physical call that will forever be a part of their nature, like a bird's need to fly or a deer's need to run. The overweight former athlete is like an abandoned child: the worse the carcass, the deeper the fall from grace. If you're a fit player, you're a happy player, no matter how much your skills may have diminished; in a sense, by staying fit you have remained loyal to the deepest truth inside yourself. It was that same inner loyalty—call it professionalism in an active player—that I admired so much in Stefan Edberg. Gross excess weight in the stars of yesteryear is not so much a sign of age as a sign of unrequited competitiveness and personal disappointment bordering on self-hate. I turned back to Bob Brett, who had kept himself almost as fit as Tony Roche.

"Every player," said Bob Brett with a coach's slow, thoughtful manner, "every player has some things that are easy to overcome and things that are really difficult to overcome. Everyone has them."

I nodded. "That's the beauty of tennis, isn't it? The other side tries to isolate in you the things you are worst at, and you keep trying to show the world your better side."

"That's why in coaching you have to know the individual. Coaching is just so . . . so personal. If you can't understand the individual, you can never really be of service to his or her game. As a coach you really have to know a player at least as well as he knows himself. Because a player can be insistent and persistent and still make no progress."

"Ivanisevic," I said, perhaps a bit too bluntly for Brett's taste.

"You said that," the Australian said. "What I mean, really, is that each person comes to the battle with a body and a mind all their own. For instance, Boris. He's heavier set than Goran. So to give him the same sort of work as Goran would be a mistake."

"On the other hand, Boris is heavier muscled," I said. "And when your legs are built more like those of Pat Cash or Becker, you have to be prepared to really run a lot in training to make those legs light as well as powerful. You are going to have to do some things you don't like to do. If you're Becker, maybe you have to run some long distances when maybe he would rather just run up stadium steps. And Goran is probably the reverse. But, really, you have to spend most of your time practicing the opposite of what you are good at."

"Yeah," said Brett. "That's right."

"And I think the reluctance to do that on Boris's part after a while reflects what changed in him as a person."

Brett nodded. "Of course. Everyone is reluctant to do what they're not good at. But in terms of *composure*, it's important that you understand the capabilities of the individual. It is virtually impossible to send someone like Boris on a ten-mile run. You have to look at their assets when you have them. I try to find a compromise between what they like to do in a workout or practice and what they don't like to do."

There is an aspect of horse training to all human sports. Coaching itself had changed. Harry Hopman was a fitness fanatic, and Laver, Emerson, and the other Australian players were his beneficiaries. Some coaches are pals, some taskmasters. Mercer Beasley, the non-playing but famous coach of Ellsworth Vines and Frankie Parker in the 1930s, left me with the impression that some coaches get to be like bad barbers who cut everybody's hair the same way. Beasley, a smoker, wrote in his book for the basic player, *How to Play Tennis,* "Do not indulge in intoxicating liquors during your training period. Refrain from drinking water during the course of a match. A slightly cooled glass of pure orange juice or grapefruit juice is best for you," and, "If you must smoke, make it a definite rule never to smoke in your tennis clothes." Beasley's book now seemed basically wrong in many sections, but both Vines and Frankie Parker had sworn by him and won. Believing in a coach is still as important as anything a coach may say. I listened with great interest. Bob Brett was like a chief mechanic who worked exclusively on repairing Grand Prix cars.

"What about Goran Ivanisevic? What does he like to do and what not?"

"It goes back to what makes you comfortable," said Brett. "Australian players in the past used to spend twenty or thirty minutes straight up at net. They just liked it there, whereas the European players for the most part still tend to spend just five minutes at the net, if that. The tendencies are all there in their practices."

"You were trying to slow Goran down on his serve in practice. It was quite beautiful to watch you work. You didn't say anything, but you were about ten feet behind him, and whenever he needed another ball, you just tossed it to him overhand on one bounce but very slowly, and Goran began to get the message. He started to slow down his motion, and he found his rhythm and improved his pace."

Brett smiled. "You noticed?"

"Absolutely. You were just trying to say something to him about his rhythm without saying anything verbally, because Goran doesn't take too kindly to criticism, I suspect, even when he's paying for it. I'm interested."

"Goran is the kind of player who would much rather rush than take his time. Even in warm-up, he'd like to hit for five minutes and play a set."

"And finish the set in twenty-two minutes."

Brett laughed. "It's not that he's wrong. But the coach provides eyes and ears for what you're doing. Often . . . [the players] are so far *in* it that they can't see it themselves."

Brett nodded, and so did I. Bob Brett coached champions, and he had just defined what all great coaching was.

"But," said Brett, "in another sense, a coach can be dangerous, because a coach may try to exert too much control and the player will rely on him to such an extent that he or she stops thinking for himself or herself—and that's no good either. Then you come to areas when they are playing to the best of their physical abilities, and that's another stage in the development of a player, because then you have to think of what to do to improve performance. Sometimes it comes down to mental things, sometimes to an additional physical thing. Maybe you need to be stronger, maybe to move better. At that stage, to improve just a little bit when you are near your peak takes an enormous amount of extra work and concentration, and some players find, consciously or not, that it's just not worth it for them. Those players hit their plateau and eventually slide down the other side.

"The thing that's most important is that not only is the coach looking for it but the player is also looking to discover what it is that's missing. That's where you go to find out about yourself. That is where a player like Lendl was so good. And it's one of the reasons Lendl survived in the game so long. You always had the impression that Lendl, who was less talented than McEnroe and Connors, was always looking for some way to improve. He wasn't popular, but check his records against McEnroe and Connors. He had the obsession."

"What are the final stages of a player's development?"

"The first thing is that they go up in the rankings. That's what often happens. And then something happens, an injury or a bad patch, and they drop down in the rankings. *That* is when you have to learn how to play tennis. You have to learn why you fell. Then they motivate, go up again playing well, get almost to that same position." Brett smiled. "And then something happens again."

He made it sound so brutal, so arbitrary, so uncontrollable, and yet somehow so magical, as if in competition you could joust among the planets and the stars.

"The first time you make a mistake and go down is acceptable. But the second time it happens the reason for it happening is often very similar. That's a problem. The second time you must know why and correct it, or in all likelihood you will not advance again."

"It's that dramatic."

"Yes. And it's mental, but so powerfully mental that a lot of times I think it can actually induce a physical injury." Bob Brett nodded. "As they get further along in their career, and unfortunately sooner or later it happens to all of them—McEnroe, Lendl, even Edberg—as they start to lose a few matches, they start to have doubts. They don't talk about it, but it's in their subconscious and eventually their conscience, and *that* is when they begin to think about retirement. The higher they are, the better they are able to deal with it. But all the same, serving at 30–40, they double-fault. They did not do that before. They've become afraid of what the other guy is going to do. It's not just mechanics. They get afraid that their next shot is not going to be good enough."

"Then they need time off to develop again."

"Right," said Brett. "The other factor is that these are kids becoming people. And it doesn't always happen easily. Some coaches want that dependence from their player—they even try to prolong it."

"The way Bollettieri was with Agassi?"

Brett shook his head. "I just said, 'Some coaches thrive on dependence.' "

"That's what I liked about Brad Gilbert and Jay Berger. They had good coaching, but they also knew what to do on court for themselves. When I see a player always glancing over to a coach during a match, I know I'm still looking at a child."

"That's right," said Brett. "The money is not a factor with most players until the end of their careers. I mean, if ten thousand dollars was top prize in 1968, and it was one hundred thousand dollars in 1978, and five hundred thousand dollars today, the number, whatever it was, was always the top prize. It didn't affect the champions one bit. Laver or Connors would have gone out and played you for five dollars. They had that fight in them. The danger of money only really comes in toward the end of their careers, when they're just trying to bring in a few more good paydays." Bob Brett nodded. "The real danger is always when your dreams are forgotten."

"At the end, the dreams are forgotten—or can be," I said, thinking back on Borg, McEnroe, Lendl, and even Connors. I wondered if the dream was still alive in Stefan Edberg.

"In anything, if the dream ends," said Bob Brett, "that's the very end of all the levels we've been talking about."

We smiled and shook hands, both still believers in the dream. And I was still a believer in Stefan Edberg.

A LATE NIGHT IN PHILADELPHIA

Jonathan Stark's quarterfinal match against Michael Chang in the 1994 U.S. Pro Indoors in Philadelphia did not start until 10:30 P.M. Echoes of Bobby Clarke's slap shot and visions of his toothless Stanley Cup smile were forever a part of the Spectrum's vast interior. The single blue tennis court sat over the ice rink, and the hushed sounds of tennis balls bouncing off the carpet rose up into the orange, steeply banked seats. One taut tennis net had replaced the loose-fitting hockey goals. By the time Stark started, I had traded in my press box vantage point for a far corner of the front row next to nobody. It was a great seat.

I was all excited. Stark had been playing very well since his U.S. Open loss to Volkov. In Bolzano, Italy, he won the tournament, defeating the 1993 U.S. Open finalist Cedric Pioline in the finals. "Pioline gets mad," Stark had told me by phone when discussing the handsome, dark-haired Frenchman with the formidable topspin backhand and forehand. "I attack him a lot, and that kind of pisses Pioline off. He likes to stay on the baseline and roll over a lot of balls. He tries to get in a groove and dictate play like that. Pioline likes to be real flowing out there. But I sense he doesn't like me coming in on him a lot on my serve. I make sure we have shorter rallies, and that seems to get Pioline really frustrated, at least against me." Stark's win over Pioline was his first tournament win on the ATP Tour, and he had lost only one set the whole week. His ranking rose to number forty-four in the world. And he earned $42,000 for the effort.

As the new year began and Stark flew toward Australia, he played in the Hawaii Open and reached the semifinals, defeating the up-and-coming Alex O'Brien in the first round and the aging war horse, Brad Gilbert in the quarterfinals, 7–6, 7–6. Gilbert used to win matches like that even a year or two before, especially against David Wheaton, but Stark simply served too well in the tiebreakers for the thirty-two-year-old. Gilbert, a master of competitive psychology rather than understatement, said, "Losing sucks. Anytime, anyplace, anywhere. It doesn't get any easier as you get older." Asked if his one-hour training sessions were enough, Gilbert snapped, "I figure if I haven't learned it by now, I may as well forget it."

Not twenty-three until April, Jonathan Stark continued his streak into the semifinals where he played the number-one seed, Wayne Ferreira of South Africa. He almost beat the freckle-faced world-top-twenty player but lost 4–6, 6–4, 6–4.

In Australia, Stark again played well but lost to the talented Paul Haarhuis, who had been given his own baptism by fire three years before on center court at the U.S. Open by Jimmy Connors. But Stark reached the final of the Australian Open in doubles with his short but fiery partner, Byron Black of Zimbabwe. Black was the set-up man with lightning fast hands; Stark was the big, easygoing gun of the team. Stark earned a cool $25,000 for his share of the doubles prize, plus $11,200 for the second-round singles loss. He and Black hardly had time to share a pint of Foster's Lager before they were back on the road again.

Stark was young, the world was small, and his potential still seemed limitless. The tour was going so well for Stark that he wanted to play every event he could. Playing well, with the potential prize money that good, makes it hard to resist going to the next event. However, Stark's coach, Larry Stefanki, who had coached John McEnroe, wanted Stark to take a break after Australia and come train in Palm Desert to get his mind and body fresh and honed for the beginning of the American season. Eager to earn, Jonathan Stark disagreed with Stefanki—the first but not the last time that season that player and coach would disagree. But in tennis, unlike baseball or football, it is the coach who takes orders from and gets paid by the player.

The day after Stark flew back from Australia, he played the tournament in San Jose, California. There he lost to Jeff Tarango, a former Stanford star, a tough journeyman with a quirky disposition, a difficult left-handed serve and prior knowledge of what Stark did not like on court. Stark's loss to Tarango was his worst loss in months. But Stark was insatiable. He took no time off, and flew from San Jose to Memphis, which each year is one of the most popular stops on the tour because of the huge old-fashioned gala ball for the players and the town's leading lights. On the court, Stark again drew Paul Haarhuis, who had defeated him in Australia. The result was the same but the scores were closer, 7–6, 4–6, 6–4. Stark and Byron Black won the doubles over Jim Grabb and Jared Palmer. One of the strange aspects of the tour was the luck of the draw. In singles, Stark kept meeting Pioline and Haarhuis. They got to know each other like cousins who quarrel.

Stark had traveled the tennis highway for seven straight weeks, going from Hawaii to Australia to San Jose to Memphis. He was a bit tired by the time he pulled into Philadelphia. His first-round match in the Philadelphia Spectrum was against Italy's Stefano Pescosolido, a relatively unknown but hard-serving former Junior Orange Bowl finalist who as a pro had twice defeated Michael Chang. Stark beat Pescosolido 7–6, 7–6.

"Did you sense Pescosolido getting tighter than you in the breakers?" I asked Stark later.

"I did," Stark said. "So many matches seem to come down to how you play in the tiebreakers. He's a very good player, kind of streaky, but he's got a huge serve, and he was putting it in. We were both 'on' with our serves. In the two tiebreakers, I just seemed to have the better shots. Larry told me later he was really pleased with the way I stayed calm the whole match. Staying relaxed under pressure in the breakers was probably the difference."

Stark's next match, against Ivan Lendl, was a sterner test. Lendl was still a tennis enigma, but at age thirty-three, his best tennis was behind him. A strange combination of the perfectionist and the dictator, Lendl complained of the wind and the sun at the Lipton; he had imported English sod to his home in Greenwich, Connecticut, in a bizarre, costly effort to simulate Wimbledon's conditions in order to win there. Lendl's tennis game was as aggressive as the eight Doberman pinschers patrolling his house. I had watched Lendl beat Jimmy Connors 6–0, 6–0, an incredible display on wet, green, En-Tous-Cas clay at Forest Hills one chilly April afternoon in the late 1980s. Connors may have been a couple of years past his prime, but Lendl was just awesome. Still, despite Tony Roche's claim that Lendl had a great sense of humor, the aura around Lendl was dark and Czechoslovakian, with a tinge of sadness. This did not mean he was not a great player. Those who claimed he was not extremely talented and was merely a fitness freak with an aggressive streak did not understand how beautifully Lendl hit the ball. Few players have ever hit a tennis ball as cleanly and as hard as Lendl. No one looked forward to playing Ivan Lendl indoors on the blue synthetic carpet that was his surface of choice because the bounce was perfect for him. In this setting the only natural elements were the beating of two hearts.

When he played against Stark in Philadelphia, Lendl's back was like a rusty gate. After all those years of torque on his phenomenal backhand and his high-tossed serve, Lendl's hinges were about to fall off. The ATP Tour trainers, Bill Norris and Todd Snyder, worked feverishly on Lendl, but this time the dark circles under Ivan Lendl's eyes were prophetic. He had seen a ghost, and it was himself. Yet even as a ghost, Lendl was a threat.

"I was nervous in the warm-up," Stark told me later. "I knew his back was hurt, because before the match he had practically everyone in the trainers' room working on him. When Lendl went out to hit before our match he could hardly walk, and after about two minutes he said 'No way' to his hitting partner and came right off. But in my warm-up with him before the real match, let me tell you"—Stark let out a very respectful laugh—"Lendl just hit the *crap* out of the ball. I didn't realize just how hard he hit the ball. *That* made me nervous. People think a guy like Jim Courier, whom I practice with all the time, hits hard. But you have no idea until you are right down on the court with Lendl just how much harder he hits the ball than even Jim. Lendl's ball was much heavier. I grew up watching Lendl. In terms of prize money, he's been the most successful guy ever on the tour, so it was a real honor to play him even, like you said, at this stage of his career. I played really well and won that first set 6–3, but it was a very close set. If Lendl had won it, he might have beaten me in straight sets. That's how close it was. But I made a few big volleys when I needed them. When I won the first set, he shook my hand." Lendl would not retire for another six months, but his back never got better. Lendl was very gracious in his final interview, conducted on an around-the-world phone hook-up. Mike Dickson, an English journalist, asked Lendl, who never won Wimbledon, if he ever regretted not changing his game.

"Maybe for grass I needed to have a different style of game," said Lendl, not dodging the question as he used to. "But it is very difficult to take that risk. For that very reason I admire Nick Faldo tremendously. I met him first before the first Australian Open at Flinders Park, so it would be early January 1988 at Sanctuary Cove, and he was there working on his game. I said, 'Nick, what are you doing there?' He said, 'Well, I am reworking my game.' I said, 'Come on, Nick, you are twenty in the world. What is wrong with your game?' He said, 'I can get better. I know I am going to hit rock-bottom before I get better, but I'm willing to take the chance.' That seemed very courageous to me. Maybe if I did something like that in '82 or '83, it could have been a different story, but being number two or three in the world at that time, I did not have the same courage Nick showed." Lendl was being modest as well as revealing. "But life is not always fulfilling everything you wish," he added.

Stark was happy with the win over Lendl. Now he faced Michael Chang. There are only so many opportunities in a year to play major players ranked ahead of you when you are playing at or near the top of your game. And Jonathan Stark was exactly at that point. His ranking would be up to number thirty-six in the world, his highest ranking ever, even if he lost the match to Chang. But Jonathan Stark's ranking would rise even closer to the top twenty if he could pull off the upset. That was never an easy proposition against Michael Chang.

The match at the Spectrum between Jim Courier and Andrei Chesnokov—the only male player with a female coach, Tatiana Naumko—preceded Stark–Chang and was incredibly good. Chesnokov's game, a fine remnant of Communist Russia, had been modeled on Bjorn Borg's at a time when copying the West was the key to much spying and other activity behind the Iron Curtain. Chesnokov was like a model capitalist worker now, with a lunch bucket and newfound heart. When Chesnokov was "on," as he was that night against Jim Courier, few people other than Michael Chang and Miloslav Mecir were smarter on the tennis court.

Jim Courier had been struggling. He had climbed the mountain to become the number one player in the world at the end of 1992, but he soon lost his crown to Pete Sampras, who had fathomless talent, not mere determination, in his well. Still, Courier was the only player in the world to have Andre Agassi's "number," and they both knew it. Courier was tougher though less talented, and he seemed to have a direct feed into Agassi's psyche from their junior days when Agassi was the sensation and Courier the determined overtaker. The junior matchups went deep, for Courier had always struggled against his friend Pete Sampras, while Andre Agassi, with all his talent, handled Sampras as no one else on tour could. Courier had had to fight so hard to become champion that, once there, he discovered he had left much of his fight in the gym. Jim Courier was from the volcanic school of victory. After reaching the summit, a part of him collapsed inwards. Like Joe Frazier after beating Muhammad Ali, Courier had had to fight hard too many times.

As a fourteen-year-old, Jonathan Stark had beaten Courier, and together they had won the junior doubles at the French Open 1987. Stark had beaten Courier again in Japan in 1993 when Courier was still number one in the world. Courier's mother had described Jim to me at their home in Dade City, Florida, and her description fit his playing style to a tee.

"At first kids at the tournaments didn't know who this guy in the long sweat socks was. But pretty soon they knew who Jim was and did not want to play him. Jim would never quit, and word about him got around in the junior tournaments. Jim was not a star right away the way Pete Sampras was. Jim had to fight for everything. He learned not to back up on the baseline from his father. They were playing baseball together one day when Jim was about six or seven, and he kept backing up to field the grounders his father was hitting to him. My husband got out the garden hose and put it right behind Jim and said to him, 'Now you stand your ground, and don't you *ever* back up behind that hose. Come *forward* to field the ball!' "

In the three long sets of side-to-side banging it took to put away the Russian Bjorn Borg clone, Jim Courier did not back up once. Chesnokov won the second-set tiebreaker 12–10, and it was great tennis. Courier said later in the interview room, "Eventually I just wore him down with my power. But I kept saying to myself, 'Gee, that was a great point!' " Courier shook his head and smiled. "We were playing at a really high level tonight."

When Michael Chang and Jonathan Stark came out onto the bright blue carpet at 10:30 P.M., the time most great boxing matches start, the circumstances of the match were disconcerting. The weekday crowd in Philadelphia seemed to have jobs to go to the next morning—some people were actually leaving. I moved down to the front row. Only the diehards, the college kids, and the funny-looking guys who liked to blow up their popcorn bags and explode them on their fists in the upper deck were left. I felt right at home.

Jonathan Stark had reason to be nervous as he took the court with Chang. Tennis requires that you become a good actor because, as Tilden said, you must appear civil at the same time you are trying to take out the other player's heart. I read Stark's emotional body language for the opposite of what he was trying to project. As he took the court against the short, thunder-thighed, black-haired piece of lightning, Stark acted supercalm as he walked. He had probably hit the men's room five times. Chang had more than Stark's attention. He had his respect. But showing too much respect is a dangerous thing, for you are on the court to dominate—or be dominated.

Jonathan Stark deposited his rackets by his changeover chair and pulled out two new ones, banging them together to try to get the one with just the right tension. He winced at the sound and dropped one.

Chang was bouncing up and down and Stark seemed unable to get his legs moving during the warm-up. A large part of the crowd continued to exit. It takes a very strong psyche not to take such an exodus personally when you are ranked thirty-eighth in the world and the

player you are facing, Michael Chang, is ranked eighth and is, by nature, something of a zen master.

Stark put all his nervous tension into his warm-up serves. Usually
the ball boys like to try to field serves in warm-up, but Stark started
hitting his serves so hard that the balls exploded off the blue carpet
and thundered in one great leap through the ball boys' arms into the
backstop. He hit the ball so hard that after one of the ball boys got
hit in the head, the others wisely just turned their backs to catch the
served balls as they fell off the weighted backdrop curtain. Michael
Chang's serve had more kick, which was more practical for a short
man like him. Chang moved coolly between his practice serves. He
understood that power in a warm-up may actually show more fear
than power.

Stark won the toss and elected to serve. Michael Chang stared
across the net, small but unafraid. On successive points, the six-foot-
two-inch Stark hit two first serves in a row right into Chang, who put
them both back into play before they reached his body. The third time
Stark hit a first serve, Chang, already anticipating the side correctly,
stepped out into the forehand alley and took the skidding bullet on
the rise, hitting a winner that had curved inside the back corner
before the net-rushing Stark had taken two steps off the baseline.
Stark looked across the net. Chang's right hand was jerked way up
into the air as if he had broken a brick by coming up underneath it
with his thumb. Stark was passed. Then, trying to serve too hard,
while down 15–40, Stark double-faulted. Three thousand people had
stayed in the huge arena, and 2,700 of them now made for the exits.
I wanted to tell them all it was no time to leave!

Michael Chang marched as he changed sides and cut right in front
of his much taller opponent at the net post. An exceptional small car
was on the highway with a big, powerful car. Stark took a deep
breath, bent low at the waist, and swung his trunk side to side before
he returned the serve. He wanted to get into the rhythm of Chang's
strokes, but Chang's mind would not permit him that pleasure. The
points still all belonged to Chang. Stark tried showing Chang two
speeds off different backhands, a hard two-handed thumper and a
one-handed slice, but Michael Chang, a student of life, ignored the

ploy and insisted on introducing the Oregonian to all four corners of the court. Chang hit looping forehands and backhands that seemed to have so much topspin they were dripping with chocolate. Then Chang drop-shotted Stark, then topspin lobbed him, and in general made Stark know what it feels like to be trapped in a blue-and-white rectilinear American world. The better Stark started to play, the worse Chang started to kill him.

There was a kind of tacit respect in what Chang was doing. It was respect, more polite than fearful or deferential. Michael Chang was great in part because he was the type of player who would crawl in order to win. Chang knew that all the players with world rankings from thirty to fifty should *never* be encouraged. Stark was at that level now, and Chang gave him respect by trying to pulverize him. Players like Stark, Chang's game seemed to say, are a mere shot or a bit of self-confidence away from potential stardom. Chang played Jonathan Stark as if he were playing Sampras or Courier and it was working. Watching Michael Chang, I felt that drive, fear, and intelligence are the perfect ingredients for a great tennis player. Lose any one of the three—and Boris Becker seemed to have lost both fear, which is partly respect, and drive—and one can never hope to be or remain a champion.

"Blowout," said a fourteen-year-old Philadelphian to his doting father. "Let's get out of here, Dad."

They did not know what they were missing! But more people streamed out of the vast building when Chang won the first set 6–2. Greatness is not something you see very often, and Michael Chang was close to being great. Chang and Borg were the two fastest players I ever saw. Chang shared Borg's court savvy and much of his strength, but like Bitsy Grant, tennis's "Georgia Peach" six eras before him, Michael Chang was probably four inches short of being the best player in the world. Still, Chang had whittled Stark down several inches during the match.

Stark was in tennis hell. He was no longer playing instinctively. He was thinking. And Chang was always a move ahead of him. Chang was like an A+ student who would not share the secrets of his academic success for the test. Suddenly Stark got furious with himself, and it worked. He belted a ball into the upper deck, took the code violation, and got going. Stark hit three enormous first serves, put away each first volley, and held his serve at love, cutting in front of Chang at the net post as they changed ends. It was a nice touch: need before beauty.

Momentarily humiliated by Stark's obvious advantage in size and power, Michael Chang ducked his head down before he served, bounced the ball twice as if checking to make sure it was perfectly round, then looked up across the net at Jonathan Stark like a Chinese-American Richard III. Chang had many favorite meals, but in my observations through the years, Chang's favorite dish was heart of All-American-boy.

It was an excellent match from that moment on. Stark rode a wave of fury, breaking Chang and going up 2–0. But Chang did the champion's thing and broke Stark's big serve right back. At 3–all in the second set, they separated like stages of the same rocket. Stark tried to come up to net on what the tennis rivals in Florida call a "West Coast approach shot," one part length, three parts instant gratification. Chang, a West Coast baseliner, frowned as if to say to the desperate serve-and-volleyer, "you can't come up on *that* against me." All bounce and business, Michael Chang blew the passing shot by Stark, broke him to go up 4–3, then broke him again to win 6–2, 6–3. As the remaining hundred or so fans cheered at midnight, Michael Chang leaned over the net, shook hands quickly with his fingertips as if Stark had leprosy, and then reached over into the seats to give his stocky brother-coach, Carl, six rackets to be restrung for the next morning's practice.

A young Chinese-American reporter wanted to speak to Chang and waited for forty-five minutes by the changing rooms, but Chang, we learned, had left fully clothed thirty minutes earlier by another exit. The attendant had assured us all along that Chang was still there. Stark, a huge towel draped around him in the cold locker room, never saw what hit him. He didn't seem upset at the loss, and that bothered me. I half expected him to get down at half past midnight and do a hundred push ups and two hundred sit-ups as a kind of penance, an insurance policy for the body toward the next battle with a wonder like Michael Chang. But Stark stayed calm in defeat.

"He just played too well," said Stark, soon to be the thirty-sixth-ranked player in the world. There are certain players a competitor will never beat, and Michael Chang seemed likely to be one of them for Jonathan Stark, who left the Philadelphia Spectrum well after midnight with no visual signs of damage and a check for $16,400 for beating Pescosolido and Lendl before losing to Chang.

By the time I got to the train station, all the regular train service to New York was finished for the day, but I caught the milk run to Trenton and transferred to the four A.M. mail train into New York City. Making a living at what one loves does not always come easily or quickly. As I shook back-and-forth on the tracks, I thought about Stark's calm, smiling face after the loss. He appeared to take it like a pro, but it might not really hit him until he got back to the hotel alone or started to travel the next morning. A loss like that could be tough if you did not have the stomach for competition. But Stark was twenty-two and already a pro. He was doing what he really wanted to do. There is a great freedom in that.

"How was it?" asked my wife, suddenly awake as I slipped in bed beside her at five A.M.

"It was definitely worth the trip," I said. "Stark is playing well, but Michael Chang is just at another level. I wonder how Stark will react when he realizes it."

Jonathan Stark came from a world dominated by pears, lumber, and the law. For over a hundred years, the residents of Stark's hometown of Medford, Oregon, had made their living from the trees of the Siskiyou Mountains and the sweet fruit down in the valley orchards. The fruiterers Harry & David were one of the largest businesses in Medford. The Oregon town had retained its small-town friendliness despite the recent influx of Californians seeking in Oregon the California of old.

Many transplanted residents, including the lawyer Richard Stark, Jonathan's father, had realized their dreams in Medford. The tall trees, fresh air, and the Pacific Northwest weather were just one step outside. The valley, where the pears grew and the Stark family lived, was covered in dense fog for most of the winter. The Oregonians walked in the fog, drove in it, and went indoors for tennis in it. To the Starks, the Pacific Northwest was another, generally gentler world, and they loved it.

With his earnings from the first two years on tour, Jonathan Stark bought a house outside Seattle. It was away from home but still in the Pacific Northwest. Stark's parents were amazed by their son's financial success. They told me he had been a good student and a natural athlete in school. Richard Stark remembered a time when Jonathan was six or seven years old and was playing Wiffle ball with his grandfather. Already tall and blond, the boy ripped the Wiffle ball over his grandfather's head on almost every pitch.

Diana Stark recalled watching Jonathan in a high school basketball game. It was the biggest game of the year, and the score was very close.

"All I remember," said Diana Stark, "is that the ball was loose on the floor and time was running out in the game." Jonathan dove for the loose ball at the crucial moment. "I just remember seeing his face as that basketball was rolling away. He just *had* to get it. He ran that ball down, dove on the floor, and practically crawled to grab it away. And he got it."

"What did he do with it?" I asked.

"I don't remember exactly," said his mother, "But he did what he was supposed to do with it. I can remember that. . . . [His team] won the game."

There were two high schools in Medford: South, where the Stark kids went, and the new high school in town, Medford North, which was built in the 1970s when the town grew to forty thousand residents (with over one hundred thousand in the surrounding area).

"North was ranked number three in the state in basketball," remembered younger brother Ted, a quarterback for the Washington Huskies. "And we weren't supposed to beat them. But we did. At the very end of the game, Jonathan dove for a ball and got fouled. He went up to the foul line very confidently, and he made both shots. The game was on the line, and he won it. We wouldn't have wanted anyone else taking those two shots."

In the elite group of the top forty tennis players in the world, of which Jonathan Stark, ranked thirty-sixth, was now a member, being an exceptional athlete is just a prerequisite for admission, a mere license to compete. Many of the European players—Michael Stich and Paul Haarhuis, for example—were exceptional soccer players before turning to tennis. Stark sounded like the type of player Dennis Van Der Meer had said he wanted to find when we talked at the Orange Bowl. If Jonathan Stark really liked pressure situations, like the free-throws he made at the end of the basketball game, he was going to be in luck in tennis.

For every fine hotel you stay at once you have started to make it as a tennis player, there were five or ten dumps along the way. Basically all you need when you are very young and hungry is a room with a firm mattress, clean sheets, and access to a washing machine. To save on expenses, some satellite players slept six or seven to a room with a mattress in the bathtub. There are a lot of good memories and sore backs to be had out on those circuits, the minor leagues of big-time tennis. The players with dates are not encouraged to return to the motel room—though it happens—because some of the roommates are still competing in the event and need their sleep. Most of the players in the challenger and satellite events have stayed in enough small hotel rooms to be sick of the sight of the TraveLodge's little bear logo. But as the players' rankings rise, they begin to stay in places where the maid leaves a mint on top of the pillow at night.

Jonathan Stark had left most of the worst hotel rooms behind him. At the Lipton Championships in mid-March, Stark was staying at the lovely old Biltmore Hotel in Coral Gables, a Florida-style Spanish mansion turned into an expensive Xanadu. Pete Sampras and Mats Wilander, old hands at hotels, were also staying there. There was a special "player's rate." When the top pros are playing for big money, the thing they want more than anything else is a quiet after-practice nap and a really good night's sleep. After travel and a few long matches, the players are generally too tired to sightsee. Every chance they get, they go back to the room, close their eyes, and nearly drink in the sleep.

It was almost noon when I knocked on the door to Stark's room.

He appeared in a huge towel, hair wet, unshaven. His face had an unhealthy pallor, and although he was too young to have dark circles, his eyes had turned purple below the lids. He had flown in the day before and had just completed a two-hour workout with his coach Larry Stefanki, who was staying in the room next door.

It was bright and sunny in Florida that day, and the birds outside were chirping gaily. Stark's open windows let the sunshine pour in at an angle and afforded a direct view of lush lawns, trees, and five dark green, hard courts. Stark seemed relaxed as he sat down in the big white towel. He had spent a week in San Francisco with a friend, and then he played very well in the desert at Indian Wells, where he beat Cedric Pioline for the second straight time since the French star had reached the U.S. Open final against Sampras. Stark then beat Andrei Chesnokov, who had played the great three-set match in Philadelphia against Courier. Stark finally lost, again in the third round, 6–4, 6–4 to Thomas Muster, but Stark's ranking had gone up to number thirty-sixth in the world after Indian Wells, and the maid had put a mint on his pillow the night before.

Stark exuded the happy confidence of a star on the rise, a player still young enough to believe he can go much farther in the game. But even though he was in the top forty, few people outside of tennis's inner circle knew who Jonathan Stark was.

Stark's loss to Chang had not stopped him in his tracks. On the contrary, it seemed to have propelled him into his wins the following week. For each fall and slide backward, Stark seemed able to pick himself up and keep going. That strength is what makes a professional athlete different from a college player. The pro with a future knows he or she is moving forward.

"What has been the toughest thing for you since you came out on the tour?" I asked.

"Well"—Stark shook his head and laughed—"there have been a few things. When I was in the juniors and in college. I was always one of the top players. Coming out on the tour, I wanted the same thing."

"It doesn't always happen that way."

"No. It doesn't," said Stark, no fear or tension in his voice. "Not to say I think it cannot happen or won't happen. But it just takes some time. You really have to have some confidence in yourself. Believe in your own game. Keep working really hard. Then, hopefully, one day, it will happen."

"What was the first big blow to your ego?" I asked. "When you first came out on the tour, do you remember a moment when you said to yourself, 'Whoa. It's not going to be so easy.' "

"Yeah, I do. I've been out on tour almost two and a half years. The big change was getting used to having tennis as your business, your everyday job. . . . Very quickly you realize that, hey, this is what a thousand other guys are doing the very same day. We are all fighting for the same rankings and the same money. And there are another thousand guys behind us who are wishing they could be out doing the same thing. That hit home early and pretty deeply. There are people working out there now just as hard as I am who are really good tennis players but never make it to where I am right now. It took me a while to get used to that. Tennis was always one of my main focuses in life, but it was always important in my mind for me to do a lot of other things."

"Such as?"

"Well," said Stark, "growing up in Medford, Oregon, which is not a real tennis hotbed, I loved the whole school thing. I wouldn't have traded it for anything in the world. I never really considered going to a tennis academy. Well, maybe when I was thirteen or fourteen, I thought about Bollettieri's." Stark shook his head and laughed. His friends Courier and Agassi had started at Bollettieri's, but eventually, as their individual games evolved, they moved away. Stark had never gone that route. "It wasn't me. I stayed in Medford. Little things were important to me: Graduating from high school. Going to the senior prom. Going on to college for at least a couple of years. I wouldn't trade those for a tennis camp life, though I know that's worked for other people."

Stark seemed whole and genuine.

"When I first came out on the tour, I was pretty excited. I wanted pro tennis so much. But it was a shock, they way it is for everybody, I guess, when they start to go to work. I'd spent the first twenty or twenty-one years of my life in school. It's like saying to yourself after graduating from college, 'Now what do I do?' I felt like that. I knew what I wanted to do, but I wasn't sure if I could do it. I know that a lot of my friends who aren't athletes are feeling that stress, too, right now, after graduating from college. They're saying, 'Jesus! What now?' That's what it felt like for me coming out onto the tour. The uncertainty. The fear of failing. Even though I felt lucky to have found something to do that I loved doing, it took a lot of getting used to. I was pretty lucky. I won a challenger tournament quickly the first year I played. I may not have come on quite as fast as some of the others I was juniors with—Pete, Jim, or Andre. But slowly but surely it's coming around."

"What about the constant travel? Edberg says it doesn't phase him."

Stark shook his head in admiration. "He's amazing. It affects me a lot. Lately, the traveling has been more taxing. Since I've gotten my ranking up to a certain point, there's good money in each event, so you want to play every week. But you can't be greedy, or you'll pay for it later. You have to take time off. That's between Larry Stefanki and me. I've had some physical injuries—hairline fractures in both my feet—so I shouldn't push it too hard. Of course, this is the part of the year when I really am pushing it hard."

Stark and Byron Black had suddenly become a very hot doubles team. I was of two minds about modern doubles, which was so different from the game of angles and positions that Bill Talbert and Gardnar Mulloy had played. Most of the really top singles players no longer played doubles on the tour. Travel had taken some of the fun and value out of doubles, though it remained a good source of potential income. McEnroe, perhaps the greatest doubles player ever, and a notorious nontrainer early in his career, had used doubles to stay fit and razor sharp on his volleys. But McEnroe had to give it up because eventually it made him too tired for singles. With the travel schedule Stark was keeping, I did not think he could play both singles and doubles well for long.

"I feel great right now," said Stark, who would turn twenty-three in two weeks. "But there have been some times in the last few weeks when"—he shook his head—"I was just *really* tired." He paused, talking as if he were in a dream. "Lots of matches. I've been in the final every week in doubles, too. There's lots of waking up every day just having to prepare for something. Everything in your life depends on what time you played the day before. If I played a night match, I'll sleep in, wake up at nine, relax, have a nice breakfast, go out and hit some practice balls with Byron, relax in the afternoon, then get ready for the night match. If it's doubles, indoors, sometimes we don't get on court until after midnight. Mostly, you're alone. It's hard to do much when you have a night match."

"So what do you do to stay sane?"

"I read," said Stark, and we both smiled in appreciation of the implication: athletes who read a lot are a rare, fine breed, but the habit can be dangerous. Deep thought and quick reflexes do not generally go hand in hand. McEnroe and Becker were big readers. And Becker in particular was derailed by his questioning intellect. I believe tennis became for Becker a series of repetitions that eventually drained his mind and spirit. Tennis is an intellectual game but its patterns, emerging through countless repetitions that do not overly trouble repetitious souls, eventually broke Becker down where he was most vulnerable, in the head.

"I read fiction," said Stark. "But what I really like are biographies. Politicians like Truman, movie stars, sometimes athletes. The book about Muhammad Ali, *The Greatest*, really impressed me."

I nodded encouragingly. Stark was young, and he had left college. His dreams were unjaded, not yet nicked by the doubters or the naysayers in life who hang around every sport, sometimes writing about it, feeding on the energy but unable to return the happy light.

"Were travel expenses a big factor for you at the start?"

Stark took a deep breath and whistled. "Terrible. It's definitely different, having to pay a thousand-dollar airfare or two hundred dollars a night for a hotel room in Paris or New York. You're used to school when you might not have a penny to your name, but you get in matches and play them for free. I was lucky. Nike signed me, and I had some success with them. And the prize money! Gosh. If you win a couple of matches a week, you're really going OK."

He had said an awful lot there, and I couldn't help but smile and like him more. Only the top hundred players in the whole world could win two matches a week with any regularity. Any player on a college team knows exactly how difficult it is to do what Stark had done. But

could he go on, could he become a household name like his contemporaries Courier, Sampras, and Agassi?

Nike Sportwear plainly thought so. The fact that Stark's older sister
worked for Nike could not have hurt. But unlike many other new
players with endorsements, Stark didn't falter when he got out on the
tour. Tommy Ho had signed for a big bonus but then struggled to live
up to the endorsement. At the age of sixteen, Ho got more than
$400,000 to turn pro as a "can't miss" national junior champion. At
twenty-one, Tommy Ho was still struggling in qualifying events. The
endorsement money had hung like a psychological millstone around
his neck. Tommy Ho was a good left-handed player, but he had lost
some incredibly close matches, including one against Brad Gilbert in
the third round of the U.S. Open: Ho led Gilbert 6–1 in the fifth-set
tiebreaker only to crack and lose. Some players just cannot quite pull
the final trigger, while others, like Gilbert, always found a way to win.
It was that reminder of the goal at hand—*to win*—that was the greatest and simplest tip that Brad Gilbert as coach would eventually pass
on to Andre Agassi.

Jonathan Stark, unlike Tommy Ho, had made more money on the
tour than he had been given by Nike. He had made $724,249 in his
first three years on tour, $442,802 of it in his third year. I was curious
about how the players handled their money. Part of winning on the
tour was money management. It was like poker at times: they had to
learn the business of when to play their hand and when to fold it or
go practice for a week or two and leave the money alone.

"If you lose 'first and first,' you're still OK," said Stark, referring to
twin first-round losses in singles and doubles. "You don't want to do
that too often, but money-wise for someone my age and coming from
where I come from, it's . . ."

"It's fantastic."

Stark's face broke into a wide grin. "Yeah. It's fantastic."

"Larry Stefanki told me that last week at Indian Wells you won
$45,000. You got to the third round of the singles and the final of the
doubles. If the money is that good for getting to the third round and
doing well in doubles, could you get complacent?"

"Obviously I'm aware of it. But if you only aim for the third round,
believe me, pretty soon you won't make that. I try to let my dad take

care of the money. I try not to think about it. Well, I did buy a new house in Seattle. And I bought a car. Those were big moves for me."

"How does the money you win get into your bank account?" I asked. "Say last week at Indian Wells? You get your checks for singles and doubles. What does the tournament do, send the checks home for you?"

"There's a Merrill Lynch program that the ATP Tour runs. You just tell the prize money person each week that you want it put into your Merrill Lynch account, and they put it straight through."

"Does your money go into stock investments or—?"

"They do whatever we want to do," said young Stark. "I should be a little more aware," He laughed nervously, "But I know somewhat what I'm doing. I mean, I'm pretty conservative with money. Some of the players are real stock guys, and they go out and get pretty wild on the stock market."

"Is that right?" I laughed. "They go after the stocks?" If these young guys made investments the way they played tennis, I could picture someone like Richard Krajicek, known for his 127-mile-an-hour serve, buying most of his stocks on margin and selling Snapple Soft Drinks short in the last bull market.

Some of the tennis players had lost big. Back in the days when the agents tended to do much of the investing for their player-clients, players like Stan Smith and Arthur Ashe did very well. Others weren't as fortunate. Gene Mayer, who had been ranked number four in the world, lost almost everything he had made as a player through investments and he sued his agency, Pro Serv. Whether the fault ultimately lay with the agents or with the players who tried to become real estate tycoons before they turned thirty-five, I did not know for sure. I did know that Mayer, for one, was upset about losing more than a million dollars. The cases like Mayer's remind me a bit of boxers' bad luck stories. Tennis players are supposed to be better educated than boxers, but education doesn't necessarily lead to financial savvy. Bjorn Borg, whose father had been in the textile business in a modest way back in Sweden, tried marketing his own line of clothes instead of letting Fila pay him to wear its sportswear. Borg made a huge mistake, and it wiped him out financially. The most outstanding exception was

Ken Rosewall, whose investments were apparently as solid as his backhand.

"Sometimes the guys hit with a stock, sometimes they don't," continued Stark, still grinning as if describing roulette. "With stocks I live vicariously through the other guys, the ones who really play the market."

There is an excitement about big-time tennis akin to gambling. The players come in all shapes and sizes, but the thing they all have in common, the reason we watch them, is that they are young, highly skilled, and, for whatever reason, are out there taking risks most people are no longer willing or able to take. It is a short, passionate lifetime within a larger life. And it is the thrill of battle and risk that older warriors like Jimmy Connors had tried to cling to. Younger players like Stark are just beginning to feel the magic, the allure of playing matches for a living. Sooner or later everyone spins off course into retirement. But when we talked that day in Florida, Stark was still like a young gambler who had come up to the casino tables early in the evening and stayed till well after midnight playing the game of his choice.

"I prefer gambling to the stock market," confessed Stark. "It's fun. I don't want to get into the heavy, heavy stuff, but I could. I can feel myself really enjoying it."

He liked to gamble, but what was the bet? Making it on the pro tennis tour is as unlikely for most players as stepping up to the roulette table, betting on double-zero and winning. And how long do those early winnings last? Tour players, men and women, seem to have placed their largest bets on the early years of their lives, when their bodies and instincts rule. They tend to forget what comes after age thirty-five. That is perhaps the biggest gamble of all, for it is tough to make the second half of a player's life pay off, too.

When you spend the best part of the years from six to thirty-two playing tennis, a large part of you remains forever a tennis player— even when you try to go on to other pursuits. It can hurt when others never think of you as anything but a tennis player. With the label of athlete or ex-athlete comes the suspicion that you have remained a type of prodigy all your life, an "extended child." Eventually, even great athletes are faced with living in more conventional ways.

Instead of the smiles of admiration you got as a young player, now that your tennis career is over, you may get blank looks as others watch you stumble ungracefully into their world. *That* is what makes pro tennis such a gamble for the young.

"Is it lonely for you out on the road?"

"It can be," said Stark, getting my drift. "It can be. But I have a real close relationship with my whole family and my community back home. So when I'm out there and lonely, I think of all of them, and I still call home." He looked around his hotel room and frowned. "It's usually kind of like this. Nice hotel room, very quiet and isolated. You've got your hotel key and your rackets. You close the door, and you're pretty much by yourself the whole day until you play."

"Your coach, Larry Stefanki, travels with you, too."

Stark's voice relaxed. "More this year than last. I can afford him this year. He's with me a high percentage of the time now. It's really not so bad. I've been doing this since the juniors, but I'm more on my own as a pro. I'm also close to Byron Black." Stark took a deep breath and exhaled. "We're friends as well as doubles partners. In fact, I think it's almost impossible to play good doubles if you don't like your partner. We're like very different brothers."

"What about women on the road? Is it lonely that way, too?"

"Aaah." Stark hesitated. "It can be."

"Is it celibacy time?"

"Not quite that extreme. But *cumulatively*, it can be tough." He laughed nervously.

"You can go out and have a decent time?"

"That's right."

"But you can't spend too much time trying to meet new people?"

His voice grew concerned, earnest. "It's hard sometimes. I'm really committed to tennis, and if I'm playing matches the next day, it's hard to go out and carouse."

"I don't know if you're quite ready for sainthood," I said with a laugh. "I hear you and Patrick McEnroe were a big hit in Portugal. And I have this one phone number you gave me for somewhere in San Francisco. I called up for you there, and there were about seven women all sharing the same house. They all seemed to know you."

Stark smiled. "They told me you called. There's this one girl I've been staying with and seeing regularly. Dana's her name."

"Is she a steady girlfriend?"

"She's becoming a steady girlfriend."

I nodded. "Do you feel you still have an emotional anchor back home with your parents in Medford, or do you feel you're your own man now completely?"

"You know, I was just talking to Larry about that today. It's slowly changing. I don't mean to get too personal, but it is hard, because you grow up for so long with your family and then to kind of change your part in the family. . . . I'm out here by myself. And obviously now I have some money of my own. Suddenly, if I really want to do something, I don't have to call them to ask for permission. I can just go do it. That makes me worried sometimes. It takes a while to get used to all that freedom. I still think of my family while I'm making my mind up what to do."

"I guess for a while you must have been like a kid in a candy shop?"

"Yeah. Suddenly I could do anything I could want to do. But if you do it too much, you're a fool. You'll start to lose."

"Have you done anything you've really wanted to do?"

"Well. After I lost to Chang in Philadelphia, I flew out to San Francisco to be with Dana for five or six days before going down to Indian Wells. After this one, I'm going to go to Mexico before I go down to play in South Africa. Side trips might seem little, but they're big for me."

"No. You need to get away. It's good for you. Borg never got away until he had to leave the game entirely. The tour is like a big Ferris wheel. You've got to get off it once in a while. Go bake out a little in Mexico and get some heat in your bones."

"Exactly. And it's independence. That's what I like. I'm almost twenty-three now. I guess I'm old enough to be doing these things."

"What is your family like?"

"My parents turned fifty last year," Stark said in a rush, the way the young almost universally seem to like to skip over talking about their parents altogether. "My father's a lawyer in general practice. My mother's a housewife. She does some substitute teaching. Eric, my older brother, is an attorney working for the public defender's office in Medford. My older sister, Gretchen, works for Nike up in Portland. She's getting married soon. And Ted, the baby, is six feet, four inches tall and still at college at Washington."

I smiled at the fact that the Stark siblings had scattered in such different directions to seek their identities. I thought I would like to meet Eric, the public defender. What wound was in there, what call to the defense? Was it the call to the defense of all those not immediately recognized as gifted? Did Stark's older brother have the deep determination of those not strikingly handsome or prodigiously athletic? *Public defender or private defender,* I wondered. For every athlete of distinction in a family, there are usually two or three other children somewhat less physically gifted who eventually find their self-expression in other ways, sometimes with an unspoken vengeance in later life that surprises everyone, especially those who at one time held the throne.

"We're kind of a diverse group," said Stark a bit uneasily.

"Strong opinions?"

He smiled. "Yeah. We're all very opinionated and have some serious family debates once in a while. My father always plays the devil's advocate."

"He stirs things up?"

"Exactly. It drives my sister crazy."

"He comes on like the big conservative?" I guessed.

"Exactly. I mean, he is, but he isn't *really* conservative. He's funny. He just likes to get us pissed off. Like on the Rodney King thing, he'll say ridiculous stuff like, 'If you were a cop, you don't know what you would have done.' He drives us nuts on purpose to make us think. But in the end we know he's joking. Mostly."

"Your brother Eric, the public defender, is going crazy?"

"Pretty much. But sometimes, on other things, he will take my father's side."

I paused for a moment, beginning to get a feel for Jonathan Stark as a person. He was certainly likable, with a quick and engaging smile, open face, and still open mind. He had a streak of West Coast conservatism tempered with the healthy high spirits of a young man nearing the top of his game. Stark's world was full of places not yet visited, intensely bright and beautiful backdrops to a foreground full of darker focus, desire, and talent where the ultimate task is to get the most out of what you are.

"What is the difference between college tennis and the initial steps into pro tennis?"

"There's *a lot* of good players out there in college." Stark said with genuine respect. Yet Stark had taken the risk to turn pro, and it was working for him, at least for the present. A touring pro needs great consistency and at least one big weapon. Stark's weapon was his big serve—which all the players on tour respected. There were college players who could play individual points better than Stark once a point was under way, but the beginning of points, the serve and the return of serve had become 70 percent of professional tennis after the new rackets were introduced.

"You can get by a little bit in college on your name and reputation," Stark said. "A lot of times in college you get some easier matches because of who you are supposed to be. That happens a little even in the pros when you'll see a guy playing really great, but, all of a sudden, when it comes to actually winning the match—"

"The guy folds the cards," I said.

"Guys like Chang and Sampras and Edberg," Stark continued. "The top guys find a way to pull it out. I mean I went to three sets with Pete Sampras and it was very close, but afterwards I wondered if it really was that close. I almost had him last year in Cincinnati. And that's what stresses you out when you are trying to improve your ranking, because close losses are just losses. Up here, nobody says 'Well played' very much. And you can't say the top guys are just lucky all the time because they *do it* all the time! Sampras and Edberg have pulled enough rabbits out of the hat to start a rabbit farm. Of course, in college, one thing I liked a lot was that you could see some real emotions flying. And you had a little cheating to deal with in college, which was also kind of fun."

"Fun? Really? Cheating in college tennis?"

"It can get really crazy in college tennis," said Stark with a laugh, as if he were describing Billie Jean King's World Team Tennis on a hot night. "You get the players hooking each other, and then the coaches are out on the court screaming at each other. I loved it. I wish one day I could get to play Davis Cup for the United States because I thrive on that atmosphere. I loved the aspect of college tennis that was like basketball in a loud arena. And it wasn't all cheating by any means. There were *a lot* of good players in college."

It was fashionable to criticize professional tennis, but college tennis had thorny issues, too. In the 1960s there was always a smattering of foreign-born players on American teams and it was a thrill to play against the University of Miami during its fifty-six-match winning streak, when Jaime Fillol and Pat Cramer were, respectively, the number one and number two players for the college and also represented Chile and South Africa in the Davis Cup. But in recent years, with college coaches under intense pressure to produce winning teams, there has been an excess of foreign players on American Division I and Division II college teams. Tennis scholarships, which Arthur Ashe hoped might go to promising young American players, are now benefiting second-tier players from Sweden and Holland, who hope to brush up on their English for free, enjoy the parties, study a little, and practice a year or two for a possible pro career. It seems to me that the only way to curb the abuses of college tennis scholarships is to take one future scholarship away from a college for each player who does not graduate. That might draw real students to the college game, which is, I think, what college tennis is supposed to be all about.

Too many valuable educations are being wasted. Paul Goldstein and Scott Humphries, the two top American junior prospects, were both going to Stanford, but I wondered how long these latest sensations would last in college—two years like Stark? The decision to turn pro had worked so far for Stark, but where would he be in fifteen years? He might have a castle and a big bank account. He might be a shell of his former self.

"If you were a young player trying to decide if you should stay in college or come out early for the tour, what is the point at which you know you are ready to leave college?"

"You just know," said Stark with enthusiasm. "I really knew. College is very important for your growth as a person, not just for tennis, but as far as leaving it, you can just tell. I knew that after my second year

I was just way too far . . . just bursting to go. I saw these guys playing on TV, and I just had to go."

"And your coach at Stanford was understanding?"

"Coach Gould . . . [has] had a lot of experience with that decision [with the McEnroes, the Mayottes, and others]. So he sat me down, and we went over the pros and the cons carefully. Coach Gould said, 'Obviously I'd love for you to stay, but go for it.' "

"What were the cons?"

"Gosh. In my mind, there weren't any. I was just ready."

"To go test yourself."

"Yeah." Stark smiled and nodded.

"To make the same move forward that Todd Martin did from the midthirties on the computer up to top twenty or top ten, what do you have to do with your game, what do you have to work on?"

"Just everything," Stark said gently. "To put it simply, just being a little more solid in every area. Not making bad mistakes. Not giving a guy a free point. I've been working real hard on my return of serve. I'm trying to block it back sometimes."

"Everyone is going for the big return of serve these days. That's probably the biggest change from twenty years ago. Did you feel there were times in the match with Chang when you ought to have tried to just chip it and put the ball in play?"

"It's a fine line," said Stark uncomfortably, as if mentally hung up on the decision. "If you're missing a lot, then you'd better regroup and get a few back. On the other hand, I want to try to be real aggressive with the way I play. And if I'm going to really beat these guys . . ."

"You've got to return hard," I answered for him, finally grasping the logic of the high-risk returns.

"Yeah. It's strange. My return of serve will be solid for, like, two weeks. And then it will go away." Stark shrugged and shook his head. "I need lots of repetition, working really hard on it. Then it comes through when I need it in a match."

"If you play Michael Chang again, what will you try to do?"

Stark hesitated and smiled. Mention of Chang made a lot of players do that. "Mmm. Well, I stayed in some good points with Chang. I set the point up well, got an easy opening, and missed." Stark shook his head at the memory. "In the second set when I got up 2–love, I said to myself, 'Come on, damn it, let's get into this! Let's stay on top of him!' But damn if Chang didn't break me right back."

"It's funny, but I think your match against Chang was like a free lesson. I bet you played better the next week out at Indian Wells because of it."

"It did help me," agreed Stark. "Up here, you have to take a lesson out of every match you lose. The ones you win, you win. But I don't think too much about the wins because when you win, you have the answers. But a year or two ago when I was just coming out on the tour, it was even tougher to play a guy like Chang because when you are starting out on tour, you think, 'God. This guy has won the French Open. These guys are on the top, and I'm not.' But it has helped that I've played some of them as a junior. And if you can stay with them just once, you'll do even better with them the next time out. Usually," he added with a laugh.

Stark is not headed for superstardom. His ground game is just not sound enough, his movement not quick or fluid enough when compared to the likes of Sampras and Stich. He seemed to sense what I was thinking.

"I've got to be able to play two or three shots in advance in my mind," said Stark firmly. "That's what guys like Chang and Agassi can do. The transition game is also something I'm definitely working on. The guy I really admire is Stefan Edberg, because he's more of an attacking player like I am."

"Edberg is not a bad guy to take as a model," I said.

"Mac would be my other," said Stark. "McEnroe loved the net, but he was also able to do what he wanted from the baseline. In my opinion, Edberg and McEnroe both have very good ground strokes. They could stay back with guys. Their baseline games were solid enough to get them into net without rushing it. They were so successful because although they were always looking to come in, they didn't have to. If you *have to* do something up here, or need to cover up a weakness in your game, they are going to find out that weakness very fast. You can't hide. McEnroe and Edberg didn't rush. They were calm and in control even when they weren't most comfortable. That's where I want to get." He laughed lightly. "It can be frustrating. I can get it for an hour or so at a time in a match when it will be clicking against any player in the world for me. Then the next time out, I'll start to feel like the most uncoordinated guy in the world. But at least I know what I do best. And there aren't that many serve and volleyers around anymore."

"And your biggest weaknesses?"

"When I start to lose, I get a little stubborn about what I'm doing. I tend to repeat my patterns. If I start to miss my first serve, sometimes I just keep trying to hit it harder and harder and it doesn't help. That's one of the things I've got to mature on in my service game." Stark nodded intently. "On the other hand, in Philadelphia, well, Michael just played awfully well." There was a great deal of respect for his opponent in Stark's voice. He was learning, perhaps not wounded by the Chang experience.

"Sometimes when I see you, it's the damnedest thing," I said. You look as if you're playing doubles on the singles court. Did you ever have that sensation? As if you were covering the court but you weren't quite there? Do you feel the natural patterns of your doubles play coming out in your singles' movement?"

"Not exactly that way. One of my problems is that not being a ground stroker my whole life and never really working on it hard, I have a tendency after I hit a shot to stand and watch it. I don't think I'm slow. I just don't move that well from the baseline. I kind of wait and react to the ball instead of anticipating and knowing where it's going to be. That's why I get there late sometimes."

I nodded. If Stark could ever get to the point where his movement improved to something approaching the quality of his serve, he would surely be one of the top twenty and perhaps even top ten in the world. That goal, though, still seemed distant.

"You've served eighty-four aces in ten matches. Right now you're listed as eighth in the world on the ATP Tour for aces. Talk to me about what goes into making a great serve. What is the serve to you?"

"It's my weapon," said Stark, lighting up. "I'm not just kicking my serve in and waiting for their reply. I'm trying to make a statement each time I hit my serve. I'm getting up on my serve and exploding forward and then getting down for that volley, and after I hit the volley getting back and ready for the next one. I serve and volley."

"How do you make your serve work?"

"I think my legs are the most important thing in my serve," said Stark. "I try to keep my right arm and upper body as relaxed as possible, and then I take a deep knee bend and explode really hard upward with my legs, and that's really it."

"Is it the explosion upward that makes the great serves?" I asked him, thinking of Edberg and the young Becker, of Gonzalez and other powerful right-handers like John Newcombe who seemed to go right up through their legs to the top of their service motion.

"Right. All big servers use their legs as much as or more than their arms. Exploding upward, hitting up on the ball," said Stark. "When I start missing my serve . . . I start pulling down on the ball and I don't get up on my legs."

"You pull the cover hand over too fast?"

"Right. And I pull my head down too fast because I'm not getting up high enough off my legs. It all kinds of goes in sync."

"Serving is an up and out motion, isn't it? When you start tennis you kind of have this feeling that you'd like to hit down on the serve, but that's not it in the league you play in. What's the difference between the first ball and the second ball?"

"I try to not make any." Stark smiled. "Energy-wise, going up for the ball, I try to go up almost harder with my second serve. Ever since I was ten or eleven years old, that was what I worked on. You can still hit a high percentage serve with cover but go after it just as hard. Just put more safety, a shade more kick, on the ball."

I could picture Stark's hand and a flurry of famous right hands from Vines, Kramer, and Gonzalez, to Hoad, Newcombe, Emerson, and Stolle, to McKinley and Ralston, Sangster and Noah, Edberg and Becker, all fanning out with their thumbs rising from bottom left to upward right like a long forward pass, the double pistons of their legs, back, and hand providing the whip, kick, and power with gathering, then exploding speed. Other, perhaps even stronger, men, could not hit their serves as hard as the players who had the powerful leap up through the legs and that confident looseness, plus hand speed, at the top of the motion. Muscle men rarely hit fast serves. Jonathan Stark was not a muscle man, but, as they say of pitchers, he could really bring it.

Stark at times reminded me of Richard Krajicek who, when asked how fast he hit the ace that brought him to match point in L.A. against Sampras said, "It would have been a ticket on the highway, that's for sure."

"Do you still think of that loss to Volkov at the Open?" I asked.

"I do," said Stark with a wince. And he described again what he had done wrong to lose the match on the two or three pivotal points in the fifth set. It is an interesting phenomenon among the top players in almost any sport: they forget their wins almost entirely yet rarely forget their losses. A loss is like a rebuke from a parent, a job not well done. To become a pro player with real longevity, you must learn to harden your heart after a loss, and go on to the next match like a salesperson going on to the next potential customer. The star athlete is selling credibility. It's a tough sale, and the first and last buyer is invariably yourself.

I knocked on the door of the room next to Stark's. There was one button I still had to push. Coaching at the very top of the pro circuit is almost as rarefied as the players themselves. Bob Brett, Nick Bollettieri, Jose Higueras, the Gullikson brothers, and Tony Pickard were among the best. There are a dozen or more very capable coaches who traveled with the top stars and the players who dreamed of joining their ranks. A lot of very good coaches got tired of the road and would not go out again for anybody. Other coaches just loved the raw freedom and the risk of it all. It was a gambler's game. Larry Stefanki, John McEnroe's former coach, was taking a chance on Jonathan Stark.

Stefanki, who attended the University of California at Berkeley, had been a pro from 1981 to 1987. He had wins over Jan Kodes, Wojtek Fibak, Phil Dent, and Adriano Panatta toward the end of their careers, and he also beat people as good as Wally Masur, Scott Davis, Robert Seguso, Paul Annacone, John Lloyd, and Emilio Sanchez. Stefanki had been what the English like to call a "very useful" player. He was fast around the court and volleyed very well. As a coach, Larry Stefanki was generally credited with having had the toughness that helped revive John McEnroe's career in 1990, the last year McEnroe really competed well.

Stefanki came to the door in a pale blue robe. He had the slick brownish hair Slavic hockey players seem to have. Unshaven, Stefanki looked like a thin, tired bear who is short on honey.

"Come on in," said Larry Stefanki.

I explained my business, and he nodded. Stefanki came from the Clint Eastwood school of charm and elocution. I could relate to him.

"What parts of Stark's game are you working on with him?"

"Basically everything."

"His serve?"

"Everything but his serve. That's a natural. I wouldn't change that. But movement, yes. Ground strokes, volley, decision making. He needs to improve in all those areas. And I think he is." Stefanki nodded.

"Is Stark a hard worker?"

"I can't say yet. So far he's doing whatever I ask him to do." Stefanki nodded in approval.

"He's been playing very well, but Chang took him apart in Philadelphia."

"I was there," said Stefanki. "Jonathan doesn't know how to play a match like that yet. Chang is not a good matchup for him, either—just too quick. The top players don't give you any time to play in. Chang is great. He beat Courier the next round in Philadelphia. Jonathan has beaten Courier, too, but he is not at that level yet. Not consistently."

"And you think he is going to get there?"

"I had a lot of people contact me when Johnny Mac hung it up, but I chose Stark. Do I think he is top-ten material? Maybe. Maybe not this year. Do I think he can make it into the top twenty this year? Definitely," said Stefanki. "Will it happen? No guarantees. But I'll tell you this. I wouldn't come out and travel with a player I did not think was going to make it into the top twenty."

I shook hands with Stefanki, and I left him to a razor and the sunlight of the dead quiet spring morning in the old and beautiful south Florida hotel.

THE PADDOCK AREA

STOLLE, MULLOY, GILBERT, EDBERG
"WHAT'S AGE GOT TO DO WITH IT?"

The two men were walking so fast through the crowds around the Lipton Tennis Stadium they seemed to be racing. Fred Stolle, many times a finalist against Emerson and the winner at Forest Hills in 1966, was out in front, followed by Gardnar Mulloy, the Miami tennis legend. The finalist in a tournament is a special beast. Stolle and Mulloy had distinguished careers, especially in doubles. In singles, only Emerson had beaten Stolle regularly, and Mulloy was always near the top. They had done everything beautifully at the moment of contact with the ball but were perhaps just a shade too tall or one step too slow against a stronger or more agile champion.

Stolle's fair skin was glowing a light lobster red that came from early mornings outside the television booth at the start of the outdoor season. Mulloy was deeply tanned, the handsome crew-cut star of an earlier generation. In short white shorts, Mulloy's long, still finely muscled legs flexed as he tried to keep pace with Stolle, who seemed in a friendly, playful way to be running away from the older man. They moved through the crowd laughing like two former vice presidents at a political convention where they are no longer trying to get on the ticket.

I sought out Gardnar Mulloy, who had won the U.S. National Doubles four times with Bill Talbert, was ranked in the U.S. top ten fourteen times, and had been a finalist at Forest Hills at age thirty-eight, losing to twenty-four-year-old Frank Sedgman in 1952. At age forty-three he had won the Wimbledon doubles, playing with thirty-three-year-old Budge Patty, beating Lew Hoad and Neale Fraser, both in their twenties, in the final. Gardnar Mulloy seemed to have drunk at the fountain of youth. He had outcompeted men twenty years his junior for so long he seemed to belong to the generation of Rosewall and Hoad, when in fact he had already been playing against their tennis heroes. His formula for eternal youth, as written up in *Sports Illustrated* at the time, was to drink great quantities of milk and avoid all tobacco and alcohol. What did he do for fun? Nancy Talbert, Bill Talbert's wife, had once confided, "Gar never met a woman he didn't want to sleep with." A "hunk" in the Miami of the thirties, forties, and fifties (and, some say, of the sixties, seventies, eighties, and nineties), Mulloy won thirty-eight U.S. titles—the last in the eighty-and-under category. I wanted to get a sense of how he had kept going. Now the tennis director emeritus at Fisher Island, Florida, Gardnar Mulloy had an incredibly soothing voice.

"What difference do you see between playing tennis when you were in your forties and playing tennis now?" I asked him.

"I don't see much difference at all," responded Mulloy firmly. "I see the ball bouncing, and I know I can still get it and hit it right in the sweet spot on my racket. It just doesn't *always* happen that way now."

"Who was the first big-name player you beat?"

"It was in the 1930s," said Gardnar Mulloy softly. "He was a guy ranked number ten in the country then."

"Gil Hall," I guessed.

"Right," said Mulloy happily.

By an odd quirk of time, as an eleven-year-old I had played doubles with Gil Hall. He was a short, strong man in long white pants who was in his late sixties when I played with him. "Great forehand, weak backhand?" I asked, trying to remember the sensation of Gil Hall.

"That's right," said Mulloy. "I beat him pretty badly, two-and-two or two-and-three. About 1937. It was an important win for me."

"What was American tennis like when you were beginning?"

"Well, there were no junior tournaments per se. Or very few. There was college tennis, but mostly we played in the men's divisions as juniors because no one had thought up all these junior tournaments yet. Eventually, if you were good enough, you broke into the men's."

"I didn't know that," I said. "It's funny. Each generation thinks it all started when they did."

"That's right," said Mulloy, laughing. "But I'm still using a Prince woodie. I get just as much power with it as they do with the new rackets. I still put a very fine gauge gut in it and string it tightly. People say today that if you string a racket loosely, it will give you more power. That's wrong. If you want power, string a racket tightly and use quality gut." Gardnar Mulloy paused. "I had a hit with Jim Courier last year at Fisher Island."

I tried to picture Gardnar Mulloy at eighty hitting with Jim Courier at twenty-three. "What was that like?"

"People on the sideline were going 'Ooh. Jim hits so hard.' But I could get to it," Mulloy insisted. "Jim's balls hit and take a long bounce. He's got that western grip. You can run those balls down. We used to hit semiflat with eastern grips, and the ball didn't rise up much. If we had hit today's balls, which are lighter, and used these big rackets with our strokes, we'd have hit everything out. That's why these kids all want to hit the way Andre Agassi does. You have to put topspin on the ball to keep it in play now." I nodded. But Courier could nail a ball pretty straight when he wanted to.

"What was all that business between Jack Kramer, Ted Schroeder, and Pancho Gonzalez? Animosity?"

"Well, Kramer and Schroeder were friends out in California. They still are. Pancho was not Jack's friend. A lot of the players on the tour hated Schroeder. Ted could get obnoxious, but he could really play. I guess Jack wanted to bring Ted along to beat Pancho."

But Pancho Gonzalez proved to be too good for Ted Schroeder. Then Kramer brought on Rosewall and Hoad. Gonzalez still prevailed. Behind the headlines there are always personalities. That edge is what puts the real acid in a player's stomach as he or she takes the court. People do not always like each other. And then they play. But as the years pass, players change. Animosities become friendships. Players discover they were on the same ball together.

"How do you rate Jack Kramer?"

"In the top ten, all-time, but I don't know exactly what number. Jack was not wildly overpowering. It was more like a controlled power. The thing about Kramer is that Jack just *never* played the wrong shot."

Ranked in the U.S. top ten for the first time in 1939, Mulloy had been a semifinalist and finalist at all the great singles tournaments in the world. Mulloy had been, and still was at eighty, an incredible physical specimen. His body had never broken down. He had never had to pull his vehicle—himself—off to the side of the road.

"A friend of mine still underlines the articles on 'Mental Toughness,'" said Mulloy. "But heck, at our age, if you have to underline it, I don't know if you'll ever get it."

"What is the toughest thing for you now as a player?"

"Getting my entries in," said Gardnar Mulloy. "When my wife died last year, I lost my best friend. She used to get me motivated. Now I have trouble filling out the entry form and sending it in. I don't care as much now that my wife isn't watching me play." The eighty-year-old paused. "But I'm heading out to the West Coast for a tournament next week. Once I get there, I'm always glad I'm still competing."

The next morning Brad Gilbert led me to a round metal table and chairs overlooking some trees and flowers at the back of the Lipton players' restaurant area, where young players were constantly being sent back to get their player identity cards because five rackets, blond hair, a big smile, and white shorts would no longer pass security since Monica Seles had been stabbed.

I had always liked watching Brad Gilbert play, in large part because playing against Gilbert would have been no fun at all. He never had Stefan Edberg's talent, quiet demeanor, or foot speed, yet Gilbert was a great competitor, leading the ATP Tour in 1993 with seven matches won in final-set tiebreakers. Like Edberg, Gilbert seemed to generate power effortlessly. And he did not choke. Though his game was outwardly very different from Stefan Edberg's, they both were able to play incredibly close to their talent's maximum capacity every time out. In a big match, the performance of many tour players is 10 to 20 percent below their real abilities. But time changes the equation.

Gilbert, who at thirty-two was four years older than Edberg, knew how to win and knew what it felt like to have been ranked in the top ten and to begin to experience the inevitable free fall toward retirement.

Brad Gilbert's face was still gritty and unshaven, pasty white in the bright sun. His chin and lower lip jutted forward as if he would march through a desert to get a win. But recently, Gilbert had had too many campaigns and not enough victories. His ranking slid out of the top thirty for the first time in nine years. He winced as we talked, like a salesman trying to exude happiness while his sales are been taken over by younger people. He seemed unsure how to reinvent himself now that the end of his career was in full sight. The summer before, Gilbert had said to me, "I'm not worried. I'm still moving just as well as I ever did. I've had a couple of bad losses. It happens." Now, the bad losses were no longer always considered upsets, and he knew it.

"You reached the final in Memphis," I said. "But in general how do you feel you are holding up this season?"

Gilbert sighed with the air of a man who had seen himself and did not like what he saw. A small patch of hair dyed tawny orange replaced a circle of gray in Gilbert's once black locks. "Unfortunately, right now, I feel like I'm battling my body more than I'm battling my opponents. I've had a hip injury. It's become more difficult to keep the competitive edge on my game. Now, instead of just battling an opponent, I've had to battle myself, too. I'm hitting the ball well, but it's just a little harder to stay healthy these days." Gilbert smiled a bit wanly, injured again near the end of his playing career. If Brad were a horse, someone might have sold him to a police department. He looked exhausted. As Gilbert said, "Losing sucks. Any time, any place, anywhere. It doesn't get any easier as you get older."

"You sound a little nasal," I noted. "Do you have a cold, too?"

"Yeah," he said, laughing, and suddenly sounded even more nasal. "I've got a wicked cold. I've had the bad hip for a couple of months. Last week I repulled a stomach muscle. It's about the sixth or seventh time I've pulled it in a year. It feels like having a chronic ankle injury, except in your stomach. Then a couple of days ago I caught this cold." Gilbert ate a french fry.

"What do you do to combat the aging process?"

Gilbert shrugged. After twelve years on the tour, Gilbert was beginning to resemble Klaus Kinski in the film *Aguirre: Wrath of the Gods* when he was lashed to a wooden raft going down the Amazon.

"Well," said Gilbert, "I'm doing a lot of sitting stretches, but I'm afraid that if I work too hard at them I'm going to rip the stomach muscle again. Basically what I do is play the same tournaments each year. I only play on courts that I already know really well. That gives me an edge. I won't go play at a new tournament site unless the court surface is really good for my game." Gilbert had played at the indoor tournament in Memphis so often that the court suited him like a favorite old chair.

"If you're having trouble beating a younger player—if he is beating you with quickness, say—what can you do to combat it?"

"I still don't feel I have lost that much speed," said Gilbert.

If Brad had been a boxer, it would have been time for the Nevada Boxing Commission to consider revoking his license. Tennis is a movement game, and tennis wisdom is only worth something if you can still get to the ball ahead of time.

Gilbert shook his head in disgust. "I lost to Goellner today, 4–6, 6–4, 6–4. It was a very disappointing loss. Before the match, I didn't think the guy had very much. He just served big. It turned out that's all he had to do—with me. He got one break in the second set and one in the third set. That's what gets me about men's tennis today. A guy like Goellner, who I don't think plays that well, can go out and serve twenty-two aces and win. I had numerous chances to break him in the last two sets. I was outplaying him, but I just couldn't convert that break point. He broke me with an overrule in the third set. He didn't deserve to break me. It was a cheap win." The second-day stubble on Brad Gilbert's face made him look even more disgruntled. He was near the end, and he knew it.

"Is that a match you would have won three years ago?"

"I could have lost it three years ago, too, I suppose. But it's something to lose like that to a guy with a game like *that*. Anyway. My idea is that you never want to lose two sets in a row the same way, and I did. If the guy is getting into net on you and wins the first set that way, maybe you try to get into net before him in the second set. If you're having no success coming in, then stay back and try to grind him down." Gilbert shrugged. He took his shades off and rubbed his eyes. The circles under his eyes were dark and deep as sand dunes. Not everybody missed the tour grind. When Mikael Pernfors was injured and then asked later what he'd missed, the Swede said, "Three foot putts."

"What else are you doing?" I asked.

"Well," said Gilbert, "Andre Agassi has asked me to watch him a little out there. Not exactly as Andre's official coach. We're just talking about a few things right now. I've still got a pretty full schedule myself, but I think I could help Andre."

I had no doubt that he could. There was very little that Brad Gilbert did not know about tennis and competing, but all the past in *pasture* seemed to be calling him now. I thanked him for his time. He was entering his thirteenth season on the tour, and most of those who had started with him were already gone.

Stefan Edberg, four years younger than Gilbert, was still running around with the best. Two days before the Lipton tournament began, I had gone out to watch Edberg practice with Sergi Bruguera. It was one of the finest practices I ever watched.

Tennis practice matches are vastly underrated as barometers of form. The behind-the-scenes work is the lifeblood of a tennis player. There are players who get reputations as great practice opponents who can't win when it really counts. But the players I watched—Edberg, Bruguera, Ivanisevic, and Sergio Casal—were all accomplished match players. Although no practice can ever fully replicate the all-out hunger and fear of an actual match, that morning the ball was being fired around the court more fiercely than in most matches.

I took a seat in the front row in the empty Lipton stadium at 11:00 A.M., when the temperature in Florida was in the gorgeous low nineties. This was spring training with a fury. The metal on the seat made my bare legs jump. The younger players I saw in the two practices, Ivanisevic and Bruguera, both took their shirts off with a smile, flicking sweat onto the green hard court. It stained briefly and disappeared.

Tennis is so much the notion of a perfectible dream. A professional tennis player must be as devoted to practice as a musician. And as with a musician, there is no guarantee that if you practice for hours you will improve past a certain stage. But if you skip the hard morning workouts before the evening matches, the fine-tuning of the match music is likely to go off. Players reveal much about themselves in the course of a practice session, and they often are very particular to whom they reveal secrets that later may be used against them. There is a trade-off in picking a practice partner. Stefan Edberg had hooked up with Sergi Bruguera, whom he could not beat on clay and did not fear on grass or hard courts. It seemed like a perfect fit. Edberg needed Bruguera to get the benefit of the tremendous overall pace generated by the twenty-two-year-old Spaniard. But at the same time, Edberg was revealing himself completely to the younger player.

Inside the big green stadium built with the help of Buchholz brothers and all those Lipton tea leaves, my reward for arriving early for the scheduled Edberg–Bruguera practice was catching the tail end of Goran Ivanisevic's practice with Sergio Casal, the blond Spaniard who was a former world doubles champion. There is such beauty to a thing well done. The two players knocked the ball back and forth across the net at incredible speed without missing, ball after firmly struck ball. At first, Casal and Ivanisevic were totally in sync with each other's play.

Gradually, by the seventh or eighth stroke of each rally, what had at first appeared as an imperceptible difference in technique began to open wider like a door, so that somewhere between the ninth and thirteenth strokes, Ivanisevic's opponent was still there but hanging on only by a strand of willpower. Casal continued to hit the ball hard but was making contact later and later until the rally became a balancing act that Casal could no longer maintain. He tried in vain to correct with power what was actually escaping him in balance. After missing a forehand, Casal cursed softly in Spanish but couldn't dwell on his disappointment because Ivanisevic was already sending the next ball toward him. They went on, lost in that beautiful rhythm, until they broke twenty minutes later for water and sat down in their chairs on either side of the umpire's tall green throne. Ivanisevic took long, satisfying swigs of water and looked up at the third person on the court.

"*Mrs. Doubtfire,*" Coach Bob Brett said to Goran Ivanisevic, whose perplexing talent had been entrusted to Brett by Ion Tiriac. "Robin Williams is brilliant in this movie, Goran—all dressed up in drag. You ought to go see it."

Brett said it lightly, trying to loosen up Ivanisevic, but the latter just stared down at the green hard court for a second, then leaped back up to go to work.

Now Ivanisevic began to punish himself as well as the ball. A moment ago he had been unbeatable off the ground, but suddenly, up at the net, he hit one volley long and he exploded. Sergio Casal began to hit lobs to him, but the lobs came over lower than the six-foot-four-inch Croatian liked, and rather than bend under them, Ivanisevic drilled three angry overheads into the back fence on the fly and threw his racket down in disgust. He was still upset about the easy volley he had missed.

"Hey!" shouted Brett. "What did you expect, you silly goose?"

Brett leaped up onto the court with racket in hand, stood ramrod straight in front of the net himself, and hit a mechanical overhead long himself, laughing, trying to get the handsome Ivanisevic to laugh and forgive himself for being human. I nodded. Brett was trying to tell his star without actually saying it in words that it makes no sense to have a great instrument (oneself) if the instrument is strung too tightly to make a reasonable sound. It was like watching a master class. Instead of pushing Goran Ivanisevic farther in an unhappy direction, Brett immediately stopped the volleys and called Ivanisevic back to the service line. Sergio Casal, now dripping with sweat, smiled in admiration. Serve after serve blew out of Ivanisevic into the corners of the service box. He was suddenly like a Ferrari again. Brett smiled briefly and turned his back when Ivanisevic looked at him for a compliment. Ivanisevic served one more game, which Casal won, and the players trotted to the net.

"I must be very good," said Sergio Casal, winking after breaking Goran's serve just once, and the remark made Ivanisevic break into a huge grin.

Stefan Edberg and Sergi Bruguera were already bouncing on their toes at the side of the stadium court. But Ivanisevic, pale board-hard stomach bare, stood there hanging over the net, sweating and grinning from ear to ear as if pleased to let Edberg and Bruguera wait.

"Okay?" asked Edberg softly.

The four players passed. Bruguera chatted briefly with Brett, who was a good five inches shorter than all of them, but the tall dark Spaniard and the blond one, Casal, seemed to have a certain rivalry or Spanish class tension and said hardly anything to each other, though they did give each other a familar nod and half-smile. Bruguera was shirtless, wet, tan, and strong. Edberg was wearing knee-length gray shorts and a dark-green T-shirt.

There is a kind of hunger in a top athlete, and the early parts of a training session are like bingeing on food, drink, or sex—you just can't get enough of it fast enough. Edberg was polished, of course, and gave the impression of taking his time. But there was such an intense expression on his face you could tell he was not there for pure pleasure or leisure. This was professional time, not to be fooled with or wasted.

Bruguera, fifth in the world, after Edberg, ranked third, went at it for an hour and a half, stopping only twice for water in the ninety-degree heat. There were no coaches, no encouragement, only all-out effort from the two of them. Their drives passed back and forth in a topspin conversation slightly higher and safer over the net but more tightly spun than Ivanisevic's flat, often wild drives. The pace was gorgeous. They seemed to come at each other in great, almost bright green waves of topspin, and follow-through. Each player tried to hurry his opponent into an error, yet they both exuded an excess of spare time in getting to the ball, which rose off them like a kind of luxury. They were two or three chess moves ahead of each bounce of the ball. Edberg glided, never chasing it. Bruguera took young, springy strides capable of covering leagues as in a fairy tale. They pushed each other so happily all over the court that at first they did not seem to be in opposition but were more like coconspirators against the ball. Then, as they started to play a set, they became like two carpenters on the same nail.

At first Bruguera hit almost every drive out, and Edberg was looking much better than the Spaniard. But in the third practice game, Edberg had to serve for nearly ten minutes, through a half-dozen ad-outs, and when the Swede lost that game, it was Bruguera who seemed to leap to life on the bright green hard court. The Spaniard's strokes were bursting with something young and sweet. Bruguera's topspin seemed as smooth as icing; Edberg's topspin drives were also smooth, but surprisingly to me, the ball was not popping off his racket quite the way it came off Bruguera's frame. Bruguera punched a backhand volley up the line. Edberg, who had hit his backhand return cross-court, raced to his forehand line and staggered slightly as he reached the ball a half bounce late and skied it. Edberg's lean, fully extended body bent over in the alley like a half-opened book nearly slammed shut.

Even the twenty-three-year-old Spaniard's errors were wonderful to behold since they were all errors of commission, not omission. As I watched Bruguera, I thought of a bullfighter because his skills were so exact, his demeanor so tall and proud yet graceful. Suddenly there was almost nothing Bruguera could not get back, even Edberg's first serves. Bruguera's pace rose to a higher level. Edberg walked in a circle behind the baseline to regroup. Then the Swede started to attack the net so quickly, so lightly that he did not seem to impose his power at all, and this was Edberg's signature; this kind of power was perhaps even more deadly than Becker's or Marc Rosset's because it was combined with pure speed, the way Pancho Gonzalez's power was.

But Bruguera had presence and a great touch, too. With both players up at the net, they hit five drop-volley angles, a great practice point that Bruguera finally won.

"I can't believe it!" roared Edberg, biting the fuzzy tennis ball and throwing it over the net to Bruguera. Truly surprised by the clay-court star, Edberg smacked the top of the net with his racket, and they smiled at each other.

"Too good," Edberg muttered moments later, after he was passed up the line off a first serve he had hit as hard as he could.

By now, Edberg's shorts were sopping wet, and Bruguera's bare upper body had turned a darker shade of brown. The difference between the two players was small, but most of those slivers of difference seemed to get collected by Bruguera. Edberg, the greatest mover tennis had seen in the past decade, looked like the superior yet the slower player. The Swede kept stretching for the ball. The volleys that he used to take a foot out in front of his body on his way to the top of the net were now hit late, with no weight behind them because

Edberg was moving sideways. All the fractions of a step slower seemed to add up to give Bruguera the edge.

Suddenly, Stefan Edberg played an awful point, ending in a wild mishit due to fatigue. Each ball in the rally came off Edberg's racket with a dull thud. I had never seen Edberg play a point like that. In his final backhand drive in response to a short ball, he sent the ball high and long into the backstop on the fly. Edberg waved his hands and bent over. He was exhausted. Bruguera looked around and stared at Edberg in surprise.

Bruguera did not say a word or show a sign of pleasure. When the practice set on the hard court was over and Bruguera had won it, they both came to the net for water and Edberg asked the Spaniard for his racket. He wanted to hear Bruguera's strings against his own racket. Stefan Edberg began banging the young Spaniard's strings against his own racket head and listened carefully. It was the sound of youth against impending age. And youth had the higher, sweeter pitch. Then, as if to be sure of what he had just heard in Bruguera's strings, Edberg played the strings of two of his own racket frames against each other, searching for the younger, more lively tension. Still frowning, Edberg discarded the racket he had been using.

They went back at it again. Edberg could not quite do it. Bruguera was sailing above the waves while Edberg was swimming through them. Two more players had gathered at the side of the stadium court for practice. Edberg played one more service point and won it, then signaled to Bruguera that their practice time was over. I had never seen Edberg look so tired. He patted Bruguera lightly on the shoulder. The quality of the Swedish champion's heart rested in the lightness of of that gesture. Once more, quickly, he banged the strings of two of his rackets together and listened, not quite satisfied.

Stefan Edberg lost the third round of the Lipton 7–6, 6–2 to Andre Agassi. Agassi came alive in the tiebreaker points. His level of play rose into the second set as he began to time Edberg's serve a little better with his each return of serve. If you put a hundred Agassi passing shots together on a piece of film, you would see in nearly each the same brief run, turn, and rapid-fire brush-up on the ball. Agassi's topspin forehands happened so fast it was nearly impossible to read which way his hand would ultimately turn the ball. This victory marked Agassi's rebound from year-long doldrums. Balding, the remaining dark hair cropped close, Andre Agassi was himself at last. Usually so mild, he roared nearly in anger when he won the match from Edberg. Agassi had fallen from athletic heights and was on his way back.

Stefan Edberg and Sergi Bruguera did not meet again until Monte Carlo, where Edberg was seeded second but lost to Bruguera 6–2, 7–6 on clay. The handsome Spaniard also beat Edberg in Düsseldorf when they played for Spain and Sweden, again on clay. Edberg's record, which had been 16–2 before he lost to Pete Sampras at Indian Wells in early March, was 32–11 two months later after the French Open, which Sergi Bruguera won, banking the $561,080 winner's share. Clay was a slow surface that favored the young, fast and patient. Wimbledon's grass was around the corner. Jonathan Stark would be in England, too. The faster surfaces, more suited to Stefan Edberg's game, were on the horizon.

ANIA BLESZYNSKI

"The behavior of the system either confirms the experiment or it doesn't. If it doesn't, it means that your underlying theory was wrong."

"Your area was the area of subatomic particles?"

"Better to say, 'elementary particles.' *Elementary* means they are the most basic particles. Not divisible anymore."

"Were both you and your husband working in the same area of physics?"

"Yeah, yeah. We met at the university in Kraków."

"And when did you leave Poland?"

"Well, if you want to be very exact . . . let me see. Seventeen years [ago]. 1977."

"And your reasons for leaving Poland were . . . ?"

"Political reasons."

"There was no freedom whatever?"

"No."

"And that was a problem?"

"Yes," said Elizabeth Bleszynski, the mother of Ania, the young tennis player I had decided to follow and use as a lightning rod for that period of transition between junior tennis and college tennis or the professional game.

"Were you feeling pressure in your work over in Poland before you left?"

"Actually no, not us. We were in a very privileged position in Poland. The reason is that if you are physicist, a mathematician or a chemist, the [Communist] Party did not exercise the pressure on you quite so much as if you were in humanities. We did not have any social influence. Our work, our teaching—very few people understood it anyway. If you are a historian . . ."

"You can get in trouble with the Party authorities."

"You can get in trouble one way or the other, but we did not feel this constant pressure."

"I went to Russia in 1980," I said. "It was pretty bad there."

"It was also pretty bad in Poland in 1977," said Mrs. Bleszynski. "There was unrest. But we actually did not think it would end so fast. It did not feel so close to the end of the empire, no."

"I remember the movies about the shipyards in Gdansk. The translation is, I think, 'Man of Steel?' "

"*Man of Iron,*" she quickly corrected me.

I winced, embarrassed. The "Man of Steel" was American: Superman. But those beautiful Polish movies showed a world of struggle in which Communist privilege was something both desired and corrupt that in its moral shadings, reminded me of parts of Antonioni's movies and of Marlon Brando's world in *On the Waterfront*. It was easier to watch such a world on a movie screen than to live in it day to day. Eventually the Bleszynskis got out of Poland, and it took moral courage as well as physical courage for them to leave. If they had wanted to accept the Communists and stay, they could have lived well. As it was, the Bleszynskis left quite a lot behind. Ania's grandfather had also been a well-respected scientist and the president of Kraków University.

"How did you get out of Poland and into West Germany in 1977?"

"My husband got a visiting position at the University of Heidelberg," Elizabeth Bleszynski continued in her heavily accented but very thoughtful and precise English. "We finished our Ph.D.s in Poland, both of us. And we had traveled a little bit before. We had had short-term positions. For example, my husband spent a year in Rome at the Institute of Nuclear Physics at Frascati. We traveled to Trieste, to the International Institute for Theoretical Physics. Then there was a well-known laboratory in Denmark. So we would try to spend a couple of months a year away from Poland, and we always returned."

"The authorities became confident in you?"

"No. But we did travel off and on to conferences. Sometimes we were refused passports. The reason was not given. When my husband received notification of the position at Heidelberg, we decided that we were not going to come back. I applied for a leave of absence from my institute, and we took both children with us, Ania, who was one, and her brother Peter, who was five years older."

"Did your colleagues know you were not coming back?" I asked, but Mrs. Bleszynski hesitated. "Maybe you don't want to answer that."

"No, I don't. Because, well, I know the situation has changed. But *if* they knew, they were supposed to report us."

"What did you take with you except your two children?"

"Basically nothing." She corrected herself. "But *books*. We took quite a few books!"

"Didn't anyone say that you were taking too many books with you for just one year away?"

Elizabeth Bleszynski was laughing. "Yes! And it was true! We took too many books. And that is exactly what they were saying to us. 'Too many books!' But we *needed* all those books. At least that is what we were saying. And, of course, we did not want to leave our books behind because they were mostly in Polish, and we thought we could never get them again."

I was laughing, too. Books. No tennis rackets yet. No extra clothes. Boxes and boxes of books. I liked these people. Books from Poland to Germany to the United States. Next to a book, a violin, and a canvas, a tennis ball was the most international thing I could think of. I smiled recalling the old saw about athletes, "He's not exactly a rocket scientist." Well, Ania Bleszynski's parents were.

"What can you say about the work you do at Rockwell International? It's in the particle physics area?"

"No. Well, OK. They call it 'Advanced Research and Technology.' So it's research. But it is not in the area of particles. It is in the area of electromagnetic phenomena. Ahh." Her voice trailed off. "A lot of this work is classified work."

"Then I shouldn't ask you too much more about it. But are you talking about planes, about outer space, what?"

"Well, when it's classified, basically we talk about aircraft and communications. When it is unclassified, we may talk about biomedical applications, for example."

"Fine. Now maybe we can talk a little more about another unclassified area—tennis—if you are prepared for that leap."

Ania Bleszynski's mother laughed again.

"But having come to the United States with not much besides books, what was it like? Was it a tremendous change for you?"

"You see, not so much. We spent one year in Heidelberg, and then we got positions here in America, both of us, as assistant professors at UCLA. So we were spared quite a lot—the feeling of insecurity, et cetera—by having a job. We knew the people we were working with to some extent. It was basically the same work we were doing before."

"But in terms of *life* in America and how your daughter got into this game played between lines. Did you notice big changes in your lives coming from Europe to America?"

Elizabeth Bleszynski seemed to inhale and hold her breath. "Yes," she said reluctantly. "Well, both my husband and I were very focused on our work. But we both noticed. There was much less stress on education in America than in Poland. This was our first observation. Well, one of the first, because when we first came to the States we did not go directly to Los Angeles. We spent close to a year at Los Alamos."

These people were not playing around with cap guns. I listened as she continued.

"Although Los Alamos is an international laboratory," she explained, "it is run by UCLA. Los Alamos is a very strange community. I mean, 80 percent of the people who live in Los Alamos have Ph.D.s, and the population is seven, maybe ten, thousand. So the change was not drastic. And the schools in Los Alamos were very, very good. But then we moved to Los Angeles."

"And the schools there?"

"Very different. My son was in the public school in Los Angeles for a year and a half, but then we had to take him out. It was a shock.

Well, the education is obviously far less structured here. My son was too young for school in Poland, but he was in school in Germany, where it was much more structured. Of course, well, perhaps American schools develop independent thinking better." She paused and did not sound convinced. "At least that is what they say."

"You're not so sure about that either."

"No. The emphasis on sports is not something I was used to. I mean, I was interested in athletics to some extent when I was young," said the mother of the sixth-ranked junior girl tennis player in the United States. "I mean, the very first thing they ask you when you apply to a college in Poland is if you are an athlete. That is because they want to make sure that you are *not* an athlete before they accept you. If they are taking an athlete, this could create possible problems."

I laughed. There wasn't a coach in the United States who could honestly disagree with that last sentence. "Problems? You mean the person might play sports instead of studying?"

"Ya. They don't want it at the Polish university. Assignments would not be turned in on time; the person will be absent. There will be many excuses. They just don't want it."

"Do you think that you can do both, sports and education?"

Bleszynski laughed and said, "No."

"OK, Mrs. Bleszynski. Now we're coming right down to it." She was laughing some more, and so was I. "Your daughter, Ania, is a pretty good student, doing a lot of advanced placements in her courses. But she's deeply into tennis. Is she out of control?"

"Well, you see"—Elizabeth Bleszynski sighed—"well, Ania is relatively bright. That's one thing. She is also athletically very gifted. But what was happening until now, she was able to achieve in tennis without practicing as much as other kids. Ania is very intensive. She practices two to three hours a day, very hard, and that is enough for her. Sometimes she does not practice at all. The other top young girls are doing maybe five, six hours a day."

"Did you and your husband have success with sports in Poland?"

"Success? Not particularly. I skied. My husband played basketball. Are we coordinated? Yes, I think I am. My husband probably less so.

The problem is that the taller you are, the more difficult it is. My husband is six-four or six-five. Thereabouts."

"He's up there." I hesitated. "You know, I decided to follow Ania in part because she still really likes school. I spoke to all the girls on the U.S. girls' tennis team at the Orange Bowl, and I asked, among other things, if they were interested in their schoolwork. They were very nice girls, but not one of them except Nicole London expressed any interest in schoolwork at all. Maybe they were just young, but it surprised me just a bit. I mean, you see somebody like Jennifer Capriati, and she's become very unhappy with tennis, and now she has no fundamental learning in anything *except* tennis. I see it in a lot of the junior girls and boys. They've put all their eggs into one basket, and there's a pretty good chance it's going to be the wrong basket."

Elizabeth Bleszynski was five foot eleven and, despite her dark hair, had something of the attractive but unobtrusive looks of Marathon runner Greta Waitz. Elizabeth spoke analytically: "Well, of course, in order to be good at something you must put all eggs into one basket. Sometimes it works for you. Sometimes it doesn't. Very often people do not put all eggs in one basket, and it doesn't work for them either!"

"That's true. All great talent is obsessive; with some of the girls it's as if their life is predisposed and set by their parents before they really know any alternatives. Their education for later life is going out the window, as it does for young black basketball players. The boys develop later and get closer to college before they make their decisions. And then there are some girls, like Amanda Basica and Meilen Tu, who drop out of school and take up home study. What do you think of that?"

"Ah, no. Learning, whether it is science or tennis, is not only reading from a book. It's the *exchange* of information. It is being exposed to someone else's opinions and ideas. School is necessary. It helps you understand the same problem from other points of view. I mean, these tennis children are growing. They are too young for that. They still need interaction. When people are thirty or forty and have certain ideas developed, they can work more by themselves. But not when they are growing. I think home study is a very bad idea."

"But surely, coming from eastern Europe, you do believe in prodigies, don't you? Chess or gymnastics prodigies."

"Or piano prodigies," said Elizabeth Bleszynski.

"Yes. What do you do with a prodigy?"

She struggled briefly for an answer. "Well, you just train the kid only in this one direction. The expectations in gymnastics and swimming—or violin—mean you must play the instrument six hours a day to meet the requirements."

Her eastern European real-life exposure was intersecting with her new American standards. The irony for me was that when I was a young boy, tennis—far more than school—had been my broadest education. Tennis, travel, and intense competition taught me to respect and accept a wide variety of people. Tennis takes one beyond the limits of one's own background. But tennis and education have both become so specialized so early that parents face a difficult balancing act between developing a child prodigy and developing an individual who can go beyond the assembly line of tennis-camp play.

Elizabeth Bleszynski took both sides of the argument. "You see, if you want a prodigy, she must play that instrument six hours a day, starting when she is six years old. It is clear. If she is very good and wants to make it a career, then she should pursue it."

She confused me a bit, but I began to see two sides to her daughter. "But how," I argued, "can children that age really know they want to make a career out of it? We say they can't drive or drink before a certain age. How can we have them making choices about their careers at that age? Most kids don't even know what they want to be when they get out of college. I didn't."

"Ah." She laughed nervously. "Well, you might have some indications. Some are not going to make it as tennis players, and more parents should be able to see this more clearly."

"Right. You can tell if they are not going to make it, but you can't always tell if they are going to make it. Take Jay Berger or Brad Gilbert, two ugly ducklings when they were young, who really came on later as players. In fact, I'd argue that the ones who peak latest peak best. Ania may be a late bloomer, but she is now one of the best junior girls in the country. It seems to me that Ania has one foot in the boat and one foot off the boat in terms of making pro tennis a career. Do you have any sense as to where she is with the choice?"

"It's difficult for me to say," said Ania Bleszynski's mother quietly. "I have watched her play since the beginning. I was often thinking, 'Will she be able to make it, or not?' And I was not sure. There were a few factors which were against her. A lot of kids started to play tennis earlier. Ania was studying gymnastics for many years, but when she became eleven or twelve it was evident that she would be taller than five feet." Elizabeth Bleszynski laughed. "She had started tennis at ten, but it got more intensive when she stopped gymnastics. And then she suddenly started to catch up with other girls who were already accomplished players. Then came another change, which was very difficult. Ania grew so fast that she started losing coordination, and this was a setback."

The setbacks. If my parents kept a list of setbacks, it would have filled several legal-sized yellow pads.

Elizabeth Bleszynski continued. "So there was this setback when she grew so fast. And from this came the feeling that Ania was little bit insecure."

"Insecurity is not always a bad thing," I said. "Look what it did for Martina Navratilova."

"Yes. Well. In Ania's case, the coach she had at that time was developing in her a defensive type of game." The Polish-American tennis mother said this with distaste, as if fine Russian caviar had been put in a microwave and turned into soggy shad-roe. "We do not like moon-balling," she said. "So we changed coaches. I think Ania plays much more aggressively now than she used to. But Ania was always fast, always strong. She could run for hours."

"Hmm," I said softly. "Ania strikes me as being strong but a little slow and still a bit defensive, at least on clay. I haven't seen her yet on a hard court, but she does lack a little confidence. This little Brazilian girl got her on a clay court in Florida and took her apart. I think Ania would have beaten her on a hard court in California if she paid full attention."

"Well," said Elizabeth Bleszynski, "Ania used to play very defensively, not attacking enough, staying way too far behind the baseline, and consistently returning the balls. Now she takes advantage of her strength, and she is very independent as a person. But as a little girl her tennis was almost getting paranoiac."

I laughed. "How so?"

"Before going for a tournament, she would have everything laid out perfectly, a towel, a water jug, et cetera. The situation was, for example, that she lost a big match once in Santa Barbara because we did not have the *red* water jug with us." The mother laughed. "Ania was also very particular about warming up before she played. It had to be the right person with just the right amount of time left before her match, or she would get upset. Thankfully, it is much better this year. Ania is seventeen. Now she is arranging her own entrance wild-card to the pro tournaments if she is able to get one. And when she was applying to colleges, she never asked me or her father or her coach to help her. When she was trying to get into Stanford, for example, she thought she would not make it. She thought Nicole London would go there instead of her, and that is why that was such a big win for Ania at the Orange Bowl. Nicole was definitely more experienced, but Ania made it on her own."

"I saw her beat Nicole down at the Orange Bowl, before the college acceptances went out. Ania played as if she really wanted to win, and she did." I paused. "She is such a good tennis player. Are you pleased Ania is going to college, or will she go out and try the tour?"

Elizabeth Bleszynski sighed. "I am not 100 percent sure what Ania is interested in. The way I see it is that Ania is always very competitive in everything. It is my impression that it is not always that important *what* Ania is doing, as long as she is winning."

"Was Ania very competitive as a child?"

"Oh, very! I remember Ania played one of her first tournaments when she was about ten. She was doing some things on court that were very unwise. So I asked her, 'Ania, why are you doing things in this way? The coach never told you to do it this way.' And Ania said right back to me, and she was really very little at the time, 'Ya, I was doing it in this way because my coach doesn't let me do it this way in the practice.' So I answered her, 'Well, Ania, at least you have learned now that it doesn't work.' Ania looked at me, and she said, 'I am not playing *to learn* anything. I am not playing *to have fun*. I am playing *to win*.' "

"Ah," I said, recognizing the symptoms. Ania Bleszynski had the winning disease, too. I pictured the little girl who had said it, now grown up into a tall, attractive seventeen-year-old. "Did she say it in English or Polish?"

"English. I talk Polish to my husband, and Ania understands. I talk both Polish and English to her, sometimes mixing it, but Ania usually responds in English."

"What do you make of other tennis parents? Do they seem normal, strange, or both?"

Elizabeth Bleszynski, a fixture for years at the southern California junior tournaments, paused diplomatically. "I think that if the kids are good players, it requires a lot of commitment from the parents' side, too. And if there is that much commitment, the parents are going to be a bit uptight, too. Obviously they push their children because children at that age just would not think to do this on their own. They are twelve to thirteen years old. You cannot expect them to have such discipline by themselves . . . to have a perspective on it, or to know what they will be able to achieve five or ten years in the future. So the parents are more strict. It is a real commitment in terms of time—and finances as well."

"Ania said to me that her father wasn't very interested in her tennis and that even you weren't that interested. Was she fooling me?"

"Well, her father does not care so much. But I would get upset if Ania did not try at a tournament. But it was in terms of, 'Well, Ania, this was a waste of my time and waste of your time.' I kept it simple: don't try, don't play." Elizabeth Bleszynski laughed, but she did not fool around.

"Do you think Ania is maturing a lot right now mentally and emotionally?"

"In the last year and a half she has matured a lot. . . . she looks much more in control."

"Self-assured?"

"Yes. Well, I hope she is able to control her emotions more now. It was a problem to some extent when Ania was young. She would cry on court. She would throw rackets. She would hit balls over the fence. I remember she once hit two balls over the fence, and the umpire just climbed over the fence to pick up the balls instead of giving her a penalty point. Well, I think the umpire should have taken from her a penalty point. There were matches when she would cry from the very first point to the end of the match. She was mostly winning, but she was also crying. She was crying a lot. I think she has learned to control that now. But at ten or eleven, it was difficult."

"She was very emotional," I said softly, recalling the Orange Bowl quarterfinal loss. Competition is highly emotional for all the players that age. "Is Ania ready for the tour yet?"

"Well, I don't think she is emotionally ready to go on the professional tour," said Elizabeth Bleszynski. "Technically being ready is another thing. About a year ago, my husband and I sat with Ania and said it would be hard for her to go to college to study and also play on the tour. We said Ania could apply to college, take a deferred entry, and go on the tour if this is what she wanted." Elizabeth Bleszynski paused. "She didn't want to do it. I don't think she felt mature enough, assured enough."

I was surprised by her answer, in part because I thought women's tennis had shot itself in the foot by turning what once could rightly be called "women's tennis" into what amounted to "little girls' tennis." My favorite women players—Margaret Court, Maria Bueno, Billie Jean King, Evonne Goolagong, and Martina Navratilova—had always made the women's game seem like *women's* tennis. Tracy Austin, Andrea Jaeger, and even Chris Evert, early on, had been little girls. I liked junior tennis, and I liked women's tennis, but I wished the pro women's game could keep them separate.

"There is a gray area," said Bleszynski. "There is an area where much exploitation is possible. But I think if you are that good, you must do it. You don't agree?"

"Well," I said, "I believe in true prodigies, not false ones. A prodigy is the one in a million. The Jimmy Connors, the John McEnroe. I saw Jimmy Connors playing at age thirteen at the Nationals at Kalamazoo when I was sixteen. And I said, 'This is one little wise guy, but he is going to be a great player.' Dick Stockton was another prodigy from my generation. The Mayer brothers were different. Sandy Mayer was a chubby little boy, and I beat him once on a red clay court in Brooklyn when Sandy was just twelve. He bloomed very late. Little Genie Mayer was the prodigy in the Mayer family. But I think there are really very few *bona fide* prodigies and a lot of impostors. Burnouts don't really count. If you're *that* good, usually you will survive for a while. But today it seems as if everyone with a racket is a prodigy in somebody's mind. A lot of them just aren't that good. It's a shame. They become little machines that just break down."

"Yes. There are very many who are not going to make it," said Mrs. Bleszynski, matter-of-factly, in that lilting no-nonsense, Polish-accented English that I liked very much. "Well, there sometimes is also the financial incentive."

I said nothing. For me, parents who lived off their children's income were a bit like Gypsy Rose Lee's mother, pimping their own children.

"For example," said Elizabeth Bleszynski, "a few years ago I was thinking that if Ania wants to play big tournaments, somebody has to travel with her. For me to travel with Ania full-time means I must leave my job. And I thought of this. But if I give up my job at Rockwell, even if I make a resolution never to bring it up with Ania, and if I try not to put the pressure on, I am sorry, this pressure is there anyway. You do not always win. There are a lot of times when you as a tennis parent are down, and then something may be said in anger. I decided that the child should not feel the pressure that would come if I gave up my job to travel with her tennis."

I told her I thought she had made the right decision.

"Yeah. I think so. So I told Ania, 'I cannot give up my job.' This means, if Ania makes it, she makes it by herself. But another big thing a child needs is a coach, and a coach is very expensive. So now there are a lot of people who approach the parents when the child is very young to strike with you a financial deal."

"You mean a Bollettieri, Macci, or Palmer Academy—a coaching system like that?"

"No. I mean investors. They came to me from all walks of life, and they said, "Mrs. Bleszynski, we will invest such and such monies in your daughter from the age of thirteen to age eighteen."

"You mean like fifty or a hundred thousand dollars?"

She chuckled. "Ya, hundred thousand. Closer to two hundred thousand dollars."

"What did they want in return?"

"They wanted me to sign a contract as her guardian saying that when Ania turned pro they would get 30 percent of everything she would make on or off the court. I don't know how legal this thing is when the girls and boys are still supposed to be playing as amateurs, but most of the top juniors have a sponsor *before* they turn pro." Elizabeth Bleszynski paused. "I could not possibly do this. One of the reasons was that my husband and I were not necessarily committed to Ania turning pro. Some parents are not particularly committed to a pro career, but they accept the money anyway. For me, for us, it was impossible. If I was not sure to take Ania out of school when she was fourteen or fifteen, then I should not take this money."

The Bleszynskis impressed me. How many others would have turned their back on two hundred thousand dollars offered in that way?

"What about Amanda Basica?" I asked. "She's a good player. But she has made an awfully big commitment just now by dropping out of high school in California. Maybe in the long run she has made the right decision, but at the Orange Bowl she looked pretty unhappy, in part because her body is starting to change and get a bit heavier. I think Amanda feels the pressure on her tennis more now that she is out of school than when she was still going."

"There was always lot of pressure on Amanda," said Elizabeth Bleszynski. "Even last year, she wasn't playing that well. Her parents are definitely, well, I would say, *obsessed* with her tennis. The father works. The mother teaches part-time. But everything revolves around the tennis of Amber and Amanda in that house." She sighed. "They were brought up this way."

"What about the pressures on the girls from the college recruiters?"

"I did not talk to many coaches. Ania handled it all. Perhaps I was not very . . . receptive. Ania was really pretty straightforward. She came down to two colleges: Stanford and Harvard. Ania visited Harvard. When she came back, she said, 'Well, I don't know.' You see, Ania could get into Harvard even if she was not on the tennis team."

I had not known that. Ania Bleszynski sounded as bright as—or even brighter than—Bill Bradley. "Ania's grades were that good?"

"Well, she usually doesn't talk about it, and she doesn't usually let me talk about it," said the physicist, "but Ania's SAT scores were over 1550."

I admit I whistled. My own 550 math was good enough to know that the perfect score, 800, times two equaled 1,600. I was not a great believer in College Board scores. My own had been middling at best, and I had not gotten interested in school until I started to write and then books came alive for me. Athletes often make great students once they find a subject they love.

My all-time favorite college admissions story involved a boy named Steve Owen, who was doing a postgraduate high school year at the Choate School. He was a short, dark-haired hockey star with a heavy Boston accent and more self-confidence than most entire teams. He wore jeans to his on-campus interview with the Harvard admissions man, who wore bifocals low on his nose and peered down imperiously at the athlete's transcript.

"Mr. Owen," the Harvard admissions man said, "with SAT scores and grades like these, what *ever* made you think you could get into Harvard?"

Owen, who had the habit of speaking in a quick, forceful staccato, said, "I put the puck in the net."

Steve Owen played hockey for Harvard—then for the Olympic hockey team—and now has a car dealership outside Boston.

Ania Bleszynski seemed like the flip side of that coin. She liked school just as much—or almost as much—as she liked tennis. I liked the complexity of that choice and how it might play out for her in the ensuing months. College was never intended to be a minor league training camp for a sports career that has more glamour than long-term meaning. But that's what it had become for many talented tennis players.

I thanked Elizabeth Bleszynski and asked her to send me pictures of her and her family in California. Two weeks later, by mid-February, the photographs arrived.

There was a picture that caught my eye, Ania at fourteen sitting on a rock on top of a mountain range with her father, Marek. Ania was smiling in a new, bright red Lacoste shirt and khaki pants with a white tennis sweater wrapped around her waist and a pair of mountain-climbing gloves over her hands. Her father was a mountain climber, tall and thin, wearing a slightly worn white Lacoste shirt. Marek Bleszynski's face was pale and attractive in the Polish way. His hair was blond, and his eyes looked very tired, as if the American dream was, like the San Andreas fault, always at risk of becoming the American middle-class nightmare. The Bleszynskis were not rich like the family of Ania's rival, Meilen Tu. The Bleszynskis were reasonably "well off," as a result of both parents working in physics for ten to twelve hours a day. They were making good enough salaries to have a nice home on an acre of good land, but when their second child, Ania, won a college scholarship, it was something of a relief.

In one picture, Ania at fourteen looked like a tennis prodigy. Her arms hung at her side and were exceptionally long. Her hands seemed to rest cupped open as if the memory of having a racket in them was never distant. She stood sideways with her chin up.

The picture from inside the house showed an elated Ania, at sixteen with a big, happy smile, her arms extended out sideways so far they went out of the picture, and behind her was her study desk, her old computer with a towel over it for a dust jacket, an open schoolbook, and three stuffed bears watching her from the counter.

The Bleszynskis' house was not shown fully in the photos, but in one of the pictures of Ania I noticed a tall rosebush that grew up the side of the house and a small swimming pool. It seemed like a bit of California heaven in Thousand Oaks, California.

There was also a photo of Elizabeth Bleszynski and her son, Peter. A would-be architect, he was twenty-two-years-old, stood six foot six, and had a gentle smile. Elizabeth was unable to find what she called a very representative picture of the house, so she described it to me in her longhand letter:

We live fifty minutes N/W of Los Angeles, approximately half way between Los Angeles and Santa Barbara. The home is a one-story, 4,000 square foot, ranch-style house spread out over one acre of land. It is surrounded by several very old and tall pines. There are also some perpetually green trees (I do not know how they are called) along the driveway and the front fence. The outer boundaries of the property are fenced in with a white wooden fence (meets local home owner's association regulations). There is also an inner-fence (meets federal safety regulations at swimming pools). The house is the so-called "home property" and there is a "home trail" along the back of our yard.

The detailed account made me smile, for it sounded as if Elizabeth Bleszynski were describing a tennis court. A week later, I got a letter from Ania Bleszynski. She had played three pro events in Texas and Oklahoma in January, and I had written her to find out how she did.

"Hi! How are you? Thank you for your letter and your phone call. Sorry it took me so long to get back to you. I have been awfully busy. I will attempt to answer all your questions and I hope my answers are satisfactory.

Our house and my family were not directly affected by the big earthquake, but I can't say the same for others around here. All the courts are still playable, but there were a few cracks.

Don't worry about interviewing me before my match at the Orange Bowl. It didn't throw me off. My loss has nothing to do with you, but with me. It was just hard being by myself, having Christmas the next day, and having a warm-up partner who never showed up. I shouldn't have let those things disturb me, though.

Robert Lansdorp asked me to think hard of how I could lose to D'Agostini 6–0, 6–0 on clay. He asked why I couldn't figure something out that would work. I think the problem is that I wasn't willing to keep trying things to find something that would work. I just wasn't motivated, which sounds like a puny excuse for the quarter-finals of the Orange Bowl. He said I have to be much tougher mentally.

My parents did not have a lot to say about the match I lost— they usually don't. My father is completely uninvolved in my tennis, and my mom wasn't there to see it, so she couldn't say too much. She was happy that I beat Nicole London. It was my first time.

Playing in Texas in early January at my first pro event was

definitely an experience. It was only a $10,000 Challenger, but I reached the final of the first tournament. My first round against Katrin Kilsch was a good draw. She is a solid player who does not do very much. It really made me work on my consistency and on my volley game, without pressuring me too much.

Second round, I had to play the number one seed, Michelle Jackson Nobrega. She was ranked 260 in the world, and I was 697. [Michelle Jackson Nobrega's ranking improved to number 134 in the world as of January 1995. She got injured and her ranking fell to 220 as of October 1995.] I didn't have anything to lose, and I thought it would be nice to beat her. After losing the first set 6–4, I realized that she was beatable if I played just a little better. In the second set, I came up to net a lot with a large amount of confidence that quite surprised me. I was playing consistently and aggressively. In the beginning of the third set, I didn't think I could keep up with her, but she gave me a lot of the first games. She was missing a lot, and I thought gradually she was giving up. But she didn't. When I was up 4–1, she started coming back and making her winners. I became nervous and began hitting shorter. She got up 5–4, 30–0. I was sure I was going to lose then, but I still gave it my best, and I won 7–6 in the third set.

That win gave me the confidence that I could repeat it against the number eight seed the next round. I did, beating Maja Wittke of Germany. I didn't play that well, but I played very consistently, and I intimidated her.

In the semis, I was up against Mamie Cenisa, the number five seed. I practice with Mamie at UCLA, and I have never beaten her in practice. In fact, I have never even come close. I was not very sure of myself. That day in Texas it was very windy. But whereas she was upset about the wind, I decided to try to work with it—and it worked out well for me. I won 6–3 in the third set.

I was feeling good about the final the next day against unseeded Tatiana Panova, a junior who just turned pro. She takes everything on the rise, and uses a lot of topspin, and she is very quick. I lost 6–1, 6–1 in the final, and I missed a lot.

I could see Ania Bleszynski trotting up to the net after the final point, shaking her head, and blowing air out of her mouth in discouragement. She got so down on herself when she lost.

As I continued reading the neatly hand-written letter, it was not surprising to learn she lost in her next pro event in Austin, this time against another Tatiana—Tatjana Jecmenica—who went on to win the event. Ania was getting a good taste of what made the pro tour so different from junior or college play. She had started so well, getting to the final of her first pro event, but after the loss to Jecmenica, she confided, it was very hard mentally to finish up at one pro tournament and have to go off to another one and face the very same people again. Ania played a third pro tournament in a row and described it to me as follows.

By this time I felt like I wanted to go home. I tried to convince myself that I had one more tournament and to do well. But staying mentally tough for three straight weeks was a whole new thing for me. I drew Kristina Brandi in the first round. She is a human backboard which sends everything back rather soft, but deep. I tried to win the points quickly in the beginning, but I had little control. I was trying to hit winners from the baseline because I had little confidence in my volley that day. Eventually, I would miss. After that match, I was extremely upset. I cried a lot when I got back to the condo room.

There were so many ways I could have beaten her, and I felt like I hadn't given it my all. It was my last match of the pro series, and I was disappointed in its outcome. Now I really wanted to go home!

Robert [Coach Lansdorp] did not have much to say back in California, except he again commented on my lack of enduring mental toughness. I just can't keep it through so many matches. I still peak for just one tournament. That is something I *have* to work on. I didn't play tennis for two weeks after that, partially because I was disappointed in my last two tournaments after nearly winning my first one. I also had to study for finals.

On Wednesday Lynne Rolley called me to tell me that they

had a wild card for me into the $150,000 tournament in Okla-homa City. I hadn't been playing for two weeks, but I didn't want to decline the invitation, because then they might not offer it to me again. I felt determined to do well.

I arrived in Oklahoma OK on Friday, and I practiced for an hour and a half. I got a really bad headache, as did most of the other girls, I believe from the weather. I played at ten the next morning and felt very good. I had to play Anne Mall, the number two seed. Her 181 WTA ranking scared me a little bit. At the start of the match, she hit many hard, low winners. I missed it whenever she didn't hit a winner. It was a sad sight. I got way down before I started getting back into it. However, it was too late. She qualified.

My general observations of the pro tour are favorable. I think the tournaments were well organized, and the housing was always good. The players were treated well, and warm-ups and court bookings were fairly easy. In order to do well as a pro, you really have to have the killer instinct—and a lot of support, too. I think it is hard without a coach or parent, just out there on my own. However, I am slowly getting used to that situation. The hardest thing for me was finishing one tournament and going right on to the next one, where the same people participate again. It is like reshuffling the cards and playing the same game over again. I don't know why, but I found it very strange.

About the other girls. I did not associate with too many of them, as I did not care to. But I felt comfortable with all of them. I knew Mamie Ceniza and I made a few other friends, but I tried to stay focussed.

My parents are not TENNIS PARENTS. As I said, my Dad is completely uninvolved and does not know even how to keep score. My Mom has been with me to many tournaments and she knows my game. Recently, she has been with me much less as I am growing up and she has *plenty* of work of her own to do. They both see my studies first, and I agree with them 100%. But I also want to be a player.

It is hard to answer everything, but I hope I have helped a little.

The letter included a P.S.: "Can you please send me that jump rope exercise sheet you mentioned at Orange Bowl? I need it!! (I'm slow)." There was another, handwritten P.S. on the outside of the letter, which I noticed as I was folding it up: "Sorry my letter is not so formal and typed up as yours was." I laughed and put it back in the envelope.

Just seventeen, ranked number 690 in the world on the WTA computer, Ania Bleszynski had been accepted to Stanford University, but a part of her hoped she would turn pro. She and Amanda Basica had been two of the top-ranked junior players in southern California for the past seven years, winning age division titles in alternate years. Being tops in California means that you are one of the best players in the United States. Bleszynski was going to turn eighteen years old in October. Amanda Basica was still sixteen. Some people said Bleszynski had a "bad birthday" for tennis, because she was younger than most of the girls but three months shy of another year of eligibility. I thought she had a great birthday. She was happy at school, and she still loved tennis.

The differences between Ania Bleszynski and Jennifer Capriati were startling. Capriati had already made several million dollars by age eighteen. Bleszynski was still worrying about having to pay five hundred dollars round-trip to get back to the East Coast that summer to qualify for the ten-thousand- to twenty-five-thousand-dollar pro challengers. Capriati seemed to have already lived—and ended—a lifetime in five years as a tennis touring professional. Ania Bleszynski at age seventeen had her whole life in front of her.

There are levels, I suppose, to being a prodigy, but make no mistake about it, Ania Bleszynski was a prodigy, too. When all is said and done, the bottom line is not money but life. In most cases, unhappy people self-destruct by getting rid of their money, as if that in itself is a type of cleansing process by which they can get back to a point in time when they can remember themselves as being innocent. Capriati had lost that very innocence out on the tour. She had seen too much too soon—and she got a lot of money to do so. (Tracy Austin and Andrea Jaeger were likewise blessed and afflicted.) There was an element of child pornography to Jennifer Capriati's appearance at thirteen and her disappearance at eighteen on drug charges. Her loss touched my understanding of Ania Bleszynski. In fact, there was a little bit of Capriati—that tan, smiling, hard-hitting little girl who dreamed of being the next Chris Evert—in all the upcoming American junior players.

Mentally, Jennifer Capriati jumped the gun. She was physically strong and technically very well trained, but she had a child's heart. Like most children, she wanted to please her parents. When I first saw her at the Lipton in 1990 with her father seated next to her in a press conference attended by a hundred or so journalists and photographers, I stayed for the grins and flashbulbs, and one or two meaningless questions about her future and I walked out to watch Jay Berger play (and beat) Goran Ivanisevic. It is a hard thing for me to say about someone who tried as hard and performed as well as Jennifer Capriati, but ultimately, Capriati's career, over at eighteen, was like a Shirley Temple movie without Shirley Temple.

Still, the Capriati–Seles semifinal at the 1991 U.S. Open was one of the best competitive matches, male or female, that I ever saw. Capriati served twice for the match in the third set, and the stadium crowd at the U.S. Open thought she was about to have her breakthrough match against Seles. The two young girls were playing incredibly long, hard points. Seles was losing more of the points, but she was severely working over Capriati's body with those wide side-to-side penetrations Seles is so famous for. Capriati, who earlier that summer had beaten Navratilova, was going to face Navratilova in the final of the U.S. Open if she could just get two more points against Seles. She could not do it. Capriati played almost like a champion, attacking Seles bravely. Seles hung on like a boxer who trails on all scorecards going into the fifteenth round. Seles's body language seemed to say, "You may beat me, Jennifer, but I'll never help you. You're going to have to do it all yourself."

The collapse inside Capriati was something terrible to behold. She came into the interview room forty minutes late with her father, and it was obvious she had been crying her heart out. Her face was streaked with tears. It seemed cruel to have to put her through any interview at all, but she seemed sixteen going on forty. She was a pro.

I couldn't have imagined seeing a runaway sixteen-year-old hooker strung out on crack look any unhappier than Jennifer Capriati looked after losing that match to Seles. The first question to her in the interview room was, "Jennifer, was this the most disappointing loss in your career?" That reporter's lack of imagination was frightening. Capriati was just crushed inside and outside; she was truly beaten. It was not only her toughest loss ever, it was one of the toughest losses I had ever seen any athlete take. She could barely keep from crying while she tried to answer the questions that her game could not. Jennifer Capriati was never the same player again.

Seles, who seemed on the court to have a heart as hard as chicken gristle until her near-fatal encounter with the German stabber, had been too good a player. Seles had played a little below par and Capriati a little above herself, and deep down, silently, both girls knew it. It was one of those matches where the realizations that come along with it are deep and permanent. In terms of tennis fundamentals, Seles was weird, a European original. Capriati was technically very American and straight-ahead, and she was not an original. She was a Chris Evert clone, brought up on the new rackets but lacking Evert's incredible patience and maturity. No surprise—she had been exposed to the pro game at thirteen, five years younger than Evert. Only two or three points separated Seles and Capriati at the very end of their famous match, yet those three points were a mile wide. It was easy to blame parents, but pro tennis has itself to blame, too, for losing Jennifer Capriati. The expectations on Capriati at sixteen were enough to put the hump on Quasimodo.

Why don't we learn from our heroes instead of our disasters? Chris Evert did not turn pro until eighteen. John McEnroe did not turn pro until nineteen, and he lasted. Stan Smith started national tournaments at fifteen, turned pro at twenty-three, and lasted. Borg turned pro at sixteen, and he burned out early. Andrea Jaeger and Tracy Austin turned pro at fifteen. Steffi Graf is the exception, having turned pro at thirteen and surviving to age twenty-five, despite her father. But Capriati was *not* Graf or Evert, and very few Capriatis come along. Most players have only ten to twelve years of maximum freshness and strength in their bodies. Shouldn't everyone have to finish high school before turning pro? Robbed of a childhood, a player will find a childhood one day. Look at Borg, who became a teenager at last at age twenty-six, socially immature, undereducated and used to getting lots of attention. This is the legacy that so many top young athletes carry with them into their later years. I believe in starting them late. The later the adulation starts, the more likely it is a player can deal with it mentally.

Ania Bleszynski was approaching a new era of women's tennis. I believe in prodigies—I love them for their gift and for the incredible dedication and coaching that goes into making a prodigy a star. But I believe more in school and in learning through books and other people before you turn eighteen. And so I liked Ania Bleszynski. As a tennis player, she became a kind of experiment for me. She did not fit the normal tennis mold. She was a budding female Bill Bradley in an era of American sport that tended to reward deep specialization and make a mockery of ongoing education. I thought, despite her mother's doubt, that Ania could do both.

The next time I spoke to Ania was toward the end of May. She was very upbeat, the wins and losses in her first pro events gone like rain on a sunny day. Wimbledon was just around the corner at the end of June. I wondered if she would get added to the U.S. girls junior team by Lynne Rolley; I hoped she would get to go because I wanted to see her compete on grass, a surface I thought would eventually suit her game. She was just about to graduate from high school and had been to the prom with a young guy a few inches taller than she was.

"Who took you to the prom, a football player?"

"Actually, he does play football," said Ania. "But he's not really like the football player–type. Ah, he plays basketball, too, that's more his game."

I smiled. "Those are the best kind, the ones who don't seem like football players but are. How did your Advanced Placement tests go?"

"History and my Latin went fine. The physics was pretty difficult. Luckily, I think they curve those, so I have a chance. I took the classical mechanics physics test. It's, like, velocity and objects moving, like a car on an incline, and friction and that kind of stuff. I skipped the other physics A.P. test—electricity and magnetism—that's more atomic."

"Is the test formula oriented?"

"Yeah. Formulas and theory. It was pretty difficult, but I guess I did all right. I studied a lot for the math A.P. I stayed up until 2:00 A.M. on Thursday night, and I had the test on Friday morning. I pretty much *had* to study that much on it because if I didn't, I wouldn't do well on it. It was linear algebra. The exam was mostly on matrix transformation, vector spaces, and, like, vector calculus."

"Not one of my strong points. How did your paper on Jane Austen turn out?"

"Actually, it came out all right. Usually my essays are so bad I'm embarrassed to show them to people. But this one was OK. I got my first A on an English essay on it. I was so happy. I wrote about *Pride and Prejudice*."

"Send me a copy of it if you get a chance," I said. "And if you get the chance, try reading *Mansfield Park*. That's the one."

"Well," said Bleszynski, "I'll try to, but it's getting pretty busy with tennis again."

"What are your plans in terms of tennis for this summer?"

"I've been thinking about that a lot recently," she said, concealing her disappointment that again she had not been chosen for the U.S. National Team. "Julie Scott, my doubles partner from Texas, wants me to go to Europe with her on vacation. I was thinking of going, possibly to Wimbledon, but I've pretty much opted against it. I have a feeling that we would be lost in London and spending most of our time just finding where we are instead of seeing things." Ania Bleszynski laughed like a little girl. "Considering Julie and I are both seventeen, I think I'll stay around the United States this summer. I know I'll be playing the U.S. National Juniors August 7 in San Jose and the Olympic Festival the end of June and beginning of July in St. Louis. I have a month in between. Actually, I called and asked for a pro schedule, but they never sent me one. But I have a schedule of twenty-five-thousand- and ten-thousand-dollar tournaments, and there are two tens at the end of July in Virginia and two twenty-fives in July. I called Lynne Rolley about possibly getting in, but she said I should write her a letter. She said she might be able to get me in on a wild card, but they would not know until the week right before the tournament. It's a long way to go for one or two matches. I might do better playing juniors out here. Qualifying matches sometimes are a lot harder than the ones in the main draw. Down in Texas, Melissa Gurney, Tatiana Panova, and I were all in the semis of the qualifier, and only two of us made it into the main draw."

"And you were one of them?"

"Yeah."

I paused a moment. "How did you react to the Jennifer Capriati drugs-and-dropout story? Did it scare you a little?"

"It didn't scare me for myself personally, because I know I would never do that. That's just not me. But I think a lot of Jennifer's problem was that all she had was tennis. Her parents were pretty hard about pushing her. . . . I know that my whole life is not tennis yet. If I said to my parents tomorrow, 'I don't want to play tennis,' they would say, 'OK. That's fine.' In a funny way, that makes me want to play more."

"Your parents don't expect or want you to become a world-class player?"

Bleszynski laughed nervously. "Well, I think that if I were to turn pro, I'd have to ask my dad—and probably go through a few arguments with him. I'm sure he doesn't really want me to until—"

"Until a year or two of college?"

She sighed. "Until all four years of college and I graduate. My father doesn't really care all that much about tennis. He thinks it's just a game." Ania paused. "Sometimes I think that if I turn pro, if I dedicate myself even more to tennis, I really could be good. It's something that I would like to do. I dream to be top in tennis." She paused again. "But I don't know if I am ready for the full commitment. Quitting school. I don't know if I would really enjoy that."

"What is it about the full commitment that worries you?"

"I guess just being afraid that if something happens to me, if I hurt myself, then I wouldn't have much to do. Emotionally, knowing that if I was hurt and . . . couldn't play tennis, that would really hurt me— knowing I was way behind. If tennis was my only thing, I don't know if I would have as much fun with it as I do."

"You think you get hungry to play tennis because you've been working hard at something else?"

"Yeah. I'll be at my desk studying, knowing that tennis is coming up, and it's kind of a good break to look forward to. Go hit some balls, get my frustration out. I practice for about three hours on Wednesday and Friday: an hour practice, an hour lesson, and an hour workout in the gym. Monday, Tuesday, and Thursday are easier—I just play a practice match."

"Do you play men as well as women?"

"No. I have had a lot of women to practice with. Cammy Benjamin, Mamie Cenisa, Cammie Foley, Jolene Watanabe, Julie Richardson. Julie and Cammie are ranked, like, a hundred something in the world. I'm not much of a practice-match player. I usually lose to Mamie Cenisa in practice, but I beat her in that women's tournament in Texas. But playing the professional women is still a little different for me, even though I am practicing with a lot of them now."

"What is it about their games that you don't quite have yet?"

"I feel like in practice that they concentrate more than I do. And I get the feeling that they practice to win. I still like to work on things like coming up to net in practice. I don't care if I lose in practice."

"When you were getting recruited for college, what was that like?"

"At times it was kind of frustrating. Coaches would call me and I knew I didn't want to go to their school, but it was pretty hard to just flat-out say no. They would tell me their name, talk about what the school had, they had this and that kind of program, and it was good, and could they send me some more information?"

"And what did you say?"

She laughed quietly. "At first I just said, 'Yeah, maybe I'd be interested.' Because it was just so hard to say *no*."

"Sounds like real estate brokerage. If you didn't say no, they would call back again?"

"Right. The coach from the University of Arizona, Becky Bell, she must have called the maximum number of times that she could, like once a week, for a couple of months. After a while I kind of knew I wasn't going to go to her school, but I was afraid to say anything, because you never know where you'll get in. But Becky Bell was the first coach I said no to. After that, some coaches would call for the first time, and I would just stop them before they got going and say that I had my four choices and was going to stick with them. I applied to Duke, University of Texas, Harvard, and Stanford. Some of the recruiters knew I liked the academic side, too, so when the Notre Dame coach called, he said they were a top-twenty academic school. And William and Mary called, too, and I was really thinking about them because they are an old college and good, too, and they were offering me a full scholarship."

"Did they all offer a scholarship?"

"Everyone except the Stanford coach, Frank Brennan. He told me that he had just two scholarships, and I was third on his list. Nicole London and Stephanie Chi were ahead of me. In fact, Frank told me that if Janet Lee hadn't turned pro, she would have been his first choice."

"Sounds as if the Stanford coach was playing hard to get."

She laughed. "I guess. I was kind of upset when he told me that. My personal pride told me that I was better than Stephanie Chi and Nicole London. And I knew I could beat Janet Lee. Finally I signed because the other three weren't going. Stephanie's going to UCLA, and Nicole's going to USC. About two weeks later I played Janet Lee and beat her in an open women's tournament here in southern California. Then at the Orange Bowl a week later, I beat Janet again. I heard there was a lot of pressure on her at that match because there was a pro contract waiting for her to sign after the match, and the agents and businesspeople had come to the Orange Bowl to watch Janet play. I really wanted to beat her, and when I got by Nicole, too, I got a note from Frank Brennan that said, 'Two down, Chi to go.'" Ania Bleszynski laughed. "I haven't played Stephanie Chi yet."

But while Amanda Basica, Stephanie Nickitas, Cristina Moros, and Meilen Tu were packing for Wimbledon, Ania Bleszynski was in California practicing for the Olympic Festival tournament in St. Louis, which she would win. On the horizon for her were a number of junior girls' matches: at the U.S.T.A. National Junior Girls' 18 Championship in San Jose, California, the Canadian Juniors in Montreal, and the U.S. Open Juniors at Flushing Meadows, New York. As for Wimbledon, Ania Bleszynski and the other girls playing in St. Louis had to watch the event at home and dream of one day getting there.

WIMBLEDON

The players love it and fear it. They can feel Wimbledon in their stomachs a month before they get there. The ball, like their tennis fortunes, can kick in or slide away, changing directions in unexpected ways. The uncertainty is in the turf itself. Feet make the game. Clay courts and hard courts are safer roads. The footing is more sure there. The beauty of the grass is that it breathes. It lives. It is English.

Hard courts are more like American highways, omnipresent, imposing, yet often cracking. We seem to like our climaxes straight, fast, and requiring little care or doubt. The surface in France is red like the earth itself in Roussillon. The French like longer battles and slower climaxes—and they get them on the clay. The Australians, great sportsmen and sportswomen, competitive and somewhat cost-effective by nature, broke fully with their English past in the real estate upmarket of the 1980s, building a beautiful modern stadium in Melbourne and rubberizing their court surfaces. They will save money in the long run, but in going to a more American surface, they lost part of their grassy connection to England and to the true legends of world tennis: Frank Sedgman, Lew Hoad, Rod Laver, Roy Emerson, John Newcombe, Ken Rosewall, Margaret Smith, and Evonne Goola-gong, Australian tennis heroes and masters of the grass-court game.

The English have never poured cement or rubber over their lawns. They cling to their grass and gardens perhaps more deeply than to their monarchy. At Wimbledon, the English have both a pastoral and a political memory. Rising from the tradition of eighteenth-century cultivated "wildernesses," such an integral part of the drama of Jane Austen's novels, the tennis lawns at Wimbledon remain "great lawns." They sometimes feel like the victory gardens that still dot English cities. The Wimbledon grass may appear Tory in its elegance, but what is required to win at Wimbledon is mostly Labor. If outsiders make the greatest tennis players, as I believe they do, it is no surprise that Fred Perry, the champion in 1934, 1935, and 1936, had his 1930s likeness printed on Wimbledon's paper admissions tickets. Grass tennis, like life in England today, is complicated. It not an anachronism; it is another world.

Wimbledon has always been good theater, part Shaw, part O'Neill, part American soap opera. There is no script, just players, lawns, and lines—not to speak but to be judged by. The effort is always to be "in," not "out," in tennis, especially at Wimbledon. My favorite sign in England is at Wimbledon. It says WARNING: THE GENTLEMEN STANDING IN FRONT OF THE TEA STAND MAY BE TICKET TOUTS. To a New Yorker that's pastoral.

On opening day, Centre Court was surrounded by police and guards who kept the grassy theater empty until the appointed hour. I slipped in a little early. Four large, squarish holes were sunk deeply into the lawn. White lines ran long and perfectly straight the length of the bare grass court, and the net was missing. There were only twenty minutes left to the start of first-day play, and on the famous grass court where Don Budge played Fred Perry, and where John McEnroe played Bjorn Borg, a young woman in a long, pleated summer skirt with floral designs sat sideways on a pillow, weaving grass by hand. Every so often she consulted a map of the lawn and gestured firmly to a slight, blond young man in red sneakers, indicating where to place his kneeling pad to assist her in reweaving a few errant strands which, from my vantage point, already looked perfect. I felt like shouting, "Pickett's Charge is coming!" But that would have been American of me, and I was a visitor. Suddenly a tall, distinguished-looking man in overalls appeared with an electric meter, and he took height measurements of the grass at several locations around the court. I loved the craziness of the place, this Wimbledon, though I might not want to live by all its rules.

Up in the stands, still empty just before the two o'clock start, a young woman guard, wearing bright red lipstick, a blue skirt, a white shirt, and a round white sailor's dress hat, smiled up at a slender male guard of her acquaintance. They looked like shy lovers from World War II. The sky was an English gray, and the octagonal eaves of the tennis theater's roof seemed the color of a black English umbrella. The grass was so green in this darkened English light.

The press rooms were buzzing with good cheer, pecking-order tension, and predictions. Outside the grounds, queues inched politely forward. Ticket touts and bobbies, sons of the same working class, did their English dance of disgruntlement, propriety, and looking the other way. Newspaper boys with pictures of Andre Agassi and Pete Sampras on the front pages of editions whose cover pages changed every eight hours were hawking the faces of today's heroes, much as their fathers and grandfathers had hawked editions that described Bill Tilden's unexpected loss to Henri Cochet, Pancho Gonzalez's victory at age forty-one over Charlie Pasarell, and those titillating Wimbledon "scandals" that have run happily and uninterrupted from Joan Lycett playing in bare legs and ankle socks in 1931 to the romantic interlude in 1993 between Andre Agassi and that old teenager-at-heart, Barbra Streisand.

I love the raging doubt of it all. The unknown is exciting, tantalizing, nearly sexual the first day of a big tournament. The pressure is such that every player in the draw meets himself or herself as never before. Wimbledon is a place players have to keep coming back to in order to learn the surface and the place. Even Roy Emerson lost at Wimbledon for ten straight years before he won it twice in a row in 1964 and 1965.

Some players are naturally better suited to grass, through power or agility, preferably both. Grass generally rewards big serves and the bravery of coming forward to net, but in recent years the return has become as important as the serve itself, as Borg, Connors, and Agassi have all demonstrated at Wimbledon. The real challenge of grass-court play is not just power but balance. Lefties like Laver, McEnroe, and Roche got down so low to the ball and angled approach shots and volleys so deftly they almost made the ball roll. Righties like Budge, Kramer, Newcombe, Becker, and Edberg seemed to catapult into play above the ball, drilling it down hard, heavy through the grass. Neither method of attack is foolproof or easy for mere mortals to copy. As the well-known English tennis mortal Larry Adler described his own grass-court struggles to the gossip columnist at the *Evening Standard* the night before Wimbledon, "I play Cinderella tennis . . . I can't quite get to the ball."

The opening-day crowd was finally allowed into the stands. The best-dressed people seemed to be in the Royal Box, though everyone in the Centre Court enclosure looked dressed up for a country wedding. Down below, two short men in overalls unfolded the net like a flag and tied it fast to wooden net posts the color and thickness of the wood of an old yacht's mast. A burst of applause rose from the crowd. The linespeople, clad in drab olive-green skirts and trousers under bright green blazers, were marching onto Centre Court with all the pride and panache of handlers at a dog show.

Then came the players. The two Americans bowing to the Royal Box looked sleek, dark, and handsome, like fighter pilots before a mission. Jared Palmer was wearing all white. Pete Sampras sported a loose white shirt and checked shorts. The loudspeaker indicated as they warmed up that three presentations would be made from the Royal Box.

The elegant Duchess of Kent and her impeccably tailored, chinless husband, the duke, received an award for the meritorious service of his family since 1929, but I was more interested in the little Australian who stood up shyly behind them in the Royal Box. He was royalty as I understood it. He had proven himself and was not born to it. He smiled modestly, his left shoulder slightly lower than his right, his face still freckled, his hair redder than it had been in several years.

"Rodney George Laver," said the announcer in perfect BBC English.

"The greatest player of them all," I whispered to myself—with the possible exception of Tilden and apologies to Kramer and Gonzalez. It had been exactly twenty-five years since Laver won the second of his two grand slams. Sampras, who idolized Laver, put his racket down flat on the grass and applauded with the rest of us, and we were all on our feet. Laver took the lovely Waterford crystal bowl in his right hand and gave a single wave of his famous left hand. I remember all those wooden Dunlop rackets with Imperial gut that he and the other Australians and the best Europeans used to play with against Americans, who used Wilsons, mostly Kramers. Rod Laver had had it all as a player. His eyes were a little misty and still shy as we cheered him, and he sat down too soon, which was exactly when to sit.

"It's dead-on two o'clock," said the snappily dressed Englishwoman stretching near me.

And then, in the complete silence that followed, Pete Sampras began defending his title with a huge serve that nearly aced Jared Palmer.

Nevertheless, Sampras's long, handsome body looked unhappy, as it often does early in a match. The beauty of Sampras's tennis is that he builds up to a kind of sporting orgasm over the course of a match rather than try to have it all right away in bursts of anger or nervous energy. Sampras seems at times a brilliant somnambulist. Gradually Sampras's inner smile emerged, but his basic modesty ensured that his surface would always be less electric than Agassi's. Where Sampras is quietly brilliant like a good book, Agassi is often irresistibly brilliant like television.

On the third point of the match, Sampras slipped on the lawn, turning the grass a darker shade of green but skidding back to his feet without ripping the turf. Slightly embarrassed, Sampras recovered with another ace at break point for Palmer. The serve took one heavy bounce off the grass and thumped the backstop, undeciphered, like a memory gone by. Sampras, like Laver, was modest on the surface but huge in reserves. Palmer loped back to the deuce service box.

Pete Sampras's service motion is a thing of beauty. He leans back on his right foot, and the toes of his left foot rise up. It is a deceptively easygoing motion, but lightness is the key to power.

Jared Palmer was leading 3–2 when I got up to leave, sure of a Sampras victory yet pleased with the elegance of both players. Palmer had a very neat serve-and-volley game, but I felt that eventually this talented son of a tennis camp owner would, at a crucial moment, lose his balance on a low volley and trip on his own neatness. Palmer tends to stiffen when things get close, whereas Sampras moves under pressure as if he has virgin olive oil in all his joints.

I stopped in the pressroom for a first cup of hot tea on this blustery English day. I came across my old pressroom friend from India, Commander Kailash N. Bahl, who was having a sweet, milky tea with a buttered roll and strips of Jarlsberg cheese from the overflowing press salad bar, and I joined him.

"We have very few grass courts in India," he explained in his very distinct accent. "But our clay plays very much like grass elsewhere. You see, in India, we have principally two red surfaces." He dipped his buttered roll into his tea. "Normally our courts are dirt, but then we whitewash the dirt surface with cow dung. It makes for a very fast surface, much faster than at Roland Garros, for example. The other kind of court in India is comprised of red gravel, finely ground. It looks a bit like clay, but the problem with gravel is that when you fall on it the scrapes are often very severe. In my opinion—and I have been both a player and a linesman—the cow dung surface is preferable." He put more sugar in his tea and added, "Tennis in my country is still a rich man's game."

Moving on to the topic of Wimbledon, he said, "There are two primary injustices here. Did you know that all Fred Perry got for winning Wimbledon three times in succession was three trophies and three high teas?" The old Indian tennis aficionado grinned broadly as if the depth of the injustice was almost as satisfactory as the French bread, butter, and Jarlsberg cheese. "The other injustice, is that the women players do not receive the same amount of prize money as the men. Their matches may not last as long, but it is my experience that women make up most of the paying public here at Wimbledon, especially the first week. Many people like their 'day at Wimbledon' even more than they like the tennis itself. Look at the queues for Pimm's and strawberries and cream: women. If this were football or cricket"—he squinted sourly and waved a dismissive hand at those two sports—"the women would get up and leave. But if it is tennis, they like the atmosphere, the sex appeal." He cracked an ancient Indian smile and nodded. "At Wimbledon, it is the women spectators who come, and the men who follow. Naturally that is why I consider it rank discrimination that women players at Wimbledon no longer receive equal prize money." The Indian reporter rubbed the dark circles under his bright black eyes and nodded again.

"Do you want to come out with me and watch a match?" I asked my pal with a smile when he was finished with his snack. On a warm, sunny day, he would have been outside in a flash.

"No, no. You run along," he replied. "I will join you shortly, but I think I will listen to Fred Perry on the BBC for a few sets."

Jonathan Stark was out in the boondocks on Court 8, facing Germany's bearded left-hander, Karsten Braasch. It was the kind of setting and unpredictable match that I loved. Stark's power game could be great on grass, but there was no guarantee that his personality would be up to winning there. I took a seat on the low wooden garden bench up against the railing.

The outer courts at Wimbledon are like regional theater, and they often offer better plays than the dramas on Center Court during the first week. If you can pick the right match—and I thought I could— the Wimbledon back courts are tennis heaven. I wanted to find one match and stay with it until its conclusion like the fisherman in *The Old Man and the Sea*. Everyone is equal out on Wimbledon's back pastures. It is not a place for prima donnas, and emotions are more likely to be wide-open there than in the Center Court enclosure in front of the royals.

As Stark and Braasch warmed up, I glanced down at the forecast provided the press by the Royal Meteorological Office:

It will be a cloudy day with outbreaks of rain. The main band of rain is through this morning, but there will be sporadic outbursts throughout the day. Timing of these outbreaks is difficult to put any precision on. It will be warm and rather muggy, highest temperatures around 19 Celsius. Winds will be southwesterly, becoming fresh to strong.

The winds had already gone from fresh to strong, gusting up from black seas south of Cornwall. The temperature, seventy degrees in the morning, had fallen to about fifty degrees that afternoon. Two Englishwomen seated next to me were already wearing windbreakers, and I soon pulled on my old red Adidas warm-up jacket. I had forgotten all the moods of an English summer, but I would not easily forget this match.

Jonathan Stark wanted the victory badly. The tall, handsome American's eyes were not distracted by the crowd but, rather, by the bouncy, effervescent Karsten Braasch. Stark had the long-legged lope of an American basketball star about to play the big game. Athletically, the American basketball body was about to face a European soccer player's body. Braasch, the shorter man, had had a better clay-court session. As they warmed up in the swirling wind that almost threw their lobs back over the net, Stark half smiled, half winced, knowing he had a much higher toss on his serve. They say the weather is equal for both players but not so—nothing is ever quite equal, at least not in tennis.

Stark and Braasch had met only once before, but as the luck of the draw would have it, that meeting had taken place just the week before, in Halle, Germany, and Stark had won the match 6–3, 6–2, also on grass. I thought that win worked against Stark today. Revenge is great among players. The good ones—the ones who will survive on tour—hate to be beaten twice in a row by the same player. Stark had beaten Cedric Pioline twice in a row on hard courts, but the Frenchman had avenged those losses by winning their third encounter at the Lipton. There was another factor, which I tried to anticipate as I watched Stark net a high practice volley into the wind. Already in his third Wimbledon at twenty-three, Stark had, surprisingly, never won a match here. Stark had lost in five sets to Goran Ivanisevic in the first round the year before. Braasch, a late bloomer at twenty-six, *had* made it out of the first round before, and he exuded more confidence than Stark. But early confidence does not always hold.

Winning a match at Wimbledon is not like winning a match anywhere else in the world. The emotions run so high because the tradition of playing where Tilden, Laver, Budge, and Kramer played is mind-boggling. The players know not to play against the ghosts and try to lose themselves in the heart of the match itself, but at some point they sense the past in the softness of the grass or a slanting ray of sunlight and realize where they are. The place brings out both humility and fierce pride in the players, and that in itself makes for very fine matches.

Braasch nodded to Stark that he was ready to receive. And when the battle was over, I was not disappointed in my choice. It was a great match.

Jonathan Stark opened with a huge first serve, and Braasch's red-and-yellow racket head, which had been dangling harmlessly between his legs, came ripping upward toward the sky, intersecting the downward thrust of the six-foot-two-inch Stark's 120-mile-per-hour delivery with such timing that Braasch's return passed Stark before he had taken two steps forward to the net. Stark looked over his shoulder at the quirky German with the short shorts and runner's legs. Next, Braasch dumped a backhand return of serve at Stark's feet, just the way John McEnroe used to let the wrist of his left hand go almost limp, deadening the return. This time, Stark's long legs were under him, and he played a drop volley from the top of the net that even the fleet Braasch could not quite reach, though he tried to pull the ball up off the soft grass with topspin and shanked it long by just a few inches.

Stark hit such big serves he was already taking divots out of the baseline as he twisted, bent, then reached up into his massive delivery. But before long, with a second serve struck almost as hard as his first, Stark served a double fault that put Braasch immediately at break point. The wind, gusting at twenty-five to thirty miles an hour, was blowing right into Stark's face as he served, plastering his blond hair back. Stark survived one break point, but then Braasch, just barely touching the ball—the way a golfer might float a long downhill putt—used a backhand return of a screaming first serve to send the ball gently up the line and out of Stark's reach. Stark, broken in his first service game, took a deep breath and sat down heavily.

Karsten Braasch was a kind of tennis cult hero. Bearded and wearing wire-rim glasses, he looked like a seminarian from Tübingen about to abandon the church because the prospect of a first date now appealed more to him than God did. Braasch's tennis was like Lenny Bruce's humor, offbeat, a little strange—but cool. Braasch rarely swore on court, except in rapid-fire freaked-out German. Looking far shorter than his reported five feet, eleven inches, with another five inches of leap in his bandy legs, Braash, quick and very left-handed, curled and sliced everything into the court at unexpected angles until, suddenly, he would pound the ball with his short serve flat up the middle for an ace. I had seen Braasch play before, and he was very competitive but always fair with opponents. He was incredibly fit and fast, but it was his strange unpredictability mixed with doggedness that made him so much fun to watch and so tough to play.

Jonathan Stark cut in front of him around the net post as they changed sides. Stark was that quintessential American athlete, unmistakable in a crowd, more sunny than moody even on a day like this, but scared at that very moment to the point right next to self-knowledge. Stark was a taller, blond version of Paul Newman playing the character Brick, the former football star, in the movie version of Tennessee Williams's *Cat on a Hot Tin Roof*. Stark now seemed to understand that unless he bore down with everything he had, he would lose to Braasch.

The bouncy-legged German was hell to play in bad weather. Unlike Stark, whose service windup was as long and true as a star quarterback throwing deep for a touchdown, Braasch had a short windup consisting of a very quick hop and a left-handed blur that didn't allow the toss time to rise or give Stark time to see the ball coming down at him. Before serving, Braasch seemed to look right in the eyes of his opponent as if to say, "I'm going to hit you right now with a Three Stooges bop on the top of your head." And the German's delivery was so quick it was done before it began. The speed of the windup was not Braasch's only deception. Already off his feet to strike down on his uniquely low toss, Braasch could change directions on his delivery at the last possible moment as if, with eyes nearly shut, he sensed which way Stark was leaning and curved his left wrist to the inside or outside of the ball accordingly. In this way, Braasch aced me in the crowd three times and aced Jonathan Stark twice, holding serve at love. Stark was down 2–0, and the heavy-hipped German woman who had squeezed in near my seat took out her camera and said of Braasch with an admiring smile, "*Sehr schnell* [very fast]."

Stark began game three with a double fault, but then he hit three unreturnable serves in a row, two on second serves. Up 40–15, Stark cut a big kicker off the forehand side, catching Braasch by complete surprise. In August 1993 in Indianapolis, Stark had given Pete Sampras a scare, losing 5–7, 7–6, 6–3. But losing to a great player by close scores is always easier than beating a player like Braasch in a maelstrom. Two games later, missing a second serve on ad-out, Stark suddenly trailed 1–4 against Braasch, who, like Luciano Pavarotti, toweled his beard off with a small hand towel.

For a moment, Stark's two-handed backhand seemed to steady him. He hit a return of serve with it that nearly took the racket out of Braasch's hand. But I shook my head. Ultimately, I did not like Stark's two-handed backhand. In a smaller man, a two-hander seemed like a reasonable weapon, but in a player as tall as Stark or David Wheaton, a two-handed backhand seemed an awful waste in terms of reach that was unlikely to be made up for by foot speed. I could not imagine Kramer, Gonzalez, or Alex Olmedo ever hitting a two-hander. One has to be exceptionally fast—like Pancho Segura, Borg, Agassi, Courier, or Chang—to really make a two-hander work at the top level. Except for Borg, Connors, and Agassi, who won Wimbledon in 1992 when an unexpected English summer heat had baked the grass hard, resulting in higher bounces, no one with a two-handed backhand had ever won Wimbledon. Now Stark seemed limited, a West Coast hard-court player stuck with two hands on the joystick, while the European, Braasch, hit left-handed hook serves and chip backhand approaches at him, making him hit up. Stark frowned and shook his head repeatedly. Braasch seemed just happy to be there at all, and he took the first set 6–1.

The basics are often the key to winning a first-round match anywhere. Braasch kept the ball on the court, whereas Stark kept trying to launch rockets off the glassy grass surface. He had the order backward. At Wimbledon, all players on the grass must start as willing field hands, and greatness may appear later: get that order wrong, and you are soon sent packing.

With Braasch leading 2–0 in the second set, it did not so much rain as begin to spit. The cagey German's reflexes and touch were great to watch. He played three drop-volley winners in a row of returns off his lefty kick serves, then he played a high, dangerously slow backhand floater up Stark's backhand line. A lesser player than

Stark would have missed the ball with an arm-jerk volley or watched it bounce and hoped it was out, but Stark swept in like the big bird that he was, stretched fully, held his backhand shoulder high, and firmly drilled a high backhand volley behind Braasch, who was sneaking into the net to try to cut off Stark's volley with a volley. Down 15–40 but encouraged by his own great shot, Stark saved the two break points with unreturnable serves, only to serve a double fault as the wind blew paper cups across the court. When the ball boy had collected the toppled stack of cups, the bearded German ripped a forehand up the line. Stark, his serve broken a second time, dropped his head.

"C'mon, Jonathan!" shouted a young woman wearing a Michigan sweatshirt.

Suddenly, Stark played a gorgeous game. Against the chip-and-charge pressure of the clever Braasch, Stark came into net behind every first and second serve the way players used to in the time of Emerson and Stolle. He played three half-volley winners, bending low and skillfully brushing the skidding balls up the line instead of across the court. Stark could play, *really* play, and Braasch, very quiet on the changeover, knew it. Braasch again let the American cross in front of him as if the shorter player wanted to leave a Do Not Disturb sign around the neck of the large, awakening American.

In the wind and spitting gray moisture of the afternoon, Braasch's service delivery could have cored an apple. The little German could make the ball hop straight or to either side abruptly from the exact same motion. Even the linespeople could not follow Braasch, and they, too, were aced on several line calls they simply missed.

"Come on, damn it!" Stark shouted up at the chair umpire, who ignored him.

Stark proceeded to hit three aces and survive four break points to hold serve. It was a flawed gem, but Stark managed to keep himself together when many could not have. Braasch went up 5–4, 40–15, but Stark now saved four set points. He was hanging by a thread, his will to win. At deuce, Stark stabbed a quick forehand return of serve down the line. The agile Braasch, scrambling like McEnroe, dove for the ball and in the air carved a drop-volley winner just over the net.

Stark winced. On Braasch's fifth set point, Braasch served an ace up the middle. The bearded German led Stark 6–1, 6–4.

Matches at Wimbledon have a tradition of going up and down like a roller coaster. Play long enough in a career, and one day a competitor will come back from any position imaginable.

The wind Stark faced on his serve was now gusting up to thirty-five miles per hour, but Stark began hitting the ball so cleanly on his volleys that it jutted forward, skipped lightly off the grass, and thudded low into the backstop for an outright winner time after time. Stark was a real volleyer; Braasch had to use two or three volleys to find the same opening. They cut the ball in different ways—Braasch on a sharp angle under the ball, Stark with a firmer, almost vertical cut.

"Karsten!" Braasch roared his own name in a sudden fury at what seemed to be unraveling.

Stark began to roll. He held his serve with two massive, flat-struck skidding backhand volleys that froze the fleet Braasch to the ground before he could turn and use his legs. Braasch won points now only by scrapping. Stark grabbed points now in easy bunches with sudden bursts of complete domination. On the changeovers, Stark sat down and stared, finally in that dreamlike zone, which has the happy, unconscious rhythm of sex and the lingering sensation that the world is good and the ball will always be right there.

Stark went on a beautiful tear. He began to wallop the ball. He was like a ray of California sunshine come to London. "Up, up!" Stark chastised himself quietly when he failed to reach up for his toss. But he got up on top of the next one and then thundered his serves down, having found a perfect inner rhythm.

For the first time in the match, Karsten Braasch looked unhappy. He had the uncanny inner speed and balance to block nearly anything back, but suddenly Stark was serving with such ease yet power that the ball girls and linesmen recoiled from the balls like figures fleeing. Even Braasch seemed to be ducking or getting hit. Braasch roared with tension as he netted yet another return of serve. It was only 3–2 for Stark, but the American so dominated the match now with his serves that all he had to do on his returns was become a little more flexible, a little more European, a little less stubbornly predictable and American. Could Stark adapt and accept, the way Stefan Edberg had so often? It was almost as if to be stronger mentally, Stark had to take a little pace off the return. "You've got him!" I felt like shouting out loud to Stark. "Put the damn return into play!" But, as Dennis Van Der Meer had told me at the Orange Bowl and Stark had told me himself at the Lipton, that was not the way Stark liked to hit his returns. Still, Karsten Braasch suddenly looked vulnerable.

"I tell ya," said a man from Texas, who had been watching Braasch serve for a little over an hour, "any serve that peculiar has to have kinks."

The tennis-loving Texan was right: Braasch owned tennis's most peculiar service motion. Down break point, Braasch turned his serving hand inside out at the very last moment before contact and aced Stark up the middle, causing the *f* word to fly out of the American. It was 3–all and getting colder. The English teenage girls in the crowd folded their arms across their chests.

Stark held his serve like a god, and the girls applauded. The German spectators, who had unfurled a large German flag much to Braasch's displeasure, went silent. This battle was not nationalistic but personal, at least for the players. Now down 3–4, Braasch let a Stark backhand float by him and land. The ball was in, but Braasch turned and smiled anyway. It was 15–all: a huge point. But Jonathan Stark knocked his forehand return of serve a yard long. "No good!" I scribbled on my index card. "Put that ball in play!"

Suddenly Stark fooled everyone. Braasch lunged across the top of the net to cover a drive down the line that Stark, at the very last moment, whipped up and over Braasch's head with a forehand that was a dead ringer for John Newcombe's buggy-whip topspin offensive lob. The ball spun slowly backward, just over Braasch's reach, tempting him to hit an overhead until, realizing he could not, Braasch turned and chased after it like a Keystone Cop. He nearly caught up to it, but the topspin lob, frisky as a cat, bounced once and leaped into the backstop, followed by the crashing Braasch.

Stark had to hold his serve for the third set. On set point, he hit a serve that made the ball come in with the deceptive ease of a yo-yo released at a speed of 120 miles per hour. The ball kicked crazily up off the grass and then shot out at a right angle clear over Braasch's head, two speeds and two directions on the same ball. The German's desperation reflex backhand hung the ball up the line like an overripe fruit and fell, just out. The third set was finally Jonathan Stark's, 6–4.

Stark had sped up his feet and slowed down his emotions. He was playing calmly and brutally now, finally finding that devastating inner balance between power and fear. It is fear, not confidence alone, that an athlete wants. In Stark's case, the edge of fear made him move better.

Braasch began serving in the fourth set with the wind at his back, and he aced Stark with his short, tomahawk delivery. Braasch broke ahead 1–0, but Stark was still calm inside, still "in the zone." Suddenly Stark seemed to have the German on the edge of the abyss. Braasch missed wildly, laughed at himself derisively at midcourt, and then let out a tremendous bloody yell—"Aaaaaaaagh!"—that was soon swallowed by the wind.

Stark silently wiped his racket handle with a towel.

At 2–all in the fourth set it began to rain, splattering the blue ink on my index card. The two men kept playing. Rain worthy of an umbrella in America is often simply ignored in England. I had never seen a chair umpire electrocuted, but I suspected that if this rain did not do it as the umpire sat with his microphone in his right hand, the lightning bursting in the yellow electrical storm down Richmond way might well do the trick. The umpire sat in his chair in a Burberry scarf and a baggy blue winter jacket and a tweed cap. He was dressed more for a quail hunt than a tennis match. The players in their shorts looked at each other and shrugged. I had never been so cold watching a tennis match. I hung on against my bladder's call like Admiral Hornblower fighting a gale at sea. The English umpire glanced at the clouds, nodded as if he had just returned from a rainy week's holiday in Cardiff, and said implacably, "Play on."

"Send for tea," I grumbled to the Englishwoman next to me as the wind howled: "This guy won't vacate his high chair until he gets blown off it."

"That seems like a possibility," said the woman from Nottingham.

Neither player liked playing in rain on grass, but neither one wanted to be the first to concede he wanted to stop.

"Hit the ball!" roared Stark, unable to lift a two-handed backhand off the slick grass.

Braasch continued ranting in the rain. But the leap-serving Nijinsky kept hitting aces when he desperately needed them and went up 3–2 in the fourth set.

Suddenly the court seemed to turn a paler shade of green, reflecting a change in the light above. Stark hit a huge, unreturnable serve that Braasch claimed was out. For the first time Braasch seemed to be stalling, hoping a rain delay might save him. Each point now became an isolated, contentious moment. The players became like two chickens fighting over a single kernel of corn. It was great to watch, but very hard tennis to play in terrible conditions.

Stark's serve became flatter and skidded through. The results were immediate and dramatic. The ex-Stanford player and Braasch had a great volley exchange—four volleys with both men at the net. Stark, the French Open doubles champion only two weeks before, won the exchange, flicking away Braasch's best shot with disdain and such power that it elicited a roar of "*Scheisse!*" from the bearded German dervish.

The match had shifted Stark's way completely. Eighty percent of Stark's serves were unreturnable. Feeling the pressure, Braasch missed a drop volley, then hit a volley long off the throat of his racket frame. Down 15–40, a hole Braasch's had been in and escaped from before, he blasted a serve off Stark's forehand side, and Stark, reacting perfectly, played a reflex cross-court winner at an impossibly sharp angle to break Braasch's serve and go up 4–3. Braasch scrambled back, and Stark fell behind 30–40 on his own serve. Stark stood tall, looked over at Braasch, and served a winner. Deuce.

The raindrops started to fall faster.

Stark came in behind his first serve and hit a volley that skidded away. Braasch tried to throw his racket at it. On ad-in, Stark hit an ace that almost broke the backstop, and the blond Oregonian let out a lion's roar, part fear, part triumph. He was up 5–3. Braasch nodded disinterestedly and held serve at love, ripping a topspin left-handed cross-court backhand winner on the run that reminded me again of Laver. At 5–4, Stark was serving for the set. Braasch walked in a nervous circle, and the rain continued. Stark, saying nothing, held his serve at love. He was a real pro. They both were. The fourth set, like the third, was Jonathan Stark's, 6–4. Immediately, the sky split open. The umpire stood up in his chair and waved his arms frantically like a sea captain roused from below decks, and on raced the young grounds crew to cover the court with canvas.

"What's the big emergency?" asked the woman next to me from Bristol. "They could play in this. Oh well. I think I'll go to the loo."

I felt truly happy during that rain delay. Both players were giving it absolutely everything they had. There was a bottleneck on the paths on the way to shelter, and I was forced to remind an American who bumped me three times in the back of the head with the handle of his Bond Street umbrella that he was not going to get inside any faster at all by doing that. I made it to the nearest men's room, then went upstairs to the press dining room to have eggs, sausages, tomatoes, and chips, and a very hot tea. I did not want to talk to anybody for fear of breaking the match's spell. I tried to picture what Stark and Braasch were doing up in the changing rooms. I had seen Stark's coach, Larry Stefanki, across the court, and I wondered what he would be saying to Stark to keep him loose but focused during the break.

Big servers on a roll are like powerful locomotives who get up full heads of steam on the way from London to Paris. Now Stark was being asked to stop over for a couple of hours in Calais.

Did Stark know how he could win? He must know, I thought. But did he know how to actually do it? I wondered who was getting more nervous upstairs, Stark or Braasch? I felt Stark was more nervous because he had beaten Braasch 6–2, 6–3 the week before and was expected to win here. They would both be taking a leak and a shower and changing their clothes. Nervous, pacing, stretching, a few words with the coach (but coaches cannot win matches), then a last soul-searching session on the Thomas Crapper. The blank look down, the game played by memory, the tension of a shared will to win. In a flash, the memory of every very close match they ever played would be rising in their stomachs.

I liked them both. Braasch was spunky, a go-getter, an angles-and-touch man. I liked playing angles and drops myself, but I admired Stark more for the way he fired that serve and played his volleys deep and firmly. Oh, how I wanted a great fifth set. And I got one.

An hour later, the same nine spectators as before had gathered back around the court.

"More bad weather coming?" I asked one of the grounds crew, who was shivering.

"No, mate, the tarp's coming off," replied the young man. "We've been told." He nodded toward a senior groundskeeper who looked like an English car mechanic in blue overalls.

The crew pushed the canvas back to its purple yardarms, rolling it back, straining at the ropes like proper navies, pulling it in, clipping it down like a giant square sail. The green lawn was dry and ready. The sky was puffy with shades of dark gray and black. A young cockney woman said, "Did you see that bloke pass by with his hair blowin'?"

Soon Braasch arrived brandishing a new red-and-yellow racket with fresh strings, followed a minute later by Stark.

Boxers always want to come into the ring sweating because the cold fighter can get knocked out before he gets warmed up. Braasch was sweating; Stark was not. There was an absolute gale, but Stark seemed to pick up precisely where he had left off. Braasch served up the middle, and Stark calmly blocked a backhand winner past him up the line. But Braasch, not Stark, picked up the pace, constantly rushing the American, who seemed tall again, straight and a little stiff.

It happened so quickly. Stark hit a big first serve that looked like a clean ace, but the ball was called out. Stark wisely turned away as if to let it go, but suddenly he seemed to realize he was in a fifth set, and he turned back to dispute the call. Stark argued quietly but lost the long debate and with it his concentration. On the next point, he forgot to bend on a forehand volley and went down 0–30.

"Come on! Right here!" Stark roared at himself, fear pouring out in anger.

Suddenly calm and brave, Stark played a great touch-volley winner, then made a reflex winner off a ball Braasch seemed to have knocked by him to draw even. They played ads and deuces, back and forth on a narrow precipice. Down ad-out, fourth break point against him in his opening service game of the fifth set, Stark hit a big backhand volley winner. Stark played the break points better than the deuces. Back at deuce, Stark double-faulted. The gale-force wind mocked him, blowing harder. On the fifth break point of the game, Braasch passed the net-rushing Stark cross-court and went up in the fifth set 2–0. Was the battle over? I was not sure. Stark was like a big American sedan at full throttle on the open highway, but Braasch had maneuvered him back out onto the European country side roads where sharp movement and reflexes, not power, were what counted. The fifth set started to slide away from Stark. Braasch was suddenly calm once again and gracious about everything.

"Yep. That's good," said Braasch, acknowledging a backhand that sent the ball past him down the line. And again, aced by Stark, "Oh ya. Bravo."

Braasch was up 3–0, with Stark at 30–40 serving when the heavy rain, the real English soup, came down. Even the woman from Bristol pulled up an umbrella and sat under it as if hiding beneath a giant toadstool. I pulled up my red hood and popped open a portable umbrella. The players ran back inside, but most of the spectators just stayed there under umbrellas, bundled up against the rain.

At 5:30, five and a half hours after the match began, the sky cleared. There was the smell of coal in the south London air. When Stark and Braasch appeared in fresh outfits at 6:00, it was now a question of light. This time Stark was already sweating when he came out to play. Down break point to go to 0–4 when they resumed, Stark served an ace, held his serve, and stood at 1–3. He was alive, but barely.

Lobs were no longer effective. The balls blew over the baseline too easily. I could see Stark trying to climb back into the match, one game at a time, and if he had played it like that from the very beginning, he might not have been in such a desperate position now. Each point was a battle. Braasch's eyes became startled brown points above his wet beard. They had both come too far to lose. Braasch was nervous, but he held his serve shakily to go up 4–1 in the fifth set. Braasch thought he had the match, and this made him nervous. Stark fell behind 15–40 on his serve, a point away from 1–5. Other servers might have been broken, but not Stark. He reared back and hit four unreturnable serves in a row to hold for 2–4.

Braasch, now serving, glanced over at Stark, rocked back, leaped, and bopped over the top of his short toss. Another ace up the middle. Braasch held his serve at love to go up 5–2, and before retreating to return serve, Braasch stood at midcourt, facing Stark as silently as a jury member. With his back to the wall again, Stark played a great game, ending it with a sweeping, angled, high backhand volley that ripped the ball off the side of the court.

"Yep," muttered Braasch toughly, succinctly.

Stark held serve to reach 3–5. He was heating back up. Braasch had one chance to hold his own serve and win the fifth set and the match.

The tireless German lefty slowly bounced the ball an extra two times. Then he quickly spun his first serve into Stark's body and charged the net. Stark ran around inside the kicking serve and drilled a forehand winner right off Braasch's chest. Braasch nodded at the ball boy as if it didn't hurt and, recocking his serve, came in twice more. Stark hit two huge returns of serve that were just a hair too long. Braasch then cut a crazy-perfect backhand drop volley and finally stood at double match point, 5–3, 40–15.

Stark was not done.

He saved the first match point with a forehand that hit the grass in front of Braasch and rolled to the backstop; he saved the second match point with an outright cross-court backhand winner. *He can play!* I scribbled wildly on a wet index card. This was pure Jimmy Connors stuff, straight from the heart. Braasch leaped again into his serve. Stark blocked it back up the line and the ball fell onto the line where the two back corners meet. Braasch swore rapidly in non-seminarian German. Stark, hot again, blew on his hand. Ad-out. Break point for Stark!

I will not soon forget what happened next. Facing break point, Karsten Braasch took hardly a second to consider. He aimed, reloaded, and fired an ace up the middle of the ad court, blowing it past Stark's forehand. No one could believe it. It was a *great* serve on a huge point. What a pro!

Stark held off another match point. On the fifth match point, Braasch hit three backhand volleys with varying degrees of assertion and slice, and the last one enticed Stark to go for a hard passing shot by Braasch, just long. The match was over. It was nearly 7:00 P.M. The two players, no longer antagonists but coconspirators on the same ball, walked up to the net, shook hands like old friends, then separated and slumped back into their changeover chairs, alone, looking up at the suddenly clear, English summer sky as it turned pink, black, and orange like a Turner painting with just one ship in port.

By the time Jonathan Stark and Karsten Braasch had picked up their racket bags for the first of their two rain delays, Pete Sampras had already showered. Jared Palmer had managed to stretch Sampras 7–6 (7–4), 7–5, 6–3 on Centre Court but had been unable to beat him.

A champion is a funny beast. Docile on the surface, Sampras was stubborn as a mule when it came to defeat. Real champions say, "No! in thunder," to paraphrase Herman Melville. A champion essentially says no to every single opponent. When the champions can no longer say no effectively, they retire. Chris Evert and Jimmy Connors were particularly great at denying other players' victories, and there is that willful, creative stinginess in every champion. They want something so badly, over and over again, that at least among great champions, having it once or twice doesn't begin to make that desire go away. The difference I see between Courier, Agassi, and Sampras, on the one hand, and McEnroe, Connors, and Lendl, on the other, is that the psychic need to win seems to have been more rampant in the players of the prior generation. Courier had the physical drive, but upon reaching the mountaintop, he was surprised to discover what Andre Agassi had already found out—that it is hard to keep wanting something when you have already been paid off economically beyond your wildest dreams. Oddly enough, though Sampras seems less tenacious than Courier and Agassi on the surface, Sampras is probably the most tenacious of the three for the long cross-country haul.

Scratch the surface of every champion—in any sport—and you will find the sub-surface inner cause beyond talent and love of the game that makes her or him a champion and the others also-rans. Technique is only part of it, and champions are definitely playing for more than money. They are fighters. When pushed, they push back almost every time. The immigrant, Sampras, like Agassi, hides his "no in thunder" with a gentle smile. But what is important is the depth of the fire, not the visible size of the flame. Sampras is now most like Stefan Edberg in the quietness of his fire, and that is the kind of fire that can be most dangerous because it is steady, insistent, and hard to put out.

Jim Courier was an excellent warrior, but, ultimately, the way he gripped the racket was a limitation. Like Pat Cash, Courier had to give so much of himself each time he played that often he punched himself out before he got to the finals. Edberg, Becker, and Sampras had the kind of inner glide that characterized Gonzalez, Kramer, and Budge. Goran Ivanisevic possessed that glide but not the deep pride that Courier, Cash, and Roche all had and which the great champions also have. Rod Laver would have played with matches lit and stuck into his fingertips. McEnroe would have, too. McEnroe's demon was not economic; it was invented, the underdog fashioned in a champion's quirky imagination. The irony with McEnroe was that he came from a wealthy family. Sampras plays to McEnroe's depth, and yet he is the flip side of the McEnroe coin. Sampras, like Gonzalez, is the great beauty that rises from modest, workmanlike beginnings. Sampras and McEnroe, working determinedly in opposite directions, created the professional selves they dreamed of becoming, the star and the outcast.

During that first rain delay of the Stark–Braasch match, I stopped back at the press interview room to catch Sampras talking. A handsome, overconfident young English reporter stood up and asked Pete Sampras if he was "aware of the fact" that in a recent poll of one hundred Englishwomen who were asked whom they most fancied to have strawberries and cream with, Sampras's name was at the bottom of the list. Sampras, surprised, easily embarrassed, laughed and covered his mouth with his hand as he tried to answer the question. Sampras struck me, as Laver always had, as being genuinely shy and honest, talented without the tricks. I wished I could have fielded the question for him. McEnroe would never have let a reporter get away with a remark like that. But it did not follow that McEnroe's American successor should be McEnroe, Jr. Every champion is just a little different, and the next one is never exactly what is expected. Indeed, this is one of the reasons they are champions.

A few days later in the fourth round, Pete Sampras played Daniel Vacek, a six-foot-three-inch, bullet-serving Czech who had the kind of rock-hard physique I thought Jonathan Stark would have done well to develop. Stark was potentially better than Vacek but not as strong in the legs. Vacek was a real threat on grass, and though Sampras won 6–4, 6–1, 7–6 (7–5), the scores were not nearly as close as the threat Vacek had presented in the first and third sets.

Sampras, who had served fifteen aces to Vacek's fourteen, said of his win, "Today was a dangerous match. A couple of swings in the tie-breaker, and I could still be playing. It's a match where you have to be very careful, don't get careless, concentrate and get the job done. That's what I did. Daniel is extremely dangerous. I mean, he's got huge first and second serves. He threw in a lot of aces. In the tie-break, it could have gone either way. I hit one of my better pass shots on match point."

A reporter asked Sampras if he was playing in the proverbial "zone."

Sampras shook his head. "I don't think you can really 'zone' on grass. It is so tough to return serve. It's tough to swing as hard as you like and still have every ball go in. In my mind, that's the 'zone'— everything you see and hit is on the line. You can't do that on grass. The one shot I can zone on grass is my serve. I thought I served quite well against Vacek. But not much of a zone. Just solid."

On a good day, Joe DiMaggio could not have said more, and he probably would have said a lot less.

A nervous young reporter from France asked in heavily accented English, "Pe-te! Who are some of za play-eurs who like to play za game slow?"

Sampras, who had never played tennis at the old-time clay-court pace, grinned at the Frenchman in a friendly manner and said, "I don't know. But they must be out there somewhere."

Trim in a dark green T-shirt, blue jeans, and wire-rim glasses, his golden-brown beard clean and combed, Karsten Braasch, freshly showered, walked into the tiny soundproof interview room looking like a German intellectual ready for a night out in a Hofbrau house. Braasch's voice was the biggest surprise of all. It was so deep that when he said "Hello" he sounded like Barry White coming in for a recording session with the Love Unlimited Orchestra. Braasch was five foot eleven, my height, but he actually looked a bit shorter. An odd combination of great foot speed, quick reflexes, and off-the-wall daring, Braasch seemed quiet, very calm inside, yet I felt a large part of him was more like his whirling dervish serve.

"Was that a great match," I asked, "or just a great fight?"

"We had a very tough battle. But I also thought it was a *great* match," he said smiling shyly. "I played very well. I thought Jonathan did, too."

"I loved it, too," I said. "It was great to watch. There were such mood swings in the match between the two of you. The third and fifth sets were the closest. When you won the first two sets, did you think that Stark was out of it?"

"No. He has beaten me before. But this was the best grass-court match I have ever played. In the first two sets, I got a little more lucky than he did. I mean, he served a double fault on break point off the net cord." Braasch shrugged, as if to say that Stark was such a great server that it had to have been bad luck rather than nerves. I was not so sure. "On grass," said the modest German, "you have to convert your chances." If certain players can be said to exude colors, McEnroe's would be green and orange; Borg's, yellow and sky blue. As for Karsten Braasch, there was a rich, brown quality to him, like a dark beer made by monks.

"You didn't seem to make any mental mistakes. Even when you were struggling, you were playing very smart."

The twenty-six-year-old German nodded. "That is sort of my game. But then I got a little excited because I thought I got a couple of bad calls. I wasn't as calm as in the beginning, and when you are going downhill in a match you sometimes try to find things which are an excuse, that let you down easier in your own mind. I was doing this for a while. I was complaining. We both argued with the umpire. But after the fourth set, I got very lucky with the rain break. After it, I was able to settle down when we started again."

"Stark is a big guy, a slow-building engine. He seemed to take a little longer than you to get warmed up again after each break."

"That could be."

"You're fitter. You're quicker. But Stark beat you last week in Halle, Germany, on grass?"

"Ya. Three-and-two," said Braasch. "But I was coming there from playing the final in Holland the day before, and the grass courts in Germany were quite different from the grass courts in Holland. It was very wet in Holland, just like today—windy, too. But in Halle, which is near Hanover, I went down like that to Stark because I just wasn't ready mentally to play. In Rosmalen just the day before, I lost to [Richard] Krajicek in my first tour final. I beat Jim Grabb, Wally Masur, then David Adams, all guys who play well on grass. I have been playing well." Karsten Braasch did not say it boastfully.

"So you didn't look at your loss to Stark the week before Wimbledon as a terrible loss. It didn't play on you mentally when you saw the draw?"

"No," said Braasch calmly. "I knew that what I had to do was play a little bit better. And I thought I could do so."

"How?"

"By serving a little bit harder against him. Last week against him, I was serving with more spin. I was playing a little more for the percentages. But serving more flat balls had worked for me in Rosmalen, so I tried that here. So, you see, these matches that you lose can help you. I decided not to go for percentages here at Wimbledon. I served much harder and flatter, and it worked."

"What is it that Stark lacks, if anything, as a player?"

Braasch paused, reluctant to criticize a fellow professional. "He is making some easy mistakes. It is not really mental, but some shots he misses are just too easy to miss, like when he has me wide out of the court and then gets an easy volley and misses it. I mean"—the German inflection rose—"this is what you *shouldn't* do."

"I thought Stark was volleying really well at times."

"Ya, ya he was," agreed Braasch. "But just one or two balls at the beginning of each set. That was all the difference. Sometimes the early games are just as important as the late ones."

"I've watched you play at the U.S. Open. You handled Paul

Goldstein pretty easily last year, and Paul is a tremendous scrapper a lot like you are. Smart, not overpowering, very quick. But you have a different rhythm to your game than almost anyone else I have ever seen."

Braasch spoke in his German Barry White basso profundo. "That is just the way I am, the way I come out in my game. The serve? Yes, of course it is different, but you know I never had the feeling that it wasn't like everybody else's until I watched myself on tape when I was nineteen years old. Then it was too late to change back. Believe me, I think it looks funny, too."

I laughed, and so did Braasch. "It looks funny, but it must be miserable to return," I said. "You release your hand inside the ball or outside it for slice, but you release your hand incredibly late, and at the same time you are jumping straight up in the air after a low toss. It's three-dimensional crazy. And then it's either boom"—I laughed as I turned my left hand out like a salute—"or boom like a curve, the slice Laver used to serve wide into the backhand corner. But the toughest one of yours to see coming is that little flat hammer serve right up the middle of the court."

"Ya," said Karsten Braasch. "But I am *not* thinking about it. When I hit it, whatever happens just happens. It's almost not me deciding where to hit it."

This German was quirky, kind, and instinctive. If you took the wildest public parks player, turned him into a physical fitness fanatic, and made him consistent, you would have Karsten Braasch. "You look very fit."

"I feel all right."

I laughed. Braasch understated everything. That was how he kept the pressure away. He played as if he had no expectations or delusions of grandeur. Stark had played as if the entire weight of the match was on his own shoulders. In this regard, the European seemed more mature than the American player, because the European had been kinder to himself than Stark had.

"During the rain delays, were the two of you together in the locker room?"

"No. I was in the locker room number two, and he was elsewhere. We didn't see each other. I took a shower and talked to my coach, who is mainly with me because he is also my friend," said Karsten Braasch. "We had some fun. A few laughs. Then I had something to eat after the fourth set."

Braasch knew how to stay loose *and* focused. So many coaches, perhaps nervous themselves, inadvertently stressed a self-punishing kind of focus. A pro needs calm, laughter, and a period of quiet reflection, a measure of loneliness. I suspected that Stark had gotten uptight in the locker room. The young American had played so tensely while being broken in the first game of the fifth set.

"At the end of the match, you had a string of four match points, but you didn't win it until the fifth one. What was going through your head as you began to lose the match points?"

"I just tried to stay calm and relaxed because that is how to play your best tennis. You can do no more. Remember, Stark also had a break point on me in the fifth set, and I served that ace down the middle. That was probably the hardest serve I hit all day." Braasch said this with satisfaction. It had been one of the bravest serves I ever saw. "So I can relax sometimes and do better than when I am trying too hard."

"Were the conditions upsetting?"

"Not to me. It was worse—more rain—playing in Holland two weeks ago. But I probably handled the conditions better than Jonathan did. He especially had problems with the higher toss on his serve and the wind. That was not my problem." Braasch shrugged.

"Stark plays very high level doubles—he and Byron Black won the French Open doubles. But for a great volleyer, Stark doesn't go side to side that well."

"He moves well once up at net," said Braasch. "But he doesn't get up easily enough, and he isn't comfortable on the baseline. I feel I can beat him back there, so I knew each point that he must come up soon. But"—Braasch hurried to add—"it is hard for me to be critical of another player's game. Stark was hitting some really great returns. But then he missed some easy ones. He has to work on that. He must remember to take the easy balls more seriously." The deep voiced Braasch nodded. He was tired. "I play [Yevgeny] Kafelnikov tomorrow."

Karsten Braasch pulled a granola bar from his pocket and bit into it. We shook hands, and he asked me to show him the way back out through the underground maze of BBC interview rooms. "I can't find my way out," he said.

I laughed again. On the court, he had known exactly where he was every second of the five-and-a-half-hour match. Braasch walked quietly out of the BBC studios and disappeared into the crowd gathered around the duke of Kent's Rolls Royce. I did not go looking for Stark right away. In college tennis, the other players might have said, "Nice match," or "good try," to the former Stanford star. But in the pros, they just counted prize money and computer points and went on with their business.

Andre Agassi was in a mental and emotional position that summer which was not so very different from Jonathan Stark's. Though ranked at a higher tier—but only number eighteen before Wimbledon—and possessing a superior game, Agassi had begun to realize that talent has only so much time to ripen on the vine. Different players mature at different times for different reasons. Braasch, at twenty-six, appeared to be at the absolute peak of his athletic maturity. Stark, at twenty-three, had perhaps not quite reached it. The early Agassi plan—to play as little and make as much money as possible—had annoyed most of us writing about the game but had left Agassi's body relatively fresh, whereas Jim Courier had virtually dried out mentally playing too many tournaments in the same time period.

There is such a fine balance between talent and the ability to win. Maturity is the glue that binds it all together, and the initial lack of maturity on Agassi's part was what led to his back-to-back losses to Andres Gomez and Courier in the finals of the French Open in 1990 and 1991. No one but Sampras was as talented as Agassi, but for a long time I thought Agassi might waste this gift. He was like a teenage movie actor stuck in the star child-actor syndrome. Agassi's girlfriend Brooke Shields, who was going through a similarly difficult transition herself as an actress, seemed to help Agassi stretch for perseverance rather than excuses. And time itself came to Agassi's aid. He stopped being such a kid. Agassi was not yet where he wanted to be, but he had begun to focus on his profession.

The match that may have permanently turned Andre Agassi around was his in the round-of-sixteen match against Todd Martin. He was expected to win it. He lost it, and it got him mad.

I had a somewhat distorted view of the match because I saw only the fifth set. I had gotten hooked on the Grandstand Court by the great five-set match between Bruguera and the Australian Patrick Rafter. The Spaniard would have won in straight sets on clay, but the Australian had the natural volleyer's advantage on grass. Rafter played his heart out but cramped badly and lost 13–11 in an old-fashioned no-tiebreaker fifth set. By the time I got into the Centre Court seats, Agassi had lost the first two sets to Martin, who at six feet six inches is the tallest player ever to be ranked in the top ten in the world. Agassi came back and took the third and fourth sets. I saw the last two games of the fourth set and was thrilled to watch Agassi's return-of-serve magic.

Agassi was a lot like Bobby Riggs in height and temperament. Agassi could hit the ball a lot harder than Riggs, but legs and perseverance were key strengths for both of them. They both liked to chop bigger players down to size, and they knew how to do it: by making the court wide. Big men like straight lines. Agassi hit the ball so deep to the corners that opponents ran in circles on the baseline. But the grass was not as dry this year as it was in 1992 when Agassi won at Wimbledon, and Todd Martin was not, to put it mildly, an Andre Agassi fan.

Less naturally talented than Agassi or any of the others in the top ten, Todd Martin has worked on his court movement the way I hoped Stark would. Martin believes in the old-fashioned merit of hard work, and it had served him well.

I was sure Agassi would win the fifth set. He had made Martin look so clumsy at the end of the fourth set. To my surprise, Martin wound up simply overpowering Agassi. Martin played with a tenacity bordering on anger, reducing Agassi to a put-upon, seemingly docile heart-throb who carried his drooping racket from deuce court to ad-court after each Todd Martin ace or put-away volley. Martin led 5–0 and finished the fifth set 6–1. In defeat, Agassi smiled, took his wet shirt off, and flung it to the cheering crowd; Martin, feeling upstaged, stood and clenched a massive fist in the air to indicate that he, not

Andre, had actually won the contest. Agassi left Centre Court taking tiny steps and waving as if he had won, and the crowd continued to cheer him. Lesser players take a loss hard, but Agassi, though bitterly disappointed, demonstrated his unflappable public personality.

In the interview room, an Englishman asked Martin the best question of the day.

"Todd. Do you feel as if you just shot Bambi?"

Junior Wimbledon is a great barometer of future form. The hard courts at the U.S. and Australian Juniors are familiar surfaces, but few juniors have much experience on grass, and that unknown factor is scary and makes them scrap for everything. No other tournament in the world can put as much pressure on a junior as Wimbledon. Yet nothing can match the confidence that results from surviving such an experience.

The Wimbledon junior event brings out American mothers as well as sons and daughters. The mothers of Stephanie Nickitas and Cristina Moros were dressed up at Wimbledon that hot summer day as if they had gone on a wild spending spree in the women's summer clothing department at Harrod's. They looked like a million dollars. If Princess Di had appeared, they would have been dressed and ready for tea. They were also clearly as excited about Wimbledon as their talented tennis-playing daughters. The inseparable doubles team marched off to hit a few balls on the grass practice courts.

"Excuse me," said Irene Nickitas urgently to the English guard barring her entrance to the path to the practice courts, "can't we go down there?"

"I'm afraid that won't be possible," said the guard imperiously.

"But we're their *mothers!*" roared the two American women at once, suddenly coming unglued in the stifling London heat wave that had followed the first-day rain. They finally were allowed to watch their daughters practice, and the black uniformed English guard retired sensibly to the shade of the big tree in front of the players' changing area.

It was not an easy tournament for juniors to get into. Venus Williams was not there by choice, for her father had stuck to his decision to let Venus turn pro and get the endorsement money *before* putting her tennis skills on the line against her contemporaries. But Martina Hingis, the very talented Czech-Swiss player, was there, as were all the girls on the U.S. National Team, which included Meilen Tu, Amanda Basica, Nickitas and Moros, and Stephy Halsell, the tough little Texan who would be a name to watch for if she grew just a bit. My one disappointment was that Ania Bleszynski, who in my opinion was one of the top four junior players in the United States, could not be added to the U.S. junior team. But junior tennis is not a perfect science, and someone good is always going to be left off the team no matter who is picked.

Amanda Basica's match against the young Slovakian Tatiana Zelenayova was a very close three-set match played from the baseline with looping topspin ground strokes, a few clutch volleys, and serves that were broken much more often than they were held. I watched for a little over two hours and could not tell until the very last point who was going to win.

Zelenayova seemed to have a slightly more polished game, but Basica dug in, broke serve on a Zelenayova double fault, and held her own serve for the match, no small feat in this case. Basica won the exciting but jittery match in two hours and ten minutes, 6–7 (2–7), 7–5, 6–4.

I caught up with Basica and her team's coach, Lynne Rolley, who was also looking after Lindsay Davenport. It was another bright-white, brutally hot day for London.

"What was it like to play your very first match at Wimbledon?" I asked Basica.

"It was really different," she replied with a nervous laugh, falling back behind the steadying figure of Lynne Rolley, who smiled at me like a chaperon and let me continue.

"You did some things well in terms of trying to slide the ball and keep it low on her toward the end there," I said.

"It seemed like when I mixed up the pace," said Basica, "she started sending more balls out." Basica laughed nervously again, so much happier than she had been after her first-round loss to Malec at the Orange Bowl. Since leaving school to tour full-time as a junior player, Amanda had put on about fifteen pounds.

Basica had been petrified, and she had been brave against Zelenayova. Some young players get angry in order to steel themselves against the effects of their own nerves. I always suspected that McEnroe's rages were in part efforts to bark orders at his nerves. Sometimes anger can succeed in making fear march more dutifully. Basica had behaved perfectly, but she had stayed nervous for three sets. The match was a real emotional roller coaster, and Amanda Basica held on at the end.

"Were you nervous?" I wondered if she would admit it.

"Yeah. *Very* nervous." Basica grinned sheepishly and shook her head, relieved. She was still nervous, and the match had already been over for ten minutes.

"Did you sleep last night?"

The sixteen-year-old grinned. "No. I couldn't sleep at all."

"What was it like walking out there on grass at Wimbledon for the first time? Did you feel as if your legs were going to fall off?"

"Yeah, really. Even my hands were shaking. I calmed down finally, but it took me a set to do it."

"Could you tell that she was nervous, too?"

Amanda Basica looked surprised. "I guess she probably was."

"Probably!" The dark Slovakian girl had tried to hide her nerves by being supercalm or by acting thoroughly disgusted with herself when she missed.

"She'd hit one good shot, but then she hit the next one out." Amanda Basica laughed with relief. "Eventually one of us had to hold serve."

The pretty Californian was still beaming. At 5–4 in the third set, she had served for the match at Wimbledon and held her serve. Not everyone could say that. Amanda had taken her losses over the year. This Wimbledon victory was a payback for all her hard work and a big confidence booster. Amanda Basica had been baptized.

Like Ania Bleszynski, Amanda Basica was still an innocent, if you can call dropping out of high school at sixteen and playing in Australia, Hong Kong, Rome, Paris, and London in front of adults "innocence." The thrill of competing was still there for her.

■   ■   ■

The Wimbledon practice courts have a nice feel to them, like a paddock area at a racetrack. I was looking for Jonathan Stark, but instead I spotted Lisa Raymond, who was just finishing a "fast hands" volleying drill on the practice court closest to the changing rooms. I stopped Raymond on her way in to get changed, and I was glad I did.

Undefeated at the University of Florida for almost two years, Lisa Raymond was five years older than Amanda Basica and had more experience playing at Wimbledon. I had arranged to talk to Raymond at the Lipton after she played but when she lost I decided it wasn't the best time for an interview. When she came off the Wimbledon practice court, she had a big smile on her face and looked happy and ready to compete. I wanted to hear from a young woman what it was like to go out on the women's pro tour after two years in college.

"The biggest difference for me was the mental aspect," said Lisa Raymond. At twenty-one, she had large, hopeful brown eyes, brownish-blond hair, and a few remains of adolescent acne mixed with the freckles on her nose. Raymond was only five foot five but highly coordinated. In her first six months on tour after college, she had beaten Gabriela Sabatini twice and appeared to be the next great American hope after the fade of Jennifer Capriati and just before Lindsay Davenport started to rise. For about three months—a year before—Lisa Raymond had been one of the hottest players on the women's tour, but the other women had familiarized themselves with her game, spreading word of her uncovered weaknesses like a wildfire. Raymond still seemed slightly dazed by her reversal of fortunes.

"In college, especially in my second year at the University of Florida, I pretty much dominated. I was undefeated. Every time I stepped on court I was confident that if I played to 75 percent of what I was capable of, I was going to win the match." Lisa Raymond hesitated. "It's taken me about a year now to try and reverse that psychology as a pro. There are no easy matches for me now and no way you can come out here playing 75 percent and hope to win a professional match."

"When you first came out, you did very well right in the beginning. Then you hit a patch when it got kind of tough. Is that how it was?"

Raymond smiled a bit sheepishly. "Yeah. And I'm kind of still in that tough patch. Last week I was ranked in the forties, but after this tournament, I'm going to drop to fifty-five or fifty-six by next week."

"Describe what it's been like."

"Well, it's been tough. When I first came out, people had big expectations for me to do really well. I was the new kid. No one knew my game. I had nothing to lose. I beat Natalia Zvereva. I beat Sabatini twice. A lot of the media started saying, 'Oh. This could be the next one. It could be *her*.' And that starts to get into the back of your mind every time you step on court. Even though you may not be seeded or ranked ahead of these people, you think that everyone is *expecting* you to beat them. And then the pressure started to get me."

"You start to feel it in the arm."

"In the arm, in the feet, and everywhere else!"

"Every time you tried to make the passing shot, you started to think, 'Oh my God, I've *got to make* this passing shot.'"

"Exactly," said Lisa Raymond, nodding. "It's just been tough. It is a huge transition."

"So what are you doing to try to shed the pressure?"

"Well, I think what I've done—which actually I didn't want to do—is to lose some matches." Lisa Raymond cocked her head. "The eyes are off me. They aren't looking at me right now; they're all looking at Lindsay Davenport as the 'next' American player. It's almost been a blessing in disguise for me. It's been a hell of a struggle. No one likes to lose, but now that the pressure is a bit off me, I think I'll be able to just go out and play tennis again."

"You've got a lovely game," I said encouragingly. Raymond had a neat, compact game that fit her like a glove. She had no glaring weakness and no tremendous strength other than great hand-eye coordination. Lisa Raymond's main problem was her height and the power she was being asked to face and generate in return. Her tennis technique off both sides was excellent, but she lacked a big serve or another big weapon. She was worried now that the other women had figured her out. Tennis can be a cruel profession. The other women were like sharks. Raymond was bruised, but the blood was still inside her.

"I guess part of it is not letting the other women think that they can beat you."

"Oh, yeah," Lisa Raymond said firmly. "Do you mean, beat me down mentally?"

"Yes," I said. "They get a sense out there, don't they, that when you're going badly they can have you."

Raymond nodded. "The perfect example of that is Steffi [Graf] the other day when she lost in the first round to Lori McNeil. That never would have happened two years ago, but Steffi started to lose a couple of matches, so now when she steps on court with someone, we don't have the feeling anymore that there is just no way you can win."

"Do the women players talk amongst each other?"

"Oh, sure," said Lisa Raymond. "Especially when they think you're more vulnerable, like Gabby a couple of years ago. She started losing some matches, including those to me, and ever since then people have known that they always have a shot playing Sabatini."

"How tough is it, week to week?"

"It's tough," said Raymond softly. "And it's very lonely."

"*Very* lonely?"

"Yeah. I'm fortunate that I have a coach and hitting partner that travel with me. I've got a lot of close friends out there. Well, not a lot. But a few close ones that I can count on, and that is just so important."

I spoke softly, playing the devil's advocate. "What did you get out of college besides an undefeated record your second year?"

"The friendships, the experiences. I just grew as a person. And that's what so many of these young girls are missing out on right now. They say, 'Let's turn pro, let's turn pro!' But it's not that easy. It's not all glamour and dollar signs."

"I see these young ones like Amanda Basica and Cristina Moros and Stephanie Nickitas. They're lovely young kids, but they seem somehow as if they're on a cloud. They might make it, or they might not make it, but . . ."

Lisa Raymond let out a sigh. "I think the best advice I could give to anyone is to go to college, at least for a year. I always was number one in the U.S. in juniors, but I always wanted to go to college." Her voice suddenly seemed to be quaking with emotion. "I didn't want to miss out on that aspect of my life. I'm so glad I went to Gainesville.

All my friends are still there. I mean, there's no rush for these young girls. College is such a great growing time, more so off the court than on the court."

"Do you feel that you actually learned things in college?"

"Oh, sure." Raymond nodded firmly. "I learned so much more about people by being *with* people, not just competing *against* them. There's a difference."

It seemed strange at Wimbledon—where every little tennis girl and boy dreamed of playing—to be talking about college as an alternative. But I understood what Lisa Raymond was feeling. "Do you think that these young kids are making too big a commitment before they really have a clue what life is about? A commitment so big that maybe they can never do anything but tennis later on?"

"Oh, definitely!" said Raymond. She was opening up as if she had had something stored inside her. As a former American college player, she stood apart from the European and South American pro tennis crowd, almost none of whom had finished high school. "I don't know what these young ones are planning now," she continued, "but it just seems that now they all want to bypass school."

"Some like Meilen Tu and Capriati, when she was playing, are doing this home study, which is what the child actors all did."

"That home study is ridiculous," said Lisa Raymond. "It's great to be at Wimbledon, but kids ought to finish high school before they can play on the tour. It's just a part of growing up. I think the age limit should be raised to at least seventeen, probably eighteen. I could *play* with the pros when I was sixteen, but no way I was ready at sixteen to take on the circuit. It's just wrong to let them." Her voice was full of emotion.

"There seems to be a particularly tough attitude on the women's tour. What is it?"

Lisa Raymond looked me right in the eye. "I think it's just women," she said. "As bad as that may sound, that's how it is out here. Guys go out to play, beat the hell out of each other, and then they'll go out together that night. The very top ones don't, but a lot of them are friendly with each other on the way up." She paused. "But the girls are just catty. They'll take the first chance they can to stab each other in the back."

"Is that right?"

"Oh, God!" moaned Lisa Raymond. "You really have to pick and choose your friends out here because there are so very few girls who really are your friends. Some claim it, but they aren't. They talk behind your back—just little things like that—but when you overhear it, you get really surprised and hurt by what they say about you."

"I take it that your toughness has to be up two or three notches from normal life or you shouldn't even be out on the tour."

Raymond nodded in agreement. "You don't win every day, so you have to learn to pick yourself back up quickly after a big loss."

"Are you putting a lot of pressure on yourself to make it back into the top twenty?"

"Oh, yeah!" She laughed. "That's just the way I am. I'm a perfectionist when it comes to hitting a tennis ball. Even if I hit an outright winner—if I don't hit the ball just right, I'm still upset."

"In view of the problems with Jennifer, and before her with Andrea Jaeger, and even in the way Seles did not rush to come back, do you think it has gotten as bad in tennis as it is in girls' gymnastics? Is a crack-up inevitable if you start too hard, too soon? I haven't seen one of these tennis prodigies start *that* young and last all the way to the end of an adult career in anything like a happy fashion. Isn't it because they miss out on school and don't develop enough as people, so that in the end *that* catches up to them as players, too?"

"That's what I think," said Lisa Raymond softly. "We're all individual cases, of course. But Jennifer at fourteen didn't know what she was missing. She thought it was all great."

"And it was for a while."

"Right. But by the time she got to be fifteen or sixteen, she started to see what all her friends were doing at home, including [dating] boys, and Jennifer wanted to do those things, and you can't blame her. People forget. To be number five in the world at that age, fourteen, is fantastic. But people wanted her to be number one. Who knows? Jennifer could have won that match against Seles and later still have gotten crushed under the pressure."

"Aren't you all prodigies, really? I mean, you are all at such a super level that you're prodigies. I remember in junior tennis there were guys like Dick Stockton and Jimmy Connors who were just two notches above everybody else. But *they* didn't turn pro until they were in college. They were more mature than these kids today. . . . The strategies of women players like Billie Jean King and Margaret Court and Virginia Wade are gone today, and not just because the rackets are different. Watching women with mature games and personalities was just different. There was a maturity to Evert and Navratilova, a thought process that came out in their choice of shots and the sensation of their emotions, that just doesn't seem to be there as much today in these very talented young female players who can hit the ball very well but have very short careers."

"We all play to win so early." Lisa Raymond looked out at the balls flying around the practice courts at Wimbledon, her eyes distant as if looking back at herself and all the girls she had played with along the way. "A lot of us never learned to serve and volley because it was too risky in juniors. Very few players are as brave as Pete Sampras was. They would never have discarded a winning shot as good as Pete's two-handed backhand used to be for the possibility of taking the big step up. Most people are afraid to be champions."

There was a tremendous commotion back up in the press lunchroom. Chairs were being kicked. Someone seemed to be in a wild rage. I heard shrieks and saw a man was down on the floor. I leaped up and moved toward him. Then I saw his body flipping like a fish on the hard linoleum floor. It was either a heart attack or an epileptic seizure. A crowd gathered, including on the periphery a tall blond woman whose face looked vaguely familiar to me.

Someone put a pencil between the man's teeth as he bounced. He was a journalist in the throes of an epileptic seizure. Five minutes later, some London policewomen arrived and took charge with walkie-talkies as the reporter lay on the lunchroom floor. The incident upset me, and as I turned to talk to someone—anyone—the first person I saw was the tall blond woman. She appeared to be in her fifties and had been sitting with a considerably older gentleman with a reddish face, prominent nose, and slick hair, the tennis legend Fred Perry. I realized I was standing next to Christine Truman, the Englishwoman who in 1961 had been the runner-up at Wimbledon and Forest Hills to Angela Mortimer and Maria Bueno, respectively—and in 1959 had won the French Open.

"Excuse me," I said, "are you Christine Truman?"

"I am." She beamed. Christine Truman as a nineteen-year-old had seemed so incredibly shy, in part because she was an inch over six feet tall. In 1959–62, she was considered a giant, though not perhaps as tall as Judy Tegart. In the 1990s, Christine Truman no longer had to worry about being the tallest woman in the room. The current generation was producing many young women six feet tall, and being tall was finely "in" for a woman. When Christine Truman was a player, she had had a fine serve and volley, but she was a step slow and had gotten so nervous and down on herself that she used to go to pieces just when everyone, seeing her size, expected her to be strong and win everything. She could not. Ann Haydon-Jones and Angela Mortimer had been tougher mentally, and Virginia Wade was more agile and naturally talented, but Christine Truman had been the third- or fourth-best player in the world in her window of time. The years seemed to have been very kind to Christine Truman. Her face was relaxed and very happy. She struck me now as a woman genuinely at ease with herself. And that was nice.

"The English have done better this year," I said.

"Yes," she said, smiling. Her voice was kind but strong. "At least the men have."

"What's with the Englishwomen?"

"Struggling a bit," Christine Truman said gently, with a hint of an ex-champion's pleasure when the current generation is struggling.

"Is that because they aren't getting enough training?"

"Well, they're staying in school," said Christine Truman approvingly. "Of course school does seem to flatten them for a year. In America it seems to be different. But Lindsay Davenport matriculated, and it doesn't seem to have bothered her play at all."

"It may be harder to play tennis and go to school in England," I said, "because at least from what I saw when I taught over here, American high school is not nearly as tough as English O- and A-levels."

"Oh, well, right," added Truman, "school does seem to be something girls over here want to finish."

It was just a brief moment in a cafeteria.

"Very nice to meet you," I said and meant it.

"Please give my best to everyone in America," Christine Truman said. She was lovely.

She went back to sit down with Fred Perry, her BBC colleague, and I overheard her say, "Fred, they took that poor fellow away, the one who fell down there on the floor."

Fred Perry nodded perfunctorily and turned back without further ado to a fried tomato and sausage he was busy eating. His reaction made me grin. He had reached the age when he was interested in no one's problems but his own. I wanted to talk to him, but I sensed I would need an introduction.

Stefan Edberg came onto Centre Court with the big, blond, left-handed Dane Kenneth Carlsen, whom he had beaten in straight sets in March when Sweden eliminated Denmark 5–0 at the Davis Cup. Edberg was ranked third in the world, and Carlsen, twenty-one, was ranked one hundred thirteenth. No one expected it to be a great match, but it was. That afternoon, the Royal Box was full of women secretly admiring Edberg's legs, yet most of the press seats were empty at the start of the match.

In their day, John Newcombe had a more penetrating serve, Rosewall a better backhand, and Roy Emerson a stronger body, but Edberg combined elements of all three great Australian champions with a gentle smoothness and quickness all his own. Edberg's legs alone seemed capable of making him one of the greats of all time.

In the first set with Carlsen, Edberg fell a service break behind; then, on cue, Edberg broke right back and won the set in a tiebreaker.

"Ah," said my old Indian friend from Delhi, "it is often the same when the lower-ranked player plays the star. The young one plays well, maybe wins a set, but gets very nervous and gives the match back to the star."

He was right. In Connors's great U.S. Open run in 1991, the aging pro had been able to upset younger players good enough to beat him in part because they were not quite sure how to do it, and

Connors was not about to tell them. Carlsen was a moose, but Edberg still looked like the hunter.

"Of course Edberg is married now with a child. And marriage is a strain on almost any player. I myself could not sustain it," confessed my Indian colleague. "Mrs. Jimmy Connors. Mrs. John McEnroe. They all have stated quite clearly that they preferred *not* to accompany their husbands to tournaments. They did not like the hotels, the traveling with children. However, if they did not accompany their husbands, they also stated that there was often a long line of women waiting to meet their husbands. I do not believe this has been such a problem for Stefan Edberg. He is different. He is not made up that way. Of course, Edberg's wife is very beautiful, and they are still in the early stages. Did you know she used to seriously date Mats Wilander?" He squinted in the bright sunshine as Edberg netted a volley. "But let me talk frankly. The other problem with marriage and babies, if you are a player, is that you cannot concentrate as well on your business."

In the next game, Carlsen served two big left-handed aces, a bullet up the middle and a Laverlike curve ball off the side of the backhand court that Edberg never reached. The big Dane, as blond and clean-cut as an army sergeant, seemed to me to be posing more of a threat to Edberg than Edberg's marriage and ability to concentrate.

But marriage was a thorny issue on the tour because it tended to undermine both the tunnel vision required for winning and the championship-sized ego that went along with it. "You see, when you are a married player, you must now ask permission to do things," said my Indian colleague. "But if you are single, you may please and think of yourself first all the time. I find that is the primary difference between marriage and being single. With a wife, this selfishness must change. But if you are still playing tournaments, you *must* think of your task first, and everything, including a wife, must revolve around it. That may not be a popular version, but I believe it to be true."

The second set was an interesting struggle. Edberg swung a serve wide into the forehand court with so much tongue to it that the grass changed color in a streaky curve as the ball ripped off the side of the court for a near ace beyond the Danish lefty's vulnerable backhand.

Stefan Edberg did not seem the same to me. He went down a break point in a game in which he had served two aces. But then Edberg, the instinctive survivor, tough as a police detective's son, rose up again, and Carlsen never saw another forehand until long after Edberg had crawled out of the hole and saved his service game.

Still, young Carlsen consciously rushed Edberg with everything he hit. It seemed a strange tactic to try against the player whose incredible reflexes had helped him serve and volley Sampras off the court at the U.S. Open just two years before. Initially the ploy did not work for Carlsen. Instead of rushing Edberg, Carlsen seemed only to be rushing himself. Edberg rearranged one of Carlsen's ill-advised net rushes and, like a teacher, held the stroke and lofted a topspin backhand lob that left the tall Dane hanging over the top of the net. Encouraged, Edberg played his own classic running point: a low chip return of serve, a forehand whipped down the line, another forehand rolled deep to the backhand, and his own rush to net. Edberg was in perfect flow. When the workmanlike Dane sent a high lob up into the bright blue sky over Wimbledon, Edberg, loping backward, let it bounce on the grass, held his swing to the last moment, freezing Carlsen, and then drilled the overhead away from just inside the baseline. Edberg had broken the young Dane's serve to go up 4–3 in the second set, serving for 5–3.

"You see," said my Indian companion with the assurance of seventy years' experience on this earth, "as a girlfriend, it is a kind of hero worship. But as a wife, it is something else again. As a wife, there is no more hero, by and large, and women in no countries that I know of like to subordinate themselves when they are no longer girlfriends." He nodded for emphasis.

After breaking the Dane, Edberg got broken right back, and he looked miffed with himself because Edberg never used to give up a break after breaking his opponent. Champions never return the favor. They take the favor and expand on it. The champions—from Perry, Budge, and Gonzales to Laver, McEnroe, and Lendl—were all stingy and greedy that way—proud of what they had just gained and able to hold onto it like a lion's prey. But as in boxing, a player is always most dangerous right after getting hurt. Carlsen began to run his big, bending lefty serve away from Edberg. In past years Edberg would have taken that same serve at the very top of its low bounce rather than trying to flick it up from behind him. Suddenly it seemed as if Edberg was only winning the long, beautiful points, and this was not a good sign because he was also losing all the short, scrappy points that make the real difference in a close match. Carlsen went up 5–4. Angel-faced, angry inside, Edberg hit two tremendous long, flat back-hands right at Carlsen's chest and then screamed a forehand winner into the open grass. But that point seemed a waste somehow, because the point Edberg really should have won was the unimpressive point before it, which he lost on a serve return that put him down 15–30 instead of up 30–15. Matches turn on such forgotten, undramatic points as the second serve Edberg failed to return. And a champion makes all those fundamental returns *before* he or she finds through further hard effort the imaginative responses that thrill us. 6–all. Kenneth Carlsen led the tiebreaker 4–1, 5–1, then 6–3, triple set point.

Edberg did not blink. I had seen him win from double match point down to Jakob Hlasek at the Lipton in 1990, and if I could remember it, he could, too. Edberg's experience stood up like a wall. Edberg hit a huge first-serve winner, then hit the top of the net with a backhand drop volley that fell over and sank in the grass. Edberg was unapologetic. Carlsen, now up 6–5, served a third set point and drilled Edberg's chipped return cross-court at a wide angle; Edberg chipped it back up the line. Carlsen hit a great angled, backhand volley, but the exaggeration of the slice was rejected as too pronounced by the dried-out English grass and the ball sat up for a moment. This was just enough time for Edberg, bending like an acolyte so his face was within six inches of the blades of grass, to loop the ball back with a desperation forehand cross-court that found a patch of empty grass just behind where Kenneth Carlsen dove, rolled, and fell away empty-handed.

Edberg had saved three set points and was back at 6–all in the tiebreaker. Edberg had to dig Carlsen's next serve out of the turf with a low backhand chip reminiscent of the way Vitas Gerulaitis used to play the low return of serve on a line from a quarter inch off the grass. Carlsen hit a good but not definitive volley, and Edberg, tearing forward before the volley landed, hit a low forehand lob for an outright winner. The crowd roared as Edberg came to a stop with a skip, a quick turn, and a sensuous pump of his fist. Back from the brink, Edberg had one set point of his own. It was all he needed. Champions do this. Other players require three or four chances to win a set, and sometimes even that is not enough. A champion gets one chance and does it. Edberg did it, and when he did, he leaped into the air as Carlsen's drive landed in the alley. Edberg had come back to win the second set 7–6 after being down 5–1 and 6–2 in the tiebreaker. He led two sets to love.

There is often such a fine line between winning and losing, especially at the highest level. Edberg's serve was immediately broken at the start of the third set. Great athlete that Edberg was, he seemed instantly to understand what he had just done, and he began running in place, practicing a backhand return with a short backswing and long follow-through. Now Carlsen's first serve, encouraged by the gift, came in so hard Edberg could not get it back. In a flash, the scoreboard read 7–6, 7–6, 0–2. I looked at the grass. The grass inside the service boxes was still four solid green squares smudged different shades of green by the serves and movement, but it was not yet sharply cut open and brown. It would be by the end of the match.

The Dane won the third set 6–2.

Youth was surging. Edberg's head fell down, as it used to in the mid–1980s before his coach, Tony Pickard, taught him to feign indifference and look up when it really hurt.

"We play our best tennis when we are out in front," Edberg had told me in 1990.

A silence fell over the court. The tennis became very beautiful. Edberg, bending low to a ball on his backhand, hit a gently rolled topspin lob winner; the ball seemed to hang just over the fully stretched Carlsen, whose swing struck only air. Edberg led 3–2, but Carlsen held his serve. Now through consistency, not brilliance, Edberg held and tried to finish Carlsen off. At 30–all, 3–4 in games, Carlsen served a double fault to go down 30–40, break point. Carlsen was a troubled Dane. But the very young and the very old don't give a damn where they are. Young Carlsen brushed his wavy blond hair out of his face and thumped a Clydesdalelike ace up the middle, saving break point and going on to hold his serve. Edberg shook his head and frowned deeply. It was 4–all in the fourth set.

When the expected separation into levels does not occur, both parties feel it and reassess the situation. At 4–all, 30–all, it was Edberg who double-faulted. On break point, Carlsen mishit his backhand return of serve, but he did so quickly, and Edberg, leaping forward, took a full swing and blasted it just wide. Both players looked surprised but Carlsen less so. The big Dane held his serve at love and took the fourth set 6–4. A Nordic dogfight was occurring on an English lawn.

"The atmosphere here today is very good," said my Indian pal in his clipped English accent, nodding his head to one side as if he had just tasted something delicious. "It reminds me of the atmosphere here in 1974, when seats cost eighty pence apiece and Borg was the hero of all the girls. There was standing room down there where all the seats are full today." He squinted in the sun and changed glasses. "I would say, judging from the Royal Box, that most of the women are rooting for Stefan Edberg and his legs. And that their husbands are rooting for Kenneth Carlsen." The old Indian smiled.

There did seem to be a flutter in the Royal Box as the fifth set began. The duchess of Kent, still turned on by competing bodies after all those years, was nearly beside herself with anticipation. Stefan Edberg had once possessed such speed that he could literally rush an opponent off the court, as he had, for example, rushed Jim Courier in the final of the 1991 U.S. Open. As if calling on his body memory to set things right, Edberg started to rush the younger player, and it worked. Early in the fifth set, the Swede held his serve with a series of volleys struck from way up at net, the fear in him pumping his speed back up near to what it once had been. Edberg went up 1–0.

"Who are you picking?" I asked a jovial, goateed German reporter sitting next to me.

"Always the younger one," said the German.

"I think Edberg will pull this out," said my Indian colleague with a sideways smile. "Carlsen, like many young players, will suffer from nerves when the match must be won."

All eyes were on Carlsen as he held serve, riding a wave of adrenaline. Carlsen swelled up like a bully out for a streetfight after herring, beer, and schnapps on a cold Copenhagen night. I nodded. It was precisely that fear you wanted in a tight match, a taste of panic and self-loathing to keep your eyes sharp. Then Edberg started double-faulting. It was devastating, like a case of hiccups at a speech. The serve and volley that had so devastated Jim Courier and Pete Sampras at the U.S. Open finals just two and three years before had the same motion, but when Edberg followed his serves up to the net like a man looking for directions, the tall Dane absorbed the kick and hit down on the ball with all he had. Edberg, his face pale and blotchy from the effort, was twice passed up the line. Edberg returned to the baseline in a wide, unhappy circle, looking for another route.

The fifth-set grass was all ripped up, torn, and cut by turning. Edberg was late to the ball. Lunging a fourth time after a return of serve was nearly blasted by him, Stefan Edberg was broken at love.

The sun was a large orange ball behind the stadium. Carlsen was like a ship coming into port ahead of Edberg. They rode together to the very edge of the horizon. One of them would not make it back. Edberg was down 3–5, and he fell behind 0–40, triple match point. Edberg's position was beyond precarious. He looked down at the shadow across the lawn, the blades of grass now cut open by feet dragged on serves and diving stabs at volleys. Edberg served an ace. At 15–40, Edberg bravely followed a second serve up to the net. Carlsen, feeling the pressure coming right at him like a wave, hit a jammed forehand over the opposite baseline in self-defense. Edberg came to rest with a rush of light feet and he seemed to bow to the net as he came to a stop. Down 30–40, Edberg came in behind another second serve and put a firm backhand volley away. Deuce! Three match points saved.

"Stefan Edberg has the heart of a lion," I scribbled.

But Edberg was driving on a tightrope. He could not win the ad-point. On the fifth match point, Kenneth Carlsen hit a big forehand into an open spot on the court. Edberg, diving to the right spot, played a backhand volley winner just over the net. It was incredible. At his first ad-in, Edberg won the point like a champion and looked across the net at young Carlsen.

Survivor of five match points, still down 4–5 in the fifth set, Stefan Edberg skipped from side to side like Muhammad Ali ready to come out for the fifteenth round. He awaited Kenneth Carlsen's attempt to serve out the match.

Carlsen bounced the ball low into the lawn and began to serve as if he was mad at the world. Anger and fear are part of the same competitive emotion, but in the Dane only the anger showed until, waiting as Edberg jogged in place between points, Kenneth Carlsen served out the match at love. When it was done, Carlsen dropped his racket, held his head in disbelief, and then rushed to net to embrace Stefan Edberg, his onetime hero. Edberg walked forward slowly to greet him, shook hands, and sat down alone. More than half the English court was in shadow. Edberg could not quite understand the defeat, but he could feel it.

It was the passage of an athlete's time. Edberg's face, pale and lined with fatigue, was still pouring sweat. Carlsen, the winner, seemed fresh enough to play another two sets at least. Edberg came off the court quickly to thunderous applause he did not seem to want, a towel around his neck, a big racket bag over each shoulder, like an actor who suddenly realized he was no longer the leading actor on England's grassy stage.

"I am not surprised, but I am very disappointed," confessed the Indian reporter. "You see, I think this was Edberg's last chance to win at Wimbledon. Next year he will be twenty-nine and an old man." He chuckled softly with the irony of a true senior, but in competitive terms it was true.

Back inside the interview room, John Parsons, *The Daily Telgraph*'s respected reporter for thirty years, used his seniority to break the silence and ask Stefan Edberg the first question.

"Stefan. What happened?"

"I lost the match. I know that." Edberg laughed his gentle, half-embarrassed laugh. His eyes dropped as he spoke. His life was changing right in front of us. Twice a finalist, twice a winner, four times a favorite in the hearts of the English, Stefan Edberg would never be so high on the mountain again, and he knew it.

"I don't know what to say," Edberg continued, his eyes distant. "I mean, I had my chances, and I didn't take them. . . . He played a good match, but, you know, I played a sloppy game the first game of the third set to let him break me. Then I had a break in the fourth set, and I was up 2–0 and I played another bad game to let him back in the match. You can't really afford to do that."

It was the closest I had ever seen him come to tears.

"Do you feel there's still another Wimbledon inside of you, Stefan?"

"Maybe one more, who knows. . . . Unfortunately I am out of it, and I just have to accept it." Edberg shrugged. "It's my own fault— nobody else's."

It would hurt more when the interview was done, for Edberg had begun to see the shadow line himself, having gone through all the stages of a career in that one match: First there was youth and all its freedoms, volleys as instinctive and penetrating as the best kisses in one's life, serves as strong as the best China tea. In the second set, he had had to become a survivor too soon in order to win it. He showed too much need and struggle, and the younger player, feeling these emerging shortcomings across the net, just kept on banging, not so much physically as mentally. That is the way a great older player loses a match to a younger player. The older player has to call too early on his magic, and then it is gone.

"Does it hurt?" a reporter asked.

"It always hurts when you lose. Even if you are playing in a small tournament, it hurts. Obviously it hurts more at Wimbledon, and I am probably going to hurt more this evening and when I wake up tomorrow morning. Sometimes it's really tough to face. Sometimes it's relatively easy. You just have to try to forget about it as soon as you can. The only thing I can say is that I tried my best, and it did not succeed. There's really nothing else that I can do. I fought for every point out there, but I didn't take my chances well. That's the end of the story."

"Questions in Swedish," said the Wimbledon official softly.

The loyal Swedish press gathered in the front row began to go through it all again, and Edberg answered it again in a singsong Swedish so gentle and under control that one would think he had just begun to be interviewed. God, I admired him. He was the most remarkable of athletes, a player who remains on an even keel even when time tears down his sails and rips up his centerboard. At twenty-eight—still in the prime of his life but no longer in the prime of his tennis career—Stefan Edberg told a light joke in Swedish and got up with just a hint of back stiffness.

"It was hard," he added in Swedish, "because Wimbledon is such a nice place to play."

"Will you come back to watch the other matches?" a young Swedish reporter called out.

Edberg stopped on the old wooden stairs, turned, smiled, and said gently, "Normally I do not do so."

Geraldine Fitzgerald, the Wimbledon press liaison, was a fairly short woman with a soft face and the kind of cute, short hairdo popularized by Karen Hantze Susman at Wimbledon in 1962. It was eighty-five degrees outside. But Geraldine, cool in the air-conditioning almost all day, was wearing a sharply pleated gray flannel skirt. I liked her. Geraldine told it like it was. She had a schoolteacher's slightly irritable disposition that she turned on and off toward the reporters she ruled with the alternating care and disgust that comes from looking after three hundred adult-looking children who all want exactly what they want immediately—big smile, please, right now, thank you so much. I was no exception.

"Excuse me, Geraldine," I said. "I would like to talk to Fred Perry. Could you help me out?"

The Englishwoman looked at me quizzically, her head tilted to one side, as if waiting for me to back off. Finally she righted her head and said to me with no explanation or hint of facial expression, "Well, you'll need an envelope."

"An envelope?"

"Of course. For the letter you must write to Mr. Perry requesting an interview. You don't expect we'd have you just tack a note up on the bulletin board?"

I smiled in pleased disbelief at the English niceties that remained.

"Here's an envelope," Geraldine said gruffly, passing me a heavy white envelope across the counter as I started to compose a brief note to England's greatest player.

If he got it, he did not respond. I tried to reach him through the BBC. I even called him at the Hotel Rembrandt in Knightsbridge, which seemed to me the perfect name of a hotel for a player of Fred Perry's caliber. I finally reached him by phone, but Perry was noncommittal in that gruff way of his. Meeting with him became my number one goal. Then early one morning at 9:15 on the Wimbledon grounds, hours before most of the radio and television commentators ever arrive for the 12:00 P.M. start, there was Fred Perry, and there was I.

Six foot one, his large head still an incredible profile, Perry said to me, "Look. I'm sorry. I just can't talk with you now. Sky TV wants me this afternoon. This German TV crew thinks I can open the door for them at Wimbledon if I let them interview me this morning, but I can't and I won't. I'm doing BBC radio at noon for the rest of the day. It's just not a good time to talk."

I liked thinking of Perry, who came from the radio generation, doing the BBC radio instead of television commentary. I smiled, and I think that smile, while he was trying to blow me away with his verbal serve and volley, got to him. Then he stared at my blue shirt: a Fred Perry.

"Oh, all right," Fred Perry said. "But I can give you five minutes, no more. Let's go down to one of the BBC studios, if we can find one down there that's free."

A Wimbledon guard smiled deferentially at England's world champion. Perry nodded and pushed ahead. A metal staircase, four feet wide and as perpendicular as a fire ladder, greeted us. Not missing a beat, Fred Perry turned, grabbed the metal railings, and climbed down quickly backward. I followed, admiring his easy athleticism. He moved like a man in his late sixties. In fact, he was eighty-five. When we got down the stairs, we discovered the door was locked.

"It was terrible weather that first day when Steffi Graf lost to Lori McNeil," I said, hoping to salvage the interview.

"Champions shouldn't have to play in weather like that," said Perry calmly as he began opening some mail he had brought along. He waited with the patience of a man on the deck of a ship traveling to Australia in 1934 rather than one stuck on a piece of linoleum over concrete at the foot of metal stairs in 1994. "I suppose you think I know every inch of this place," Perry confided, "but I don't. There are places they won't let me go here."

We had to climb back up the stairs. I was happy to be in the presence of an eighty-five-year-old tiger. We passed the four training tables in the women's locker room. "That's not for us," said Perry. Finally the man whose bronze statue stood near the entrance as tribute to his three consecutive Wimbledon victories, from 1934 to 1936, found a room he liked—the back of the big interview room where Edberg went out the day before—and he sat down next to me and frowned.

Fred Perry spoke with the intense but slightly peevish voice of a champion who believes, as a great painter or a great musician believes, that there really is no point in trying to explain how it's done because if you have to ask there really is no hope for you.

"Look. This game is not complicated," he began. "If there is no footwork, there is no tennis."

I smiled and nodded, repeating what he had just said out loud. This pleased him.

"See, if you're not secure in your footwork, you're in trouble," Fred Perry continued in a gentler voice, and I could picture him playing against Budge, Borotra, Vines, and Gottfried von Cramm. Fred Perry had been a champion greyhound in slick-black hair and long white pants. He had moved better than any of those four illustrious opponents and was perhaps the best mover before Borg and possibly including Laver, Edberg, and Chang. Perry was more than graceful—he was fast, slim, and very strong.

"Grass is now such a specialized game," he said. "We used to play more of it, but it got too expensive." Fred Perry nodded, as if to say that this was simply the disappointing way of the world and that he did not necessarily disapprove of change even though grass-court tennis remained his love and his forte. "Still, there are grass courts now in Holland and Germany. The Germans, who were basically a clay-court nation, have even played a Davis Cup match at home on grass." Perry chuckled at the idea.

"You handled von Cramm," I said. Perry had beaten von Cramm 6–1, 6–1, 6–0 in the 1936 Wimbledon final, still the most one-sided

Wimbledon final of all time. In his three consecutive Wimbledon finals, Fred Perry did not lose a set.

"Well, it was almost a certainty when I played von Cramm," he said very matter-of-factly. "von Cramm was a European clay-court player."

He had opened a window for me to the past. I had always assumed that von Cramm, because he reached so many finals on grass, was essentially a grass-court player. "What was wrong with von Cramm on grass?"

"Long swing. Long follow-through," said Perry succinctly.

The cover of the September 12, 1936, edition of *Newsweek*, which I bought from my on-the-street bookseller in New York just a week before Wimbledon, carried a full-body shot of a powerful bony-faced Fred Perry hitting an overhead in long white pants, eyes squinting into the sun. I pulled it out for Perry and opened it to the article that showed Kay Stammers, the beautiful English champion of the day, smiling in her white tennis visor, legs crossed in white culottes, and a lean and beaming Bill Tilden sitting at a bridge table in long sleeves and a tie during Wimbledon. As he saw himself on the cover and his old friends pictured in their youth inside the magazine Fred Perry's voice changed entirely, as if I had brought him back his real friends, most of whom were dead now.

"Here's a picture of Tilden," I said. "You played with him."

"Oh, sure," Perry said softly, staring down into the magazine. "I played over three hundred matches with him."

"That many! And your result was?"

"Well, he was older than I was," said Perry, coming to Tilden's defense, then, quietly after a pause, "Bill was six or seven years older." (I looked it up later; Tilden, born in 1893, was actually sixteen years older than Fred Perry.) He paused again. "We played together on the pro tour, but . . . Bill was finished by then. We had Vines, too. Did I have the edge on Tilden?" Perry laughed. "Well, if I didn't have the edge on a guy who was over fifty, I wasn't very good, was I?"

"What was Tilden's serve like?" I had heard that he had a powerful cannonball first serve, but the French, starting with Rene Lacoste, feared Tilden's spin serves more, because when Tilden started hitting his cannonball it meant he was in trouble. When Tilden spun the ball, the French players said, they knew he had lots more in reserve.

If he hit the big one, especially on clay, they knew he was tiring. Suzanne Lenglen, the Nijinsky of the tennis courts in the 1920s, famous from the Côte d'Azur to Los Angeles, had reputedly told Lacoste that he should hope to see the Tilden cannonball on the grass at Forest Hills in 1927. Lacoste did, and he defeated Tilden 11–9, 6–3, 11–9 for the first time. But in 1928 the thirty-five-year-old Tilden, serving Lacoste nothing but spin serves on the Frenchman's native red clay in Paris, lost the first set 6–1 but defeated Rene Lacoste in five long sets, prompting Lacoste to say, "Is he not the greatest player of them all?"

"To me," said Fred Perry, "when you talk about who was the best player I ever saw"—and now Perry's eyes lit up, because he literally had seen them all—"I say Bill Tilden. These professional boys today do not realize how much they owe to Tilden. He *was* tennis. He won this tournament three times. He only played here four times. The first professional, about 1928, was Suzanne Lenglen, the French girl, who got twenty-five thousand dollars. They toured in the United States with Murray K. Brown, Vincent Richards, who had won the Olympics in Paris in 1924, and the Tinsey Brothers. The first year they made money. The second year they broke even, and the promoter said, 'That's it.' It was 1929, and the stock market crashed. The next year, Tilden turned pro anyway after winning Wimbledon, and he really started the pro circuit as it is known today. Bill persevered. He had a chap called Karel Kozeluh, and the only place you could play professionally was America." Fred Perry nodded, fondly. "You could not play as a professional anywhere else in the world. They wouldn't have you."

"Tell me about Tilden. What was the outstanding feature of his game?"

Fred Perry did not hesitate at all. "His head. When you played Bill Tilden, you had to think. I learned a great deal from him. See, when you played Bill, you never got anything you wanted. If you wanted it low, he gave it to you high. If you wanted it wide, he gave it close. If you wanted it fast, he gave it to you slow. If you wanted to talk, he shut up. If you wanted to play silently, he talked."

I laughed out loud in delight. Bill Tilden. Ty Cobb had had very unkind words to say about Tilden at an awards dinner in the 1920s, but Bill Tilden lasted as long as Ty Cobb did and had at least as great an impact on his sport.

"You were always thinking, and you *had* to think against Tilden," continued Fred Perry. "Today's game, because of the equipment which limits them to certain things, is lacking a bit in thought. They use the technology to the absolute utmost for their own game, which is wonderful in its way. They play extremely well, but there are certain things they just *cannot* do anymore with this equipment. We could never play like they do with our equipment, but they can't play like we did with our equipment because we had to work for the opening much more. They can force it. Now when you force something and you make mistakes, you fall over. We never used to fall over. We never knew where the ball was going to come back; we knew where it *wasn't* going to come back." He smiled at the distinction. "See, we had the fellow on the run by the time he moved in. It's a different ball game completely. The tournament tennis played today is show business. You're advertising this. You're advertising that. At the age of twenty you have a manager, you've got a lawyer, you've got a coach and a trainer, you've got a mother, you've got a father, a girlfriend." Perry grinned, then frowned. "It's an absolute business. They are *extremely* lucky today. And basically, they owe it all to Bill Tilden. A few other people came along later. Frank Hunter, then Jack Kramer and his tour. But really, Bill was the one who started it all. You played maybe 104 or 105 one-night stands in four or five months. We played indoors in America with the snow up to you-know-where. You're driving three hundred miles in between. It was tough. And everybody hated you. Because it was something new. You were a 'dirty pro.' When I turned pro in Britain, it just wasn't the thing to do. My membership at Wimbledon, which I had won through winning the Wimbledon title, was rescinded—and rightly so, because I was no longer an amateur. You had to be an amateur to be a member of the club. And"—he said this with pride—"I was definitely *not* an *amateur*."

"There was this rivalry thing between you and Bunny Austin at that time—"

"There was never any rivalry between myself and Bunny Austin," snapped Perry imperiously, raising his voice slightly, as if I had compared Noel Coward to Joseph Conrad. "No. When we started on the English Davis Cup Team, Austin was number one, and I got better and better and won grand-slam tournaments, so I became number one."

"If the English establishment was so against professionalism, why did you turn pro?"

"Why does anyone turn pro?" snapped Perry. "To make a living. We couldn't live on tea parties. I couldn't turn down what they were offering me in America at that time. And I didn't want to."

Fred Perry had been about fifty years ahead of his time. "You had won three Wimbledons in a row."

He nodded. "I won three Wimbledons in a row. I won three Americans in four years. I won the French and the Australian. I was the first player to win all four championships," said Fred Perry. "But not in one year."

"But didn't you almost do it all in one year, except for the French?"

"Oh, the French," said Perry a bit disgruntedly, recalling 1934, the year he won the other three—the year before he actually won the French, beating von Cramm on clay in the 1935 French Open final. "I sprained an ankle in '34 at the French." Clearly it still irked Perry, sixty years later.

"Who were you playing when you sprained your ankle?"

"I was playing Georgio di Stefani, the Italian. I sprained the ankle early in the match, and I said, 'Georgio, I can't win. And I don't want to quit. I don't want to walk off. So don't make me run.' But he made me move enough. He said, 'I'm sorry, Fred,' you know, this sort of thing. But I knew he didn't trust me." Perry laughed and nodded. "When I came to the net in Paris after I lost, I said, 'Georgio. Next time we play: 6–love, 6–love, 6–love." Perry remembered it fiercely, as if it were yesterday. "And Georgio was in the world's first ten. At every subsequent tournament where we saw each other, no matter where it was in the world, I would say, 'Are you in the top half or the bottom half, Georgio?' If he'd say, 'bottom half,' I'd say 'lousy final then,' or 'lousy semifinal,' or 'lousy last eight.' A year and a half later, I finally caught up with him at Melbourne on a grass court in the semifinal of the Victoria Championships, and I beat him love, love, and love."

I grinned. "You gave him one back then, did you?"

"Because of Paris," said Perry, laughing in 1994 about 1934.

If Perry hadn't sprained his ankle in Paris in 1934, he would certainly have been the first to win all four major titles in one year. And he did win the French the following year.

"I think we had more fun. There were no airplanes. You didn't play in New York on Sunday and have to be in Paris on Monday. You had six days on a boat. When we were in Australia, we had five weeks to get back to England. So it was a different ball game and era."

"Today's players seem younger, don't they?"

"Well, they're only twenty years old. The girls are sixteen," said Perry in disbelief. "They've got baby-sitters *and* hairdressers. Capriati at fourteen was worth two and a half million dollars *before* she hit the first ball. You can't ever compare the old game with the new game."

I found that I kept wanting to go back to Tilden. I had interviewed modern players, but Perry was my link to a distant past. I had read Tilden's great, out-of-print book, *How to Play Better Tennis*, but I had never felt him firsthand on a court the way Fred Perry had.

"Tell me more about Tilden. What were his serve and forehand like?" I wanted Perry to get specific about Tilden's strokes.

"Tilden was very difficult to play," said Perry thoughtfully. "He dominated the whole thing. When two players walked on the court, Tilden was always the dominating figure."

"He had a presence."

"Right. If you walked into a room, you immediately knew he was *there*. Bill just didn't walk into the room, he took it over. It was his personality, see."

"Was Tilden a funny man at all? Amusing?"

"No, no. Bill was just such a great guy. We used to talk for hours. He couldn't volley, but one day he'd volley you. You never knew what the hell he was going to do. So it was interesting playing Tilden because you knew the wheels were turning. But I find now that there's not the same . . . fire in the players. Against Tilden you always had a feeling that came from inside Bill of 'I am *not* going to let you beat me.'" Perry paused. "I don't see that as much today. Not as intensely as it was with Tilden."

"I heard a story," I said. "In 1943, when Tilden was fifty, Gardnar Mulloy arranged a pro exhibition match between Tilden and Ted

Schroeder for the U.S. Navy. Tilden won 6–2, 6–2, and after the match Gardnar Mulloy asked Tilden how at age fifty he could possibly have beaten Schroeder, the reigning U.S. champion, and Tilden said to Mulloy, 'I never lose to people I hate' and walked away."

Perry laughed. "Yes, that was Bill! I remember we were on a summer tour with Kozeluh, Vin Richards, Tilden, and myself. It was about a hundred degrees, and we were going to play that night at a very nice country club in Independence, Kansas. I had to play Bill. He called me at about ten-thirty in the morning and said, 'What are you doing?' I said, 'I'm going to drive my car to the country club. I'm going to park under a tree. I'm going to take out my golf clubs. I'm going to hit a few balls. I'm going to sit down. I'm going to smoke my pipe. I'm going to hit some more balls. Then I'm going to sit down and smoke my pipe under the tree for a while, hit some more golf balls, have a bit of lunch, come home to rest, and play you tonight.' " Fred Perry smiled at the memory. "Tilden said to me, 'I want you to come out this morning and hit a few tennis balls to me.' I said to him, 'Bill, you're nuts. We've been playing for four weeks already, seven days a week. And we're going to play tonight.' Tilden said, 'Please come along with me. I want to show you something.' So we go down to the club in Independence, Kansas, in 1946, thereabouts, and he says, 'Fred, I want you to hit me low forehands, half pace—we practiced half pace because if you made mistakes, you wouldn't hurt yourself in practice. So I did what he asked, and he hit them back with a perfect continental grip." Perry grinned. "Now when I first turned pro, I didn't turn pro with Bill, although he'd made me an offer, and when I didn't go with him then he said to the press, 'I didn't sign Fred Perry because he's only got a lousy forehand that doesn't work anyway.' My forehand was my big shot." Perry laughed. "So [during practice] Bill said, 'Do you notice anything?' And I said, 'Am I supposed to?' And he said, 'I'm using a continental forehand grip.' I said, 'But I thought it wasn't worth a damn,' and Bill said, 'After playing about 180 or 190 matches with you, I realize that for a low ball wide on the forehand side, the only grip to use is a continental grip because I can still go down the line, up the middle of the court, and way across the court with it from there. Can't do that with the eastern grip.' " Perry's voice grew quiet. "And then Bill said to me—and I will never forget it—he said, 'I felt that until I mastered that shot, I would never be the perfect player.' " Fred Perry looked up. "He was fifty-three years old when he said that."

I felt a shiver of goose bumps go through me. It was as if Tilden himself, tall and smiling, were sitting there behind us, checking over our shoulders to be sure we got the story right. Fred Perry had not forgotten that morning in Independence, Kansas, with Bill Tilden in the intervening fifty or so years. Tennis is such a beautiful learning game, and Tilden was its greatest and deepest study, still trying to perfect his game at age fifty-three. For some reason, perhaps because I knew the personal and financial problems Tilden was having in his life at that time, the story just about made me cry.

"Today," said Perry, "these boys don't seem to learn much after the age of eighteen or twenty. They can't. See, to learn a new stroke and put it into your repertoire, there's always a chance that it might not work anyway, and it means two months of hard work without any money or sure results. Well, in two months playing the tour, they can make a lot of money. So they don't fill in the gaps." Fred Perry nodded. "Players of today play now the same way they did five or six years ago. Same patterns."

"And it's very straight," I said. "Almost rectilinear."

"It practically has to be with these rackets," said Perry. "We had twenty main strings and a smaller-headed racket. In England, we used nineteen-gauge gut, which was very light gut. The Americans had the same size racket heads, but they had eighteen main strings and used seventeen-gauge gut, which was thicker. If we were in America and ran out of strings, we had to use the seventeen-gauge American gut, and we couldn't use it because there was no feel." Fred Perry's right hand started to move back and forth in the air as if he wanted to let it do the talking. "Today they have the bigger racket heads but only sixteen main strings, so the ball is on the racket and off again too quickly to feel it. So they have to force the ball all the time. The harder you hit it, the more mistakes you're going to make. Most of their mistakes come from the service line. I don't see these people going into the net on short, angled shots anymore because you can't make those plays with these rackets. So when you talk tennis today, you have the 2,500 players who play the tournament circuit, which is show business, and then there's a game that seventy million people play that is much closer to what we used to play."

I asked him about Rene Lacoste. They had just missed each other.

"Lacoste was captain of the French team when we played Davis Cup in Paris in 1931. He had just quit, and I never played him. But I did play Cochet and Borotra and all those boys."

"And how did you find Cochet and Borotra? Cochet was spectacular?"

"Well, I had copied Cochet," said Perry. "I had the same style Cochet had, but I was stronger than he was, I was bigger than he was, I was faster than he was, and I hit the ball harder than he did." Perry held up a hand. "Playing Cochet was like playing a mirror."

"But you were the better side of the mirror."

"Well, I was younger, don't forget.

"Cochet unfortunately has passed on, but he would be about eighty-eight today," said Fred Perry, eighty-five himself.

I smiled, knowing that Cochet, born in 1901, would have been ninety-three. The younger player always thinks the gap in years between him or her and the older player is smaller than it actually is. There had been, in fact, nearly eight years separating Perry and Cochet. They had had different primes, but Perry's record was better.

"How would you characterize your particular strengths as a player?"

"I had the continental forehand and took the ball very early. I had all that from table tennis before I took up lawn tennis. The angles . . . [are] the same; the parameters of the ball are the same; the spins and counterspins are the same. Except you can't volley on the table."

"Was your backhand a slice, or did you come over the ball?"

"My backhand was designed to keep the ball in play until I got the ball I wanted on my forehand. I was fitter than anybody else. And I think I was probably fitter than any of these boys today, because I trained for three years with the Arsenal football club. In 1932 I lost four matches. I lost the Davis Cup in Berlin in the fifth set; I lost in Paris in five sets, Wimbledon in five sets, and at the U.S. in five sets. I came back from America and a dear friend, Sam Hardy, who used to be Spalding's in America, said, 'Well, where do you go from here, Freddie? Australia again?' And I said, 'No, Sam. I'm going back to

England.' And he said, 'What the hell for, to freeze to death?' But I was going back to train with the Arsenal football club. I made a deal with them that for the next three years, rain or shine, any day I was in London and not playing tennis I'd be at the Arsenal. They used to have me run up the stand and come down. I went up and down those stairs all day long, then I'd have a lap with so-and-so. Well, I was running about ten to twelve miles a day that way." Perry smiled. "In the next four years, I lost only one five-set match. My whole game changed, because by that time my game was good enough so that very few people were going to beat me in straight sets anyway. My game plan was to win the first set at all costs or lose it 16–14, which you can't do today with this 7–6 stuff. I knew that if I won that first set, they weren't going to win three sets in a row, and they knew it, too."

I looked at Fred Perry. Underneath his long white pants of the 1930s had been legs that had been able to keep pace with the best soccer players in the world. I said, "I've always thought you have been slightly underestimated when compared to Don Budge. You beat Budge so often and then you turned pro, and Budge won his slam the next year against a weaker field that no longer contained you."

I thought Don Budge had the better all-around game and certainly the better backhand, perhaps the greatest ever, but I felt even now sitting next to Fred Perry at age eighty-five that he had been far more fit than Budge, faster, and, in a tight spot, a better competitor. I always recalled my father's stories about watching Budge play Bobby Riggs almost every day out at Hickam Field in Hawaii during World War II, and how Riggs had beaten Budge over and over again on the hard courts only a couple of years after Budge's prime.

"In America," said Perry, "they like to write about their own. I suppose it's natural. They write about Agassi. He's a good player, but Becker is the only foreign player who has gotten real publicity over there recently. Edberg just happens to be there." Fred Perry shook his head. "Well, Don Budge was an American. So naturally, they always thought he could beat me. Don't forget that the grand slam did not exist when I was playing. It was an invention of the Americans. It was started by Allison Danzig of the *New York Times*, who called it that when Budge won it. It had never occurred to us to try to win all four in one year before that." As Perry paused, thinking back to an era when his reward for winning Wimbledon three years in a row consisted of three gold coins and the Renshaw Cup. Second prizes were ten pounds sterling. "Nobody said a word when I won four slams in a row but not in one year. Then Budge won the grand slam and Laver won it twice. But I wonder how many Americans know that Roy Emerson also won all four slams but not in one year."

Some people liked to dream about Babe Ruth and Ty Cobb. I preferred Don Budge and Fred Perry. The old rivalries intrigued me as much as the new, and I thought Fred Perry historically had been given short shrift. It was actually Fred Perry who had dominated tennis—and Don Budge—until Perry turned pro. Perry was nearly thirty years old before Budge, twenty-three, beat him in a pro tour, eighteen matches to eleven. Perry had beaten Budge often in other years, but Budge has gotten far more credit for that one pro series after Perry had already crossed his own shadow line. "Do you recall playing Don Budge?" I asked.

"Oh, I played Budge many times," Perry said with complete ease. "I played him in the Davis Cup. I played him at Wimbledon and beat him. Yeah. The last time I played him was in 1936 in New York. I beat him at Forest Hills on a very stop-and-start day with the rain."

"Forest Hills in 1936?"

"That's right. Budge was serving for the match with new balls at 5–4 in the fifth set, and he hit his first serve as hard as he could. Old Len Richards of Spalding's was in the umpire's chair, and I looked up at Len and whispered to him, 'He can't win it.' " Perry allowed himself a smile. "Because, see, with new balls you don't hit the first ones hard, you spin 'em in. The first time you hit a new ball hard, it flies wildly. Budge should have known that, but apparently he didn't. He got very tired, and, well, I beat him finally."

Budge himself wrote of the fifth-set loss to Perry,

I got the break for 4–2. Promptly I permitted Fred to break me back. My serve was a dishrag. However, tired as I was, I was able to break him back again, so I stood at 5–3 serving for the National Championship of my country against the number one player in the world. All I had to do was hold my serve one more time. I could not. I was so exhausted in reaching up to hit my serve that I felt as if I were leaning on the ball. There was no life in my shots. The stretching and reaching for the serve particularly wore on me. He broke me again . . . held his own serve at last and tied the set at 5–all.

Budge came back to lead 8–7, but Perry won it 10–8 in the fifth. "What did you admire most about Budge's game?" I asked Perry.

"Well, Budge could steamroll you. He had a great, great backhand. He used a very heavy racket, about fifteen or sixteen ounces. He sort of dropped the racket head on the ball with his backhand, and off it went. It was a particularly great shot when Budge was standing still. So I tried to keep him moving all the time. Otherwise he'd murder you with it. Don't get me wrong; Budge was a dead good player. But the way I played Budge," said Fred Perry, "was to keep him very busy. He always said to me that I kept pushing him, that I was at him all the time. He didn't have any time with me. You know, Budge started out with a huge topspin forehand. And actually in Los Angeles when he saw me play for the first time in about 1932, he tried to copy my forehand, and he wound up with something in between that suited him." Perry smiled.

Perry's own reign had been the four years from 1933 to 1936. Budge's reign began in 1937, and he turned pro in 1938. Bobby Riggs began beating Budge in about 1943. "What did you think of Bobby Riggs as a player?"

"Well, Riggs tantalized you, you see. But he was a get-em-back artist more than anything else. He had a good head on his shoulders, Riggsie."

In 1939 Bobby Riggs threw his match at the Queen's Club against Gottfried von Cramm so he could get better odds on himself the next week at Wimbledon. He did and made a killing on his bets, winning the men's singles, doubles, and mixed. This was right before the war closed Wimbledon down for five years. Riggs never did get to play at Wimbledon again after completing one of the most remarkable sweeps in tennis history.

In that 1939 Wimbledon final, Riggs beat Elwood Cooke, who twenty years later coached eight-year-old Dick Stockton and myself at the old 168th Street armory in Harlem, New York, where the surface left splinters in the balls. I remembered Cooke chain-smoking in long white flannels as he coached us silently. Riggs won the Wimbledon title over Cooke 6–2 in the fifth set, but Cooke had almost won in straight sets, leading Riggs 6–2, 6–8, 6–3 before Riggs ran him off the court. Had something happened in that second set for which Cooke never forgave his doubles partner, Riggs? Cooke never told us. Perhaps we were too young to understand. But I sensed that winning and losing a Wimbledon final can mean a world of difference.

"The whole key to it in any era, in any job," said Perry, "is if you really enjoy something, you are going to do it better than the next person. If you lose that joy, well, the sport or the job is not for you."

I had one last line of inquiry: the difference between the tall bronze statue and the man. The affection for Fred Perry had been late in coming from some quarters. "When you were first coming up in the 1920s and the 1930s in England, you were not the darling in the press, were you?"

"I was not the old school tie," Perry corrected me firmly, proudly. "I was not the establishment."

He still wasn't, and it showed in the deferential yet somehow almost indulgent treatment this old tennis master received. He was a legend around Wimbledon, yet in and out of the Member's Enclosure, where only members could enter, I had heard there was not quite the degree of reverence I had for him. Some loved him. Some did not. "Wasn't your father a member of Parliament?" I asked.

"Yes. But my father was a Labor M.P. He was a union man in the cotton trade and . . . the first Labor governments of the late twenties and early thirties were always minority governments and *Labor* was a very dirty word. Plus, I was north country, from Stockport in Cheshire, well by a hundred and twenty yards really from Lancashire, and the north country people never understood the southerners, like the Yankees and the southerners in your country. They didn't understand me. I didn't understand them, and I never tried. See, I was in a game at the time which was very establishment, very top-drawer. Most of the players and most of the officials were all high society, Oxford-Cambridge boys. And I wasn't. But, unfortunately"—he winked—"I got good enough to beat them all."

"Do you think those differences helped to motivate you?"

"Oh, yeah. Because I didn't like to come in second. I never went on a court to lose. I lost a lot of times, but I didn't like it." He nodded, his eyes sharp and darting.

I had only one more question. "What is it about a champion, that inner fight, that need to prove something, that you and Tilden had?"

"Pride," Fred Perry blurted out, strong to the end. "Pride. Which is gone. Now it's mostly money."

Fred Perry nodded at me, shook my hand, and was gone.

The veterans Roger Taylor and Allan Stone played a doubles match with Cliff Drysdale and Owen Davidson in the scorching sun. Taylor still had the good looks of Sean Connery, and his left-handed serve in its day was perhaps the biggest weapon in English tennis since Fred Perry's forehand. Taylor could make the chalk fly the way my own favorite English player, Mike Sangster, did in all Sangster's 12–10, 10–8, 15–13 losses to Chuck McKinley. In 1970 Taylor reached the semifinals of Wimbledon, beating Rod Laver 4–6, 6–4, 6–2, 6–1. More recently, Taylor's jet-black hair had turned a steely shade of gray and his serve had lost a bit of its bend.

Cliff Drysdale was by far the fittest of the foursome. His partner Owen Davidson, the Australian doubles great, sported a walrus mustache and a stevedore's slumping belly that belied his great skill as a doubles player. Allan Stone had been a top ten player in Australia in the early seventies.

I watched them play for over two hours on the side court where Yevgeny Kafelnikov had dispatched Karsten Braasch succinctly. Roger Taylor still had the old, confident swagger between serves, but as the heat of the afternoon wore on, he seemed to trail his left foot longer and longer on his delivery. Sweat was pouring off all four of them like water, but if they ever put the ball on Owen Davidson's racket, the old lefty angled it away without another thought. It was great fun to watch them play. They knew doubles inside out. They still attacked the middle, played the sharp-angled drop, and lobbed straight over the net man, shots that were becoming virtual dinosaurs with the new rackets in the hands of the younger players. When Roger Taylor broke Stone's serve to win the first set, he smiled a pirate's smile, but toward the end of the third set they all looked ready to call it a day—or drop dead.

A very unusual doubles player, Cliff Drysdale ran around his forehand to take everything he could with his famous two-handed backhand. This backhand, unlike modern two-handers, was hit with his racket head taken back higher than the ball, so that Drysdale could drive it flatter and, I thought, conceal it better the way Pancho Segura concealed his two-handed forehand. Drysdale, the legs of his team, sent up a final series of excellent two-handed lobs. Roger Taylor, still strong as a tree overhead, handled them all, until one of his branches seemed to fall off.

There were no tiebreakers in final sets at Wimbledon, but when the forty-five-and-over Gentlemen's Doubles match went into the third set they all looked like foot soldiers in *Beau Geste*. The match ended in a strange but perhaps fitting way. Roger Taylor was serving, down match point. His first serve sailed long—tired power. He tossed the second ball high in the air, but the big Englishman was so exhausted after two and a half hours in that sun that the ball bounced off the middle of his racket frame, hit on his own service line, and dropped softly into the bottom of the net, a double fault to end the match. The four great veteran players looked at each other and burst out laughing. Taylor shook his head sheepishly. Drysdale smiled. Allan Stone kidded Taylor. And the walrus, Owen Davidson, seemed to be looking about for a pool of crushed ice. They had competed until they could not move. They had nothing more to prove, and finally they realized it.

Five days after Jonathan Stark's loss to Karsten Braasch, I could tell the defeat was still eating away at him. I tried to get right to the point with him.

"How does your game right now compare with your play at the end of last summer at the U.S. Open when you lost to Volkov in those five great sets?"

Stark smiled nervously. His face was still long and handsome with blond beard stubble, but stress had cut lines between his eyebrows and across his pale forehead. He was twenty-three but now had a battle-seasoned face. The kid in him may have died a little playing Michael Chang at ten o'clock at night in front of the three thousand remaining fans in Philadelphia. "Ah," said Stark, "that's hard to say. Aspects of my game have improved a lot since I played Volkov."

We both knew that his 12–9 record in singles since then had not really borne this out. Batting 57 percent on the ATP Tour meant good money but only one ATP tournament win for Stark. He was earning, but he wasn't burning the circuit up the way Yevgeny Kafelnikov was.

"I try to get a little better every day," said Stark. "When I lose a tough one, I try to just focus on the next tournament and go on from there."

I nodded. Stark, at least verbally, had a good professional attitude. I wanted to ask his coach, Larry Stefanki, how Stark had progressed, but Stefanki had flown back home alone right after the loss. Did Stark really want to be a champion? Did he really have the pride and inner toughness to develop his talent to the maximum? Would he, like Tilden, ever be out on the court trying to figure out a shot? Many players on the ATP tour did not do nearly as well as Stark. He was still in that neverland between obscurity and stardom, where one's peers know and respect you but the fans may not even know what you are going through to try to get yourself to the really big time.

"I'm not giving away cheap points off my volley anymore," said the doubles winner of the 1994 French Open, who had nonetheless sailed some key volleys long against Braasch. "I'm working on my—"

"Feet?" I asked. Movement was still Stark's Achilles' heel.

"My feet. And return of serve."

Stark was far more upbeat than he had been the day after his match with Braasch, when the first thing he said to me when he saw me standing there as he stood signing autographs was, "I am really struggling."

Stark *was* struggling. I knew it was fashionable to be positive about everything, but once in a while a hard, even angry self-assessment could also be helpful. I could feel something sliding away from Stark. I would have been mad if I were him. But he was calm. And he was the player.

I preferred the assessment of his game that Jonathan Stark had given me right after his loss to Volkov. He had been angry with himself, still hungry to win, and bitterly disappointed with the loss. But he had seemed complacent after the loss to Chang in Philadelphia, as if he were already so much a part of the computer rankings system that he could have let the computer play Chang. Real anger with one-self, the ability to recognize that a professional responsibility was not being met, was ultimately part of the tennis genius of Jimmy Connors and John McEnroe.

"The other day you told me you were struggling," I reminded him softly.

"Listen, I don't know what you have in mind with this book," said Stark, frowning as if ready to go silent.

"Listen," I shot back. "I really liked the way you played last summer against Volkov. I think I saw in you and liked the same thing your coach, Larry Stefanki, saw and liked. You've got a lot of good things to draw on if you could just do it and also deal with the weaknesses in your game. You're so darn good. But you could be better. What really interests me is that the tour is such a process, such a long trip of self-discovery and learning."

"It is," admitted Stark, relaxing. "It is an up-and-down process of learning. There are some slow learners and some fast learners, and I'm not saying I'm either, but, you know, sometimes you think, 'There it is! I'm right where I want to be!' And then . . ." Stark shook his head.

"Is the pro tour a balancing act between learning and playing?"

"Definitely." Stark nodded. "You work so hard on your game, but you can't carry that type of thinking out onto the court because in the matches you have to think about what you have to do to win the match. You can't still be thinking about your strokes. And that's the balancing act for all of us out on the tour."

"Your instincts have to be ingrained so deeply."

"Right. Practice enhances them. You need to have that natural instinct, and then you have to be able to let it flow. They can't be sep-arate or you break down. There is a very fine line, a very fine balance to doing that. You can't be worrying about the mechanics of your backhand when you are out there against Michael Chang; there's just no time for that kind of thought."

"On a couple of key points against Braasch and last year against

Volkov, I remember saying to myself, 'God, Jonathan has *got* to put the next return of serve on the court.' And you hit it long."

Stark, whose decided stubborn streak was both helpful and a problem at different times, dropped his head slightly. "Yeah."

"What do you think when you do that?"

"Well"—Stark took a long, deep breath and sighed—"we spoke about this subject after the Volkov match. There's a very fine line with my type of game. I am an aggressive player. If I think in my mind when I am playing tennis 'Just get this ball in,' chances are I am going to miss it. I'm the kind of player who has to go for it."

"And yet, the other day I saw Sampras playing Daniel Vacek, who's about your height, around six foot three. It was not an easy match at all. Vacek has a huge serve, too. And there were points when *Sampras* was happy to just put the ball back onto the court on his return, sometimes with a little bit of underspin. It was working for Sampras. He did not try to hit a winner on every return. He was giving himself a chance to get back into the point against Vacek, the way Connors used to do so well. You don't think that's worthwhile sometimes?"

"Oh, it's definitely worthwhile. And on the grass it is a little different—you try to just block it back a little more. But in the Braasch match, it shouldn't have made a difference. I should have won it. And no excuses. But the conditions were horrendous, and if I were to pick one person whom I really wouldn't want to face in those conditions, it would be Braasch. Still, champions are the guys who pull out matches like that. They get through it and take the tournament from then on."

It still hurt him, and I was sorry. Braasch was like a touch of late-night hell, a player he should have beaten.

"I was *really* close to coming all the way back. I won the third and fourth sets, and then there was that downpour, and that was a little stroke of—"

"Bad luck." I leaped to his defense. "That rain was a big stroke of bad luck."

"It was bad," continued Stark softly. "I didn't *want* to lose the first two sets, but what I really felt like was just, 'Hold serve. Keep on fighting and you're going to get a break because this guy is going to give you chances.' And that's what happened. By the end of the fourth set, he was pretty pissed off. *He* was struggling."

"If you had played the fifth with no interruption, you had him."

"Even if we'd played two more games in the fifth set before the rain, I felt like I could have broken him again quickly."

I thought of boxers at the start of a fight. "When you came out for the fifth set, had you broken a sweat?"

"That's a good question. I stretched but I wasn't sweating. I probably should have been, because Braasch starts so fast. He broke me that first game, and it started to rain a little, and that was pretty much it. The rain never got hard enough in the last set for them to call it. I had a few chances in his last service game, but he aced me on that break point. He hit a great serve under pressure."

"In a general way, can you describe the difference in playing and traveling between when you are struggling and when you are on a roll on the tour?"

Stark nodded. "When you have some success, *everything* seems to be easier. The traffic jams you get in coming to the courts don't bother you as much—you don't even have them." Stark shrugged. "You know, I was pretty upset about the Braasch match after the match and the next day. But then I thought, 'It's just one match. I'm hitting the ball well. I won the French Open in doubles.' Hell. I shouldn't be in a bad mood. My brother's here this week to stay with me. So why bum him out? I wanted it bad, but hopefully I'll have many more Wimbledons."

"Is tennis so draining because it is almost a direct reflection of everything about yourself? In other words, what comes out on the court is actually you. Is that what makes it so tough when you lose?"

"Yeah," said Stark, struggling to find the right words. "You really are laying yourself on the line a bit."

"It's all of you from the inside out."

"Yeah. And you are really fighting your ass off."

"And if it doesn't come out right, you feel as if it's all of you that didn't quite come out right?"

Jonathan Stark nodded with a great, happy smile that would always serve him well. "But also, don't forget, the tour is kind of a fun thing.

Two guys go out there, really dueling. Nobody else, just you two. That's what most of us like about it. The competitive part."

Stark was not a passenger. He liked taking the wheel and the big, major thoroughfares. Part of the beauty of the tennis highway, part of my fascination with the game itself, was that one shoulder of the road was talent and the other was self-discovery. The tennis highway stretched back a century, and new people were getting on and off it all the time.

"What did it feel like walking onto the court to play the final doubles match of the French Open?"

"It was really . . . great. Blackie [Byron Black, Stark's partner] and I were really pumped up to be in the final. There were definitely some major nerves flying."

"You felt it in the knees?"

"Oh, yeah!" laughed Stark, "Especially when it came time to win it. I had four match points on my return of serve before we won it. One of them I shanked way out of the court."

I laughed. "Nerve shot, right?"

"Right. Another one I hit really well, but they came up with a good volley. And the third one I hit great but right into the top of the net tape. So [Jan] Apell and [Jonas] Bjorkman held serve, and then we played a tiebreaker. There were some double faults in the breaker from all of us. But in the end we got it done."

"What happened on match point? How did you win it?"

"We were at 6–5 in the breaker with Blackie serving. Blackie missed the first serve. I was up at net, and I told myself I was going to poach no matter what. He hit a second serve, and I went."

"And how did you get the final point?"

Stark smiled. "[With a] backhand volley."

"Did you split them up the middle?"

"No. It was down at Bjorkman's feet."

"And he kicked it?"

"Yeah." He had won the match with a backhand volley he would remember for the rest of his life. "It was great to win it, especially after losing in the Australian Open final. We didn't think we'd done our best there."

"Did you go out that night and celebrate in Paris?"

Stark shook his head. "No. We should have stayed and had a celebration, but Byron was playing in England the next day and I was going to Holland to play on the grass." Stark shrugged. I liked him. What he was trying was not easy.

"I've been watching you for a while now," I said. "The only weaknesses I see are the strength of your legs—your movement—and some weakness at the back of the court on the ground. But the main problem is the movement."

"For the last year I've been working my ass off to try to develop my lower body. I'm just bigger on top."

"I see a guy like Vacek."

"He's a horse," said Stark.

I nodded. Vacek had blown away Kafelnikov, just as Kafelnikov had blown away Braasch. Then Sampras just absorbed Vacek, enormous serve and all. There were so many levels to the game. "Your serve is as good as Vacek's, and your volley is better. Become a horse, Jonathan."

"Everyone has different body types and things they do well. I'm working hard. I'm doing sit-ups. But you're absolutely right about the legs. I need work on them."

"Are you getting top guys to practice with?"

"Larry Stefanki gets me great people. I practiced with Agassi yesterday. We played a set and a half. I know all the guys. But you can't sit there and say my ranking should be higher or 'I should be there by now.' The thing is, I'm not. All I can do is put myself into the position of competing for it each week. I'm really into it. I'm eating right. I'm getting my sleep. I'm doing what I know I have to do. I just have to keep putting myself into these tough situations. I have to keep learning—not get nervous. I think I can do it."

I told Stark the story about the fifty-three-year-old Tilden learning a new stroke, and he smiled with understanding.

"Tennis is a learning process," agreed Stark, "I have always been big. I've always been a good athlete. In the juniors, even at the college level, I could just bang away and win. Some of that is OK, because natural stuff is good to have out there. But playing against the top hundred, hundred and fifty—you really have to know what you are doing. These guys are just as good athletes as you are, so you have to find an extra edge. And the edge is mental."

"It's a great game," I said.

"Yes, it is."

"Keep cookin'," I said as we slapped our hands together in a handshake. "I'll look for you at the U.S. Open. Give them heaps!"

Pete Sampras's win in the final over Goran Ivanisevic was smooth but by no means effortless. When Ion Tiriac, then Becker's coach, predicted in 1989 that Ivanisevic would win "not one Wimbledon but five," he may have put a curse on the handsome Croatian. Tiriac, who had taken over Ivanisevic's finances, and Bob Brett, whom I had watched running Ivanisevic's practice session at the Lipton, had kept their horse under tight reign. But playing Sampras in these years was a bit like running against Secretariat. Only Andre Agassi seemed capable of staying with him, toe-to-toe and talent to talent. As he had in practice at the Lipton, Goran Ivanisevic eventually bolted and ran away like a wild horse. Quiet, modest Pete Sampras had the gift of keeping his brilliance between the lines.

Martina Navratilova came to the end of her Wimbledon line in 1994. She had actually crossed her shadow line in the late 1980s when Steffi Graf and then Monica Seles began to beat her regularly, but Navratilova was still the best technician available on grass. When all the other women seeds collapsed around her, as if sensing she wanted to go out like the queen of tennis she really was, the smart money was on Navratilova to win against Conchita Martinez. And she might have. But the day was hot again, the grass almost as firm and bouncy as it had been that day in 1992 when Agassi won the final against Ivanisevic, and Martinez, a Spanish clay courter, played beyond expectations. Navratilova was en route to winning the match when Martinez fell, and in the delay for injury time, Navratilova talked to the crowd, lost concentration, got stiff, and never recovered her early advantage or momentum. Martina Navratilova was proof that if one stayed with one thing long enough with all one's heart, public recognition might finally turn into something like tenderness, even in a defeat. Navratilova seemed to have finally learned that a loss does not mean you are a bad person. In losing gracefully, she captured what Chris Evert had always had: the public's affection. But really, Martina Navratilova and Bill Tilden should have had the last dance together at the Wimbledon ball. They understood better than anybody how a body can, for most of a career, mistakenly equate winning with love.

I had a great run in Battersea Park the morning I flew home from England. The sun was burning off the mist over the river, and the two small London bridges, the Prince Albert and the Putney, stood glowing in the hazy light as barges full of coal made their way down Chiswick way, the flowing river lovely and still as English in its sense of time as the fast brown water of the Thames.

PRIDE—ANIA BLESZYNSKI
AND LYNNE ROLLEY

Lynne Rolley, the U.S.T.A. Director of Coaching for Women, had once been ranked in the top ten in the United States, and she was Lindsay Davenport's primary coach. Chestnut brown hair cut short, small face tanned to a dark glaze, Lynne Rolley had a slow smile that had seen so many tennis balls, children, and parents coming at her through the years from different directions that she had almost seen it all in junior tennis. She was the unsung czar of American girls' junior tennis. All roads went through Rolley.

Nick Saviano, the U.S.T.A. Director of Coaching for Men, had told me at the Orange Bowl that picking the U.S. National Team was one of the most difficult, stressful parts of his job. Lynne Rolley was very knowledgeable about tennis and young players, and I was determined to ask her why Ania Bleszynski was not put on the American team when she had been the only American girl to make it to the quarter-finals of the Orange Bowl.

"Do you think Meilen Tu or Amanda Basica will turn pro this year?" I asked.

"No way," said Lynne Rolley. "I would certainly discourage it. None of these young girls on the team are ready to turn pro this year. They're still learning the game. When Amanda or Stephanie Nickitas lose a match, I try to talk in terms of our goals rather than tear them down about the specific match they lost." Lynne Rolley paused and reflected. "The thing a lot of young players have to realize is that you can play as well as you are capable of playing and still lose."

Lynne Rolley had said an awful lot in her last sentence. Learning how to absorb a loss and keep moving forward was the key to junior tennis.

"Lynne," I said, "I want to ask you about Ania Bleszynski, the girl who beat Nicole London at the Orange Bowl."

Lynne smiled without much enthusiasm.

"Ania's beaten Janet Lee twice and Nicole London and Amanda Basica. She's very tall and she's not going to be the next Maria Bueno, but I can't understand why she was not picked for the American team."

"Well," said Rolley as if she'd received faxes and phone calls from a dozen aggrieved parents before I threw in my two cents worth. "Ania got some assistance from us last year at the Canadian Open. The problem with Ania is consistency. She's improving on that. But she'll still win a few matches and then just fall apart."

"Fall apart?" I said. "Every loss is a breakdown of one sort or another. But Ania has been playing awfully well. She got to the final of her first pro event in Texas."

"Ania is definitely playing better," Lynne Rolley conceded. "But the real problem with Ania is that she is too old."

I shook my head. How could seventeen be too old? I recalled what Dennis Van Der Meer had said to me at the start of the Orange Bowl, slamming the wooden table softly: "What is still attractive for me as a coach is the parent who comes to me and says, 'I've got this sixteen-year-old girl who says she can't make it as a pro because she's over the hill at sixteen.' I tell that girl she is *not* over the hill. In fact, there are instances when she may be. But I insist to all parents and girls who want to turn professional one day that sixteen or eighteen years old is *not* too late for a girl to bloom into an outstanding women's professional player. This baby boom in women's tennis is a sham!"

Now I caught myself echoing Van Der Meer. "Too old!" I said. "Lynne, she's just seventeen. She skipped her last year in the sixteens, and that was probably a mistake because the toughest matches to win are the ones you're supposed to win in your age division. But too old? I don't buy it."

Lynne Rolley smiled and said, "Listen. Ania is a very bright girl. She'll probably go to Stanford next year. If she does well, we may try to get her into a few satellite pro tournaments next summer."

I shrugged. I disagreed, but then I thought Dawn Buth should also have been on the U.S. team. But it is always much easier to second-guess the coach than to be the coach. There was one more phenom about whom I wanted to pick Lynne Rolley's brain. "Let me ask you about Venus Williams. I heard she beat Amanda Basica pretty easily."

"We had both Williams girls to our USTA camp about a month ago. They played with twelve of our players. They are good prospects"—she paused to choose her words carefully—"very good prospects. They played practice sets against all the girls, and they competed as well as anyone. But they were not head and shoulders above the field."

"The father's decision not to let them play junior tournaments seemed bizarre but interesting to me," I confessed. "I know Mr. Williams was afraid they might burn out, but you do learn so much from the experience of winning and losing."

"I agree," said Lynne Rolley. "We've seen situations where it's worked to have them start early, the way Monica Seles did, and situations where it hasn't worked." She paused. "In the end, until they are really old enough to make decisions for themselves, junior tennis all comes back to the family."

I agreed, and Ania Bleszynski had a great family. Being part of the U.S. National Team—what we used to call the Junior Davis Cup Team or Junior Wightman Cup Team—did not necessarily mean a girl or boy would become a top pro player. But in terms of getting experience, the U.S. National Team was highly desirable.

When I returned from Wimbledon, a letter from Ania Bleszynski had arrived. Her essay on Jane Austen was enclosed, and here is an excerpt:

Pride

In her book, *Pride and Prejudice*, Jane Austen presents two characters, Elizabeth Bennet and Mr. Collins, who both demonstrate pride, but in vastly different ways. Through Elizabeth, Austen shows that pride is not always a negative quality. In fact, as it exists in her character, it comes to be one of Elizabeth's commendable qualities. In direct contrast to Elizabeth, Mr. Collins possesses pride that is depicted comically and satirically by the author. In this way, Austen is satirizing society as a whole, with the exception of Elizabeth, who is proudly unimpressed by money and reputation.

Mr. Collins takes extreme pride in his acquaintance with Lady Catherine, as she is a wealthy woman. Hardly ever does he complete one of his long and eloquent speeches without having several times referred to her and her high social status. The ladyship's wealth is the only reason for Collins's pride in knowing her, for there is nothing else attractive in her. Her ladyship is an annoying, self-involved, condescending and boring old woman. However, Mr. Collins is blinded to all her defects by her wealth. Jane Austen is showing how people are so materially oriented that they do not see anything else in a person but money. Collins is amusing, but when we realize that he is simply a slightly exaggerated symbol of society, the humor almost becomes grotesque.

Elizabeth reacts very differently to Lady Catherine: "Elizabeth found herself quite equal to the scene." By this very proud statement, Elizabeth does not mean that she is equal in wealth to Lady Catherine. She is simply implying that she is not intimidated by such a display of grandeur. In her two significant conversations with Lady Catherine, Elizabeth displays no deference. Rather, she responds to her ladyship confidently, proudly, at times even haughtily. The lady herself notices Elizabeth's assertiveness when she says to her, "you give your opinion very decidedly for so young a person."

In rejecting the marriage proposals of Mr. Collins and Mr. Darcy, Elizabeth again displays her self confidence and pride. If she were to accept either of them, she would have wealth and the distinction of being married. Marriage proposals do not come too often, and, by declining them, Elizabeth is risking never being married. Despite these prospects, both proposals are flatly and decidedly refused. Elizabeth does not wish to compromise her own values and pride. The others, like Collins, are unable to deal with people like Lady Catherine in a fitting way, like Elizabeth does. They are too busy making love to money.

Elizabeth's pride is based on her discernment and observations of other people. She is dissatisfied with the great majority of her society, just as Jane Austen wants us to be. But whereas Collins proudly kisses the feet of those with money, Elizabeth looks past wealth to personality and character. In doing so, she finds few people worthy of her love. She comments to Jane, "There are few people whom I really love, and still fewer of whom I think well." Proud but commendable.

Ania Bleszynski's English teacher, Mr. Commons, had written a few comments in the margin. After her ending he wrote, "Pithy and forceful." After her line about "making love to money," he wrote, "well put." Bleszynski had once told me that the problem with school was that sometimes you had to write what the teachers wanted to hear, but her paper on Jane Austen seemed to have come genuinely from her good mind and seventeen-year-old heart.

In her handwritten letter to me, Bleszynski wrote:

Hallo! How are you? I enclose my *Pride and Prejudice* essay. Sorry it took so long to send—I hope you haven't forgotten the book. I'll try to read *Mansfield Park*, but I haven't had much time.

I just returned from St. Louis where I played the Olympic Festival. I won the singles and the mixed doubles and got a bronze in doubles. I enjoyed it a lot. I played sectionals in California right before that, and I won those, too. So far, so good. My sights are now set on the Girls 18's Nationals in San Jose. They will be tough, but I hope to do well and get a wild card into the U.S. Open.

Next week I am playing an "opportunity tournament." If I win it, I will get a wild card into the qualifying tournament of the Toshiba Classic in San Diego (formerly the Mazda Classic). Besides that I am not playing in any other pro tournaments.

They occur at the same time as my nationals or right before. Lynne Rolley was not very helpful with getting into any others. As it is though, I have a list of junior tournaments set up for August.

So, how was Wimbledon? Did you see Scott Humphries win the juniors[?]—now that is quite impressive. Also, Amanda Basica lost to Anna Kournikova—that was unexpected. What else did you encounter in England? I would like to go there some day.

Stay in touch and hopefully I will see you at the U.S. Open or the Junior Open, whichever I get into.

I smiled. Ania Bleszynski was very bright and playing great tennis. But as to "pride," the only way Ania would get into the main women's draw of the U.S. Open would be to win the USTA National Championships in the girls' eighteens.

LAVER AND ROSEWALL
TOGETHER

Rod Laver and Ken Rosewall had aged well. They go together like Campari and soda. Laver could nearly peel the cover off a yellow tennis ball with his amazing topspin strokes off either side. Rosewall had a compressed, effervescent interior that bubbled competitively well into his forties. Ken Rosewall's immaculate footwork and timing had made him the Fred Astaire of tennis. He made the difficult look easy. Yet Rosewall liked to respond rather than initiate: he had answers for every predicament. Rod Laver was the relentless attacker, up to the net in a flash and all over it like a swarm of bees. Laver went for his shots long before the synthetic rackets made a certain amount of "shooting" the thing to do. Laver took many risks but as he improved, the risks became certainties.

Laver was the only player to win two grand slams—and he could have won at least two more if Open tennis had arrived between 1962 and 1969. Laver combined movement and power in a way not seen before or since. McEnroe for a while had Laver's lightness and movement, but he never approached the great Australian's level of physical fitness. Without tiebreakers to shorten the match, John McEnroe, despite a superior serve and a more dramatic touch than Laver, would not have beaten Rod Laver.

Rosewall won the French Open in 1968, beating Laver in the final, and in 1953, beating Vic Seixas in the final. The son of a grocer, raised in Australia of the 1930s and 1940s, Rosewall had the zeal of a missionary. He gave his opponents the uncomfortable feeling that he would play forever if it meant winning. At twenty, Rosewall beat Lew Hoad in the final at Forest Hills in four sets, ending Hoad's bid for the grand slam. Rosewall beat Laver in the famous 1972 World Championship Tennis final in Dallas, 7–5 in the fifth-set tiebreaker, one of the greatest matches of all time. Laver and Rosewall could barely walk up to the net to shake hands after it. The score for one of the sets Rosewall won in Dallas against Laver was 6–0. Very few players could say they had taken a 6–0 set against Rod Laver.

Success came later to Laver than to Rosewall. A small but scrappy, freckled and red-headed kid raised in the Australian outback in the 1940s, Laver had an enormous drive fueled in part by the fact that, unlike Rosewall, he had not been an instant star. Laver worked not to discover his brilliance but to control it. Laver, the champion, was born through his incredible hard work and the need to overcome a profound natural shyness. He and Rosewall were perfect gentlemen— assuming the operative definition of *gentleman* is still one who does not show emotion while destroying his opponent in body and mind. In 1990, Wimbledon and U.S. Open Champion Arthur Ashe told me with a smile that before he finally beat the thirty-seven-year-old Laver toward the end of the Rocket's career, Laver held the edge in their head-to-head matches, 27–0. No one else stumped Ashe that way, and of course, Ashe did beat Jimmy Connors in the final of Wimbledon in 1975.

"Sure, I respected McEnroe's talent and Connors's intensity," said Pete Sampras, "but the Aussies, those guys were *great!*" The three Australians Sampras singled out were Laver, Rosewall, and Lew Hoad, who died in 1994 of a blood disease even more rare than his blond Sir Lancelot-like talent. Hoad was brave. Rod Laver was irrepressible.

In New Haven, just before the U.S. Open I sat down in a corner of the pressroom opposite my two tennis heroes, Ken Rosewall and Rod Laver. Talking together was a bit like talking to the baseball stars of my boyhood era, Mickey Mantle and Roger Maris. The Australians had remained fast friends despite their long rivalry. When Laver came on the scene, Rosewall, who was four years older, was just beginning to take over from Pancho Gonzalez and rule the pro tour. Later, Laver took over from Rosewall. But they had always recognized each other as two perfectionists lucky enough to be playing at roughly the same time. Sampras and Agassi have the potential for something similar. Borg and McEnroe could not endure as a rivalry, because Borg was already all played out emotionally and was unwilling to ever play second fiddle. The McEnroe–Connors and Seixas–Trabert American rivalries were intense but never quite as friendly. In Australia one's on-field accomplishments, like business accomplishments, are a smaller part of the measure taken of you as a person. That, too, contributed to the ease with which Rosewall and Laver could associate with each other. They were people before they were players.

I was nervous talking to them both at once, and I tried to break the ice. "The first thing I want to ask you about is playing tennis over the age of fifty," I said. "And you both qualify."

"Yeah." Rosewall, fifty-nine, said wryly in his unwatered-down Australian accent. "Yeah."

"Thanks," said Laver, fifty-five. "Thanks for rubbing it in."

Laver and Rosewall looked at each other and chucked. Rosewall's shy smile made him look a bit like Stan Laurel. They laughed that easy, unassuming Australian laugh, without pretension or signals of false pride, the absence of which had left their shoulders so free to just hit the ball and play the game. They had put *me* at ease. Yet despite their gentle exteriors, I sensed they were still fighters and great competitors. Rosewall, like Connors after him, looked as if he would play you for a nickel and gladly take it. Something in Laver and Rosewall's personalities—in part their height—had given them the champion's insatiable will to win. They made taller men struggle. Now, over fifty, they had had to make peace with that inner demon every competitor eventually must temper or reharness.

"Where did it go?" I asked, nodding at Laver's once Popeyelike forearm.

"Gone," said Laver, smiling gently. "It disappeared with the wooden rackets. I stopped playing for a couple of years in the early 1980s, and it hasn't come back since we started using these lighter rackets. It was the wood rackets that made my forearm like that."

The wood, and Laver's incredible on-court training, including Harry Hopman's famous two-on-one drills where Laver was the "one" and Roy Emerson and Neale Fraser might have been the "two." But longevity in tennis went beyond physical fitness. It is determined by the quality of your excess talent. A sports generation generally lasts five to seven years. The great players are so much more than the rest of their own generation that they play well into the next generation and even into a third or fourth generation. Like Laver, Connors and Navratilova had longevity. Tilden had it, too. McEnroe, more meteoric, did not. Hoad proved great but was a shorter candle still.

"For me," said Rod Laver, "it was over after my good run in 1974–75 when I cut back my schedule. I became somewhat of a part-time player. That was pretty much it. I didn't have a full circuit, and I wanted to break away. My wife was reminding me of it, too. She said to me, 'Why don't you put your toys away?' " Laver laughed his shy, modest laugh and looked down, his freckled, aquiline nose and eye still sharp. "I think that when you aren't just thinking tennis-tennis-tennis, you find that the concentration level, the intensity, tends to erode."

"Is that what happened to McEnroe a few years ago?"

"Yeah," said Laver. "A little bit. In the case of McEnroe, he went to trying to change his rhythm on his serve. Various parts of his game he figured he could switch. But, you know, he tried to change a winning game."

"You can't do that," I said.

"No," said Laver. "That's something you can't do. You've got to die with it when you've gone that far. You've just got to keep plugging away and believe that it's going to come back and you will find the right level, but McEnroe went in different directions. He thought that was the way to go with the new rackets and new technology."

"What about Stefan Edberg?" I asked.

"Stefan may have lost a quarter step," replied Rosewall mildly. He had lost a half step himself when, at age thirty-nine, he played Jimmy Connors in the 1974 Wimbledon final and got hammered. But people tend to forget that before he met Connors, Rosewall beat Stan Smith in the semifinals in five long sets. He had nothing left for Connors in the final. I have thought about the Rosewall–Connors matchup a lot and concluded that I would have bet on Rosewall at age twenty-five, when he was beating Gonzalez, over Connors at age twenty-five, and

Rosewall at age thirty-nine over Connors at age thirty-nine. I gave it
to Rosewall on fitness. But at thirty-nine he had not been able to give
away eighteen years to the twenty-one-year-old Connors.

My thoughts turned back to Stefan Edberg, who had never been as
heavy in the legs as Boris Becker. The naturally thinner bodies usually
survive longer.

"Edberg's only twenty-eight, but it seems as if he's lost that little
edge. What do you think he might have . . . ?"

Laver's voice was deep, quiet, and thoughtful. "I think Stefan's lost
it in his serve. His serve used to be his biggest weapon."

"Is it too much of a kick serve now?"

"It's very inconsistent now," said Laver. "It's something that he's got
to work on again. Rather than kick it in, I think he's got to almost
slice it. A flat slice. And keep it moving. Everyone's ready to jump all
over the kicker."

"It's always seemed to be Edberg curled around the ball on his
serve. But it's not as lively now."

"Yes," said Rosewall. "It seems like Edberg's missing an awful lot of
first serves. And when you're missing the first serve, there's lots more
pressure on your second serve, which means that you're not really
going to direct it that well because you're just trying to get the second
ball into the court."

"They know which side it's going to kick up to nine times out of
ten?"

"Right. So put a few shooters in there," said Laver, and the redhead
grinned, as if he had a plan, a scheme, and he was about to ace someone right up the middle or off the forehand side of the court. "Maybe
Stefan can't do that with his action. He does kind of scoop around it.
He used to be able to beat everyone with it anyway, but he may have
had a shade more power on the shot a couple of years ago when he
was in the real rhythm of his serving. I think he may have lost a little
of that rhythm, and the result is that his ball tends to lose a little tra-
jectory and a little speed through the air."

"Are the guys who hit the really hard serves like the pitcher who
loses a little pop on the fastball?"

"Yes," said Laver, "that's exactly what it is. It's just that little bit of speed. You don't see it, but you can sense it when you're receiving. You can actually feel the difference on your strings. Before, you'd get one to return and say, 'What was that!' Ooh. It weighed a ton on your racket. But when it starts to go for the server, it doesn't have the same weight. Serving is just knowing that you have timed the ball spot on. You're just rocking and clicking, and your rhythm is there. All of sudden you're putting a bit more weight into it, and that is when the ball is really flying. I shouldn't count Stefan Edberg out. But if he's forcing his serve, it means he's not timing the shot as beautifully as he always has."

I could see Edberg now, tossing the ball so high on his toss, turning to reach for it, snapping up and over on it on his headlong charge to the net. Laver had four serves he used: a curve ball into the body on the forehand side, a fast ball away, a nasty kicker up around the throat, and his trade-mark a slice that hooked low and ran away from a right-hander in the backhand court.

"What is it like for both of you to play now, as opposed to thirty years ago? Do you still get the enjoyment out of it?"

"We still get the enjoyment out of it," said Laver, nodding at Rosewall, "But we get a lot more aches and pains that go with competing over fifty, or over forty for that matter."

"You were both relatively free of injury during your careers. Do you think that was because you were both so fit for so long?"

Rosewall smiled. "We had *silent* injuries."

"Silent injuries?"

"Yeah," said Rosewall easily. "That's just the way things were."

Laver interjected. "I think the biggest thing is that if you declare an injury, you might as well pack it in. Your opponent is going to make you pay for it."

"You do hear a lot more about injuries today in tennis. Does that say something about the nonstop schedule or about the players themselves?"

"I don't think the players are any less keen," said Laver. "It's just that it's not too hard to tell who is on the training table and who is not. We never wanted to give up the edge."

"There's more strain on the players now," said Rosewall cheerfully.

His spirit made him seem fifteen or twenty years younger than he really was. "From the money side or for computer points, the players today can't afford to take time off the way we did."

"Some of our contemporaries had rotator cuff injuries or dislocated knees," said Laver. "I remember Ken made me sprain my ankle once. I was going one way and tried to jerk back around for the ball. They had to help me off the court, and I was done for the day."

Rosewall, the little iron man, smiled modestly at the memory of wrong-footing Laver into a sprained ankle.

"Have you gotten past the point of being upset that your games aren't what they used to be? Was there a period in your lives when you said, 'Damn it. It's not going the way it used to go, and it's not going to go like that again?'"

"Well, for me," said Rod Laver, who seemed closer to his actual age, "it happened at around thirty-seven to forty. I would play good matches—as good as I thought I could play—but the next day I'd come out as flat as a pancake. I was irritated because there was nothing I could do to get my game back up to where it should be."

"I think it depends on the style of the player," said Rosewall. "Rod's style was more aggressive. I was more of a counterpuncher. I may have felt comfortable just a bit longer. But keep things in perspective. In our midforties, we weren't competitive anymore with the very top players."

I laughed. No one but Laver and Rosewall would have expected to be competitive with tour players when they were in their forties.

"I did win the tour event in Hong Kong a couple of years later, [in 1977, at age forty-three over Tom Gorman]" said Rosewall without boasting. "I beat some of the young tour players. But generally, like Rod said, after forty—or fifty—you have to just keep things in perspective and know that you are not going to be able to do what you could do before."

They had dealt with the loss, or partial loss, of what they once had been. It was never easy. The same problem will face Edberg and Becker, then Sampras, Courier, and Agassi, and how they deal with that transition will determine the rest of their lives. When you play tennis at that level, you will always be Rod Laver or Ken Rosewall. But they seemed to have come out of the tunnel of their tennis egos and were both happy with their lives now. It had taken Laver longer to come out of his shell, and he struggled for a time with retirement. But Laver was too much a champion for self-pity. He was a new man, no longer bitter that the big prize money had not arrived when he was at his peak and not nearly as shy as when he was playing. Laver was that rare superplayer: a giver as well as a taker.

"What is the difference," I asked, "between a top young junior player and someone who goes beyond that to become a top-fifty world-class player?"

"You've got to have a few of the key ingredients in one body," said Laver. "You've got to have the talent. You've got to be able to come through and win matches. You need the desire, the competitive juices, and that real killer instinct that gets you to the top. But for the most part, I would think it's natural talent." Rod Laver paused. "You may not have it. You may just have the ingredient to be a fighter. But without the talent of wonderful strokes"—Laver's voice trailed off. Then he added, "Those who have won the big events have all the ingredients."

"It's a perfect balance," I said softly.

"Well," said Laver, "solid ground strokes, a good serve, volleying capabilities. It changes slightly in different eras."

"Recently," said Rosewall, "there have been some exceptional young players. Pete Sampras, Chang, Agassi—to name three. Sampras is as good as we've seen. But generally, at least on the men's side, it seems that it will take a young player a long time before he can force his way up to anywhere near the top of the pro circuit today. With women it's different."

"The man is going to be a lot stronger than the junior champion," said Laver, "whereas the women's champion, a Seles or a Graf, is not going to be that much physically stronger than a sixteen-year-old girls' champion."

I nodded, but thought there were some exceptions. Margaret Smith and Martina Navratilova had been so much stronger than *all* the other women. They had truly been the two giants of women's tennis, though Chris Evert, Maria Bueno, Billie Jean King, and Evonne Goolagong had all been fabulous players and equally as entertaining.

"Are there any things you can do to try to compensate for age?"

Rosewall laughed. "Well, I'd say it's mostly a matter of keep playing. It's when you stop that it [really] starts to go."

"The thing that can keep you rolling through those rough times," said Laver, "is to keep thinking about your game, not your self. Think what your game is doing. You've certainly got to stretch more. And you should play up on the baseline, not four yards behind the baseline, because you'll get to a lot more balls that way. There are lots of little tricks. Don't let the ball back you up. Start moving for the ball before it lands. Why hit a ball down the line in reply to a ball down the line, when your opponent will answer with a cross-court and make you run a long way? Stop the angles from coming at you. And when someone comes to net on you, why try to pass him every time when you know that the overhead is the stroke that goes first on everybody as you get older. Over fifty, *lob*! It'll open up the passing lanes. When you hit fifty, it's not enough just to show up at the courts and say, 'Here I am!' You have to show up and say, 'Here I am. Now what can I do to win?' " Rod Laver grinned and added, "Of course, if you don't care about the outcome don't worry—you won't win."

"Were there any players you emulated?"

"I guess I patterned my game after Lew Hoad," said Laver. "Lew's game was very aggressive. I was not very consistent so I could not revert to a game like Ken's. That just was not my style. And to a lesser extent I watched Frank Sedgman, the way he was aggressive on the court."

"We all had our idols," said Rosewall. "When I was a boy, and I'm just a little older than Rod, my idol was John Bromwich, who was well-known in the United States more for his doubles play with Adrian Quist. But I grew up in the same area of Sydney where John Bromwich was living. He was an ambidextrous player." Rosewall smiled. "Americans always talk of having invented the two-handed shot, but Australians had players there for years who were doing it. And then of course, Frank Sedgman, like Rod said. Bromwich and Sedgman were ideal champions, both on and off the court."

I had not heard that old phrase, "champion both on and off the court," in a long time. It was epitomized by Rosewall and Laver.

"What about Tilden? Did you see him play?"

"Aw, only in old films!" said Rosewall a bit defensively.

"What did you each think of Pancho Gonzalez?"

Laver spoke first. "He was one of the roughest competitors I ever played against. He was pretty mean," Laver said lightly. "He wanted to win. It was you against him, and he said, 'I'm not losing.'" Laver chuckled and nodded. "So . . ."

"You were a bit that way yourselves, weren't you!"

Laver laughed. Rosewall took mild offense.

"Aw, well," said Rosewall, "we showed it differently, though."

Rosewall's proper, hard working Australian personality and immaculately constructed tactics were the very opposite of the outspoken, rebellious Gonzalez, who would race to net on a surge of power, or a whim.

Rod Laver's more impetuous, red-headed fire had been closer to Gonzalez's smoldering dark flames. Laver had broken through as a pro, and against Gonzalez, after Rosewall did. In 1970, the year after Laver won his second grand slam, a forty-two-year-old Gonzalez beat Laver 7–5, 3–6, 2–6, 6–3, 6–2 in front of 14,761 fans at Madison Square Garden. It was the opening round-robin match, and Laver went on to win the event, but a five-set win at age forty-two over Rod Laver was incredible. "If you were trying to break Gonzalez down," I asked Laver, "would you try to go over to his slice backhand?"

"I only came in at the very end of Pancho's career," said Laver. "It was more Lew and Ken who played the regular matches against him. Pancho had a tremendous forehand when he was in his prime. But when I played him, inconsistency had made his forehand his weaker shot. He used to hit winners off it, but if you pressured his forehand a bit it might fold. I don't think you could do that to him when he was young."

"Pancho Segura would be the one to ask," said Rosewall, ever the diplomat. "When Lew [Hoad] and I first heard of Gonzalez—I turned professional just before Lew—we had never seen Gonzalez play much. I had the one tour with him [won by Gonzalez 50–26]. I had always heard of Pancho's weaker ground shots, but under certain conditions they didn't seem to be too weak." Rosewall nodded and smiled wrily. "Gonzalez had that way of manipulating the game, of being able to control the match. And he also had the ability, like when he played Lew, to improve his game. As the series with Lew went on, Pancho's overall game got better, especially his ground strokes and his back-hand. Pancho had to learn to hit his backhand to different areas. For a while, his favorite backhand shot was the backhand down the line, and you always saw it there. But to play Lew, who was so quick and good at the net, Pancho had to do something different." Rosewall's square chin broke into a big smile and laugh. "We might get some arguments on that from Pancho, if you decide to use that [in your book]."

Laver grinned, too. Pancho Gonzalez was apparently not easy to change.

If Gonzalez heard a phone ringing in a gas station at night along a lonely stretch of highway, he was sure the call was for him—and then say he was not going to answer it. Gonzalez was the fiercest tennis competitor I had ever spoken to, with the possible exception of Laver, but Gonzalez's competitiveness had been less happy than the Austra-lian version, because he was an *isolato*, too proud to ask for friendship and not quite sure the entire world was not as tricky as Jack Kramer had been with him. Gonzalez was the founder of the line of fiery ten-nis souls that included McEnroe and Boris Becker.

"This business of being a champion," I said. "I think of Gonzalez. Is there a quality of being a bit of a loner to being a champion?"

"Aw," said Ken Rosewall, the practical man on and off the court. "I don't know about that."

"I think you find yourself being pushed into that position," said Laver defensively. "Everyone else is gunning for you. Being a loner to some extent is advantageous. Of course, I never had the early pres-sure Ken did. I was winning the U.S. junior championships at seven-teen. Ken was winning the French Men's at age seventeen. He was far more advanced than I was. It's a long and very different path we took. I was not a very good player at a young age." Laver nodded at Rosewall for emphasis. "I was just a hacker. Ken and Lew. They were the players. They were in Davis Cup competition at that age, and you would never have seen me anywhere near that level. I couldn't win the junior championships in my own country at seventeen."

"That might speak to the type of game you had," I said.

"Yes," said Laver matter-of-factly. "It was inconsistent."

"In those days," said Rosewall, "the players did like to have their moments by themselves. Today players in the public eye will have an entourage about them. We stayed alone more, but as Australians we always had friends available to us."

"Borg was the one who really struck me as being totally alone," I said. "And I think it eventually got to him."

"When you were talking champions," said Laver, "I thought we were just talking about our own era. But I'd say that Lendl was a loner. I'd say that McEnroe was a loner. Connors less. Borg certainly isolated himself. I don't think he felt he needed any of that other camaraderie, other than on the courts and around the courts. Borg was a happy camper but a very quiet individual. And I think that it helps a lot to be brought out of your shell."

"Borg did not get out of his shell until his career was over," I observed.

"I think he was afraid to be out," said Laver. "Because he was the number one guy, and he didn't want to show . . ."

"Anything," I said.

"And he didn't," said Laver. "He showed nothing. He let his racket do the talking and was brilliant, but he didn't seem socially comfortable with people away from a tennis court. He'd be in his room certainly. He didn't think he could go down to Picadilly or King's Road without being mobbed by people. And I think he was dead wrong in that. They weren't going to mob him. But perhaps you're right [in saying] Borg became such a recluse that he couldn't pull out of it."

"He was so fast," I said admiringly. "Were you surprised Borg didn't do better when he tried to make a comeback?"

Laver and Rosewall looked at each other and laughed, and Laver said, "No. We all knew that unless he changed his racket he wasn't going to go anywhere because the game changed just when Borg left. You can't compete against these rackets. Every seventeen- or eighteen-year-old kid is going to hit the ball by me today. You don't have to be as accurate with this racket. You just have to have a lot of topspin and a lot of speed and give it a good whack."

"What do you think tennis teaches you about yourself?"

"Discipline to a big extent," said Laver. "It's part of your love for the sport. You're certainly ticked off when you lose a match, but you're a more rounded person by being able to compete on a court. It's not going to help you unless you become social to some extent off the court. I had to come out of my shell. And doing tennis clinics helped me a lot because suddenly I *had* to be able to talk to people. Bjorn will learn, but I did a few clinics with him and he would come out, play with them for half an hour, and say to me, 'You take them now' and leave me with them for another two hours." Laver and Rosewall had a chuckle at Borg's expense.

"Everyone has a different personality," said Ken Rosewall. "I was from a quiet family, a quiet background, so it took me a long time to come out of myself. When I turned professional and played the series of matches against Gonzalez, Kramer was running pro tennis and it really opened my eyes. I realized that we were just a small bunch of guys and a lot of associations didn't want us around at all. That really woke me up."

"How would you rate Kramer against Gonzalez?" I asked, sneaking one more question in before my time was up.

"Well," said Rosewall, smiling softly, "Jack was definitely the better player at that time. But, basically, Kramer had a very short career. And Jack was really very particular about where he played and when he played." Rosewall nodded. "Jack was a grass-court player and an indoor player. All his years as an amateur, Jack never played in the French. When he first played Pancho on the boards covered with canvas, he was better, but Pancho improved a lot. Of course, Jack was seven or eight years older so they never did meet at the same stage of their careers."

Laver nodded, indicating he had to go play doubles.

"I appreciate this very much," I said, standing to shake hands with Laver and Rosewall.

Ilie Nastase's big 560 Mercedes came barreling into the parking lot, and he was in such a rush that he bounced the right front wheel up onto the curb and seemed to stop the car by slamming the gearshift into park. He hit the ground laughing and running, his tennis clothes pouring out of his open bag. Nastase was heavier than I remembered him, as if carrying five pounds on his stomach for every backhand drop-volley winner he hit in his five-set victory over Arthur Ashe in the 1972 U.S. Open.

I decided to stick around for the doubles. Rosewall was not playing, but Laver was. Nastase and his partner, Roy Emerson, were paired against Laver and Vitas Gerulaitas. Last on the court as the other three champions warmed up, Nastase dropped his tennis bag on the hard court in the New Haven stadium, looked up at the crowd, and bowed. He then turned to the chair umpire, an attractive young woman whose name had been announced over the PA system, and he said in a stage whisper heard all the way to Fairfield, "Hello, Beverly baby."

I had never seen Emerson blush, but he did now, shaking his head and looking around at Nastase as if he had drawn Jack Nicholson for a partner.

I was seated in the front row behind the court, the better to hear as well as see it all. Directly below me, Laver and Gerulaitas were warming up with Gerulaitas on the backhand side and Laver on the forehand. It did not feel right to me. Laver had probably had the greatest return of serve in doubles from the backhand side of anyone until, or perhaps including, McEnroe. Gerulaitas, sixteen years younger than Laver, had been a very fine doubles player himself and knew he could beat Laver in singles now. He had won the Italian and Australian Opens. Still, there was the matter of respect.

"Which court do you want to play, Rocket?" Gerulaitas finally asked, his shorts very short, his smile very bright, his blond hair thinning.

Laver ignored Gerulaitas's question three times and continued calmly warming up his topspin forehand from the deuce court until Gerulaitas finally answered his own question a bit sheepishly with the good-natured modesty that, at bottom, Gerulaitas had had in his heart ever since he met Bjorn Borg.

"Well," Gerulaitas said to Laver, "I'm shitty off both sides. I guess I'll take the forehand court."

Asking Rod Laver if he wanted to play the backhand court was kind of like asking Muhammad Ali if he knew how to jab. By the end of the match, Gerulaitas was glad he had traded places. They were to play a nine-game pro set.

Laver ultimately stole the show, but Nastase's abilities almost always surfaced first. On the very first point, Nastase, his touch still magical, cut right in front of his partner, Emerson, and carved a beautiful forehand cross-court drop volley angled away from Laver, who scampered after the ball without reaching it. Laver tapped his netted ball gently to the ball boy. Nastase turned and bowed elegantly to the crowd.

I was close to the action, but photographer Ellen Wallop, whose subjects have included top athletes such as baseball player Mo Vaughn and boxing champion Mike Tyson, was even closer down in the photographers' pit. After the match Wallop told me, "Laver's eyes were incredible. They were so concentrated. As soon as a point began, his eyes got a *look* in them, and that look did not let up until the point was over."

Laver was still keen to win, and he was not a great fan of Nastase's. To add to the tension, Laver was fifty-five and Nastase was forty-seven, and the latter still had the uncanny ability to make everyone else on court—even his partner Emerson—look perfunctory while he looked invincible himself.

"Emmo!" shouted Nastase as he blasted a weak Gerulaitas lob down Gerulaitas's alley for a winner. "We got some *penetration* with that one!" He nodded toward Laver, who was waiting to return his serve. "I got some more penetration for this one."

Nastase ripped a huge serve right down the middle into Laver's backhand and rushed the net. Laver, fooled and stretched fully, chipped a backhand return that came over so low that Nastase could not have gotten the ball up off the hard court with a spatula. Nastase scowled in disbelief. Laver looked down at the court itself and walked mildly away from his great shot with the characteristic slight limp to the left of a man with a left arm and heart disproportionately large.

Gerulaitas served to Emerson, hooking an ace wide to the big Australian's forehand side. At deuce, Emerson sent a towering lob up into the blue, sunny sky, and as Laver positioned his body to deal with the sun and the overhead, Nastase faked an enormous sneeze that went off loudly just as Laver made contact with the sharply falling ball. He did not let it bounce. With a short backswing, Laver, not trying to do too much with the ball, firmly punched the overhead into the open slot, or weakness, between Emerson and Nastase.

The difference in the levels of excellence of the four champions on court gradually emerged. Nastase and Gerulaitas, though playing against each other, both started out hotter than the older players, the Australians, but by the end of the beautifully contested match the difference between Laver and Emerson, on the one hand, and Nastase and Gerulaitas, on the other, was clearly the difference between great champions and great talents: in a word, consistency.

Emerson was so strong and stayed on the ball so long. Laver's hand, though faster, was also firmer longer at the point of contact. Nastase and Gerulaitas were more immediately dramatic but ultimately lighter through the ball. Nastase seemed to sense none of it, or he chose to ignore it. Gerulaitas seemed to feel it, and it made him quiet and humble playing next to Laver.

In a moment of telling beauty, Emerson crunched a high forehand volley angled away from Laver. Moving his left arm across his body, fully stretched to his right, Laver angled a low backhand volley right back across the top of the net to the left, one bounce in the alley, ball last seen rolling in the direction of Bridgeport. The crowd roared with joy. Emerson's jaw fell open and locked into a smile. Nastase waved his racket as if to say, "Lucky," and Vitas Gerulaitas, as if apologizing for ever doubting which side Laver should play on, got down on the court on his hands and knees and bowed to Laver as if the shy, freckled redhead was Allah. Laver pretended not to see it. He was already on to the next point.

Laver was a walking tennis clinic. Returning serve, he was intent on leaning on the ball at all costs. Even if he was largely fooled by the direction of the big serve of Emerson and the thumper Nastase also had, Laver's body weight somehow managed to move forward rather than backward at the moment of contact. It gave great weight to Laver's replies. Laver's own serve was always better placed than struck, and he was not nearly as effective as McEnroe in that one aspect of their games. But Laver's serves were very deep, sliced, kicked, or flattened, and he moved them from corner to corner like a surveyor. Still, at his age, even for Laver serve-and-volley tennis was not easy. Laver's face turned a blotchy red and white from the effort, and Emerson broke Laver's serve once with a high backhand overhead hit, without a jump, from behind Emerson's head, his back to the net. Laver nodded, and Emerson came up with a quip that finally brought a big smile from Laver, something Nastase hadn't been able to do.

Finally Emerson, serving to the deuce-court, took another short Gerulaitas forehand and approached on it hard and deep to Laver's forehand. The response was automatic. Laver, hanging back, hit a cross-court forehand with so much topspin and forward-moving side-spin that the ball spit over the net like a snake, landed right in front of Emerson, and hissed at his feet, nearly tripping him, for the presumption of an approach shot into Laver's big forehand. Emerson simply laughed and nodded. Laver was the best.

Laver had not hit that ball out of desperation or a fit of ego. Great shots at all levels arrive when they have been earned, not merely wanted.

The match was almost over. Nastase, who possessed every shot in the book, was suddenly without answers to Laver. Everything Laver hit now turned to gold. At 8–7 in the pro set, Gerulaitas had to serve for the match. No one had any idea what would befall Vitas when, a year later, he would be asphyxiated by a poorly installed heating system at the Long Island guest house of his friend, real estate developer Marty Raines. Vitas was so alive just then, in New Haven. He was always a golden boy in an age that had almost forgotten the value of such spark in and of itself.

Vitas Gerulaitas kicked in a weak second serve and bravely followed it up to the net, trusting his reflexes. A beautiful full-court exchange ensued. Rod Laver lobbed over Roy Emerson. Ilie Nastase raced back behind the fully outstretched Emerson to run down the lob, and Nastase hit a gorgeous full-swing backhand that shot the ball over the net at about ninety miles an hour. Laver, nearly straddling the middle of the net, blasted a forehand volley right at Emerson's chest, and like swatting a fly, Emerson flicked his racket behind his back on the backhand side and reblasted Laver's acrobatic volley with an iron wrist. Laver, completely stunned by Emerson's brilliant fluke of a return, flinched down into his feet and hit a backhand cross-court drop-volley winner that barely bounced.

The crowd roared once more. The match, like the crowd, was Laver's.

RECKONINGS

In August, all tennis roads lead to New York City. What used to be the more elegant but closed grass-court world of club sandwiches and iced tea at Forest Hills gave way to an open tennis park and trade show atmosphere with binoculars for the fans in the upper decks, hot dogs long enough to be arrested, Velveeta cheese with spicy chips, and the same undeniable love a salaried ticket holder has for watching an upset. There is a raucous boldness to the place that seems just right. The Coliseum that Dennis Van Der Meer envisioned for me down at the Orange Bowl already exists, and in this place of battle in Flushing Meadows, New York, only the strongest, fastest children need apply for work.

Ania Bleszynski, Jonathan Stark, and Stefan Edberg—tennis youth, middle age, and old age—and all under twenty-nine years old, were ready. They had high hopes, but with 128 players in both the men's and women's draws and another 64 junior girls and junior boys—to say nothing of the grinning veterans—high hopes and large racket bags were not in short supply.

Boris Becker was one of the players with high hopes. I had seen him under the courts after a late-night match at the Lipton in Florida when he and his new coach, Nick Bollettieri, were just starting out their partnership. Bollettieri—an ex-Marine, a onetime Miami University law school student turned tennis guru, and, above all, a survivor and salesman—had left Andre Agassi, whose many wins over

Boris Becker he had helped choreograph. Bollettieri was image conscious for his camps. He felt Andre Agassi had lost his innocence
singing "People" in a London hotel room with Barbra Streisand the
summer after his 1992 Wimbledon victory. Earlier in Agassi's career,
everyone was telling Agassi he ought to play Wimbledon for the experience. But for Bollettieri, image was still almost everything in sports
promotion, and he thought his superstar's spring-fall affair might set
a bad example for his young campers. Agassi may have lost his tennis
virginity in the eyes of his coach, but his sponsors were still delighted
to have him: Andre had the magic.

Brad Gilbert, whose own playing career had come back to earth
gently since I spoke to him at the Lipton, had made a gradual transition into the role of Andre Agassi's coach. Gilbert had a dramatic
positive effect on Agassi. It was a question of attitude and approach
to competition: Agassi had the tremendous talent; Gilbert had the
ability to make the most of much less. He taught Agassi to respect the
gift he had. Gilbert was a pro's pro, and gradually, as if by osmosis,
Agassi began to play to win, Gilbert's ultimate message. It was interesting to watch the change in Agassi from talent to winner. Gilbert,
a master at winning the unremarkable points on which so many
matches turn, taught Agassi to be more stingy with errors.

In losing the French Open finals in 1990 and 1991, Agassi had
been full of talent but lacking in the knowledge of how to take hold
of the points that really win, the undramatic points, the points that
bring no applause. Jim Courier, winner of the French in 1991 and
1992, reached that understanding, and overall personal maturity,
before Agassi did. Now with Brad Gilbert's rough face in his corner as
a constant reminder to fight for everything, Agassi played tougher and
with more heart. Add *that* to his talent, and Agassi suddenly became
very hard for anyone to beat. I was curious as to how Gilbert had
helped Agassi.

I found, though, that the sympathetic older player I had spoken to
while he was discussing his aches and pains and munching french
fries down at the Lipton had become a lot tougher to talk to now that
he was Andre Agassi's coach. Suddenly, he was show-biz.

"I can't talk," Gilbert said up in the changing room of the U.S.
Open two hours before an Agassi match. "I'm watching Oakland and

the Yankees. Try me after Andre's match. But I can only give you two or three minutes."

I came back at ten-thirty that night. The coach-player aspect of the game interested me, particularly in light of what Gilbert had been able to do with Agassi's game. It corresponded, of course, with a period of greater maturity on Agassi's part—he was no longer a teenage whiz kid but a professional reaching the heights of his ability.

"What have you been able to do with Andre that he was not able to do before he got together with you?" I asked Gilbert in the locker room as Fred Stolle combed his hair after a veterans' doubles victory.

"Well, Andre is really focussed on tennis now. I've told him a few things. I told him you can't get anything back from the past. You can only go after the future. I told him that you don't get three points every time you hit a screaming winner—you just get one point. I told him to be more solid, be more repetitious. I told him to quit experimenting out there."

"Andre seems to have a combination now of being relaxed about tennis and being super focussed on tennis. Isn't that combination unusual in top players?"

"Yeah, it is," said Gilbert. "Definitely. That's the way I tried to be about it, too. But Andre's got an incredible combination. It's not easy to be that relaxed and that concentrated."

"If big matches are won by a handful of points, what have you done to get him to play the big points better?"

Gilbert nodded. "You know what it is? It's knowing that every point is important. Then, on really big points, what you want to have happen is what you want to have happen. What you don't want to have happen is what you don't want to happen. Maybe if the other guy's best play is getting in and getting you under pressure, then don't let that happen. If you think about it ahead of time, think of what you want and don't want to have happen on the point that is coming up, you can prevent it from happening more often than you realize. You have to be aware out there of what you want and don't want to do. That's really the mental side of the game."

.   ∎   ∎

Boris Becker had not been faring as well as Andre Agassi. Becker's game had become a stubborn parody of its former glory. Becker was now almost insistently physical on court but heavier than he was at age seventeen. He was still a formidable opponent, yet at age twenty-six, Becker had many miles on his speedometer and, like Borg before him, had shown signs that child champions, even those as nice as Boris Becker, eventually insist on discovering their childhoods. I was sorry because I liked Becker so much. By nature, he was a gentle but insistent rebel. Becker and Germany had divorced each other as many times as Elizabeth Taylor and Richard Burton. Marrying an attractive, intelligent black woman was a statement and a declaration of personal freedom. But Boris Becker did not make things easy for himself. In life, as in tennis, Becker now seemed to want to try winning from one set down.

Becker lost in the first round to Richey Reneberg, whom I had facilely referred to in *Tough Draw* as "a journeyman who painted by numbers compared to the artistry of John McEnroe." Reneberg had become a very solid top-thirty player. Becker's high hopes fell in five seesaw sets in which Becker, born to red clay in Leimen, not to the hard courts for which his game was better suited, tried at times to play the tenacious, lighter Reneberg from the baseline. Few horses are as stubborn or as well liked as Boris Becker. When he finally lost the first-round match in a fifth-set tiebreaker, John McEnroe, whose consistently high-level commentary I watched on tape almost every day when I got home from the stadium, observed at one point, "A player of Boris's caliber should be able to make the adjustment against a player like Reneberg even if Boris did think the hard court at the U.S. Open was playing slower this year."

It sounded reasonable, even though McEnroe himself had been unable to "make the adjustment" against the very same Richey Reneberg at Wimbledon in 1990. Was it false modesty or memory loss when McEnroe added, "Richey's win over Becker is by far the biggest win of his career."

With Becker down in the first round, it was clear that the U.S. Open, the most glorious grind in the world of professional tennis, was not going to be easy for anyone.

The side courts, where I liked to hang out during the first six days of the tournament, were full of great action as usual. I felt after a while as if the big stadium court was for the tennis tourists, the corporate expense-account crowd who took the best seats, the balding television executives with Agassi shag cuts down their backs. I was a bit tired of the pecking order of box seats whose prices and available locations seemed to get steeper and steeper each year. The elitism eventually complained about at Forest Hills has been replaced by a corporate domination, another kind of American royalty. But hanging out around the outer courts, which really are spaced like a public tennis park, reminded me of wandering around Forest Hills as a boy. Then and now, it was great fun to roam.

In the peak of the August sun, two giant young men were crushing serves and volleys at each other. Nicklas Kulti, the six-foot-three-inch, handsome Swede who was a former junior champion at Wimbledon, was making a stand in the second round against Switzerland's freckled giant, Marc Rosset, who at six foot seven was one of the tallest players on the pro tour. It was like a game of "Dare." Rosset and Kulti hit their serves so hard they seemed to dare each other to return them. The crowd that morning was small, with people drifting in and out of the corner seats every odd game; a hard-core group of fans remained glued to their seats as their knees burned bright pink. I stayed for well over an hour. The score rose on serve to 4–all in the first set; then young Kulti, jammed up near the head by a mishit return by Rosset, had his serve broken. The two fought for another hour and a half, through four sets of beautiful summer hell, until finally big Rosset, sprouting a goatee, walked up to the net like a pro basketball player who has had the final dunk.

I was already deeply happy and hopping with the action when Jonathan Stark took the court with his first-round opponent, Jonas Bjorkman. Stark and his coach, Larry Stefanki, had arrived in New York together. Like plays tried out in New Haven, like operas tested in Rome instead of Milan, the ATP tour stopped in Washington, Montreal, Cincinnati, Indianapolis, and Long Island before pulling into New York. Most players agreed: New York was not the nicest place to play, but it was arguably the most important.

Stark had had a curious summer. Seeded first in doubles at Wimbledon after winning that event at the French Open, Stark and his doubles partner, Byron Black, did not win at Wimbledon. Nevertheless, they were seeded first on the big, white U.S. Open scoreboard where friends so often meet. I did not like the fact that Stark had played the first round of his doubles the day before he was to play the first round of his singles, because it can take several sets of singles play to make the adjustment back from doubles. But as it turned out, Stark's singles' opponent, Jonas Bjorkman, was a top doubles player, too, having lost the final of the French Open doubles to Stark.

Stark's singles' results had been up and down. Stark always played well in Indianapolis, in August. He had nearly beaten Pete Sampras in 1993. This time Stark reached the quarterfinals, beating old nemesis Alexander Volkov and Mats Wilander before losing in the quarterfinals to Olivier Delaitre, a match he might have won.

Jonathan Stark and Jonas Bjorkman of Sweden came out together for their first-round match without a word. Stark looked powerfully fit and wore a red headband around his forehead. Bjorkman's clothes were simpler—solid white except for green around the shoulders. Bjorkman was about five years behind tennis fashion, but his legs were thicker than Stark's and highly toned. Bjorkman's father was a postman back in Sweden who worked as a hockey referee on weekends, and young Bjorkman had skater's legs, a blond crew cut, and a way of looking up as if he wanted to take on the world in a friendly fight. Like his countryman and hero Stefan Edberg, Bjorkman played with Wilson frames.

There were maybe a hundred people in the stands on either side of Court 17. I sat and watched Stark in warm-up, as I had in Philadelphia and at Wimbledon. The psychological battle started even before the first serve was hit. Neither player hit a ball into the net or long for the first five minutes of the warm-up. Stark's service motion was still perfectly timed and powerful. Jonathan Stark hit a serve the way cowboys in the old westerns rode a horse.

I saw Larry Stefanki come in and I started to gesture confidently to him, but I saw him avert his gaze as if he did not want to talk. Just before play started, Stark left the court, accompanied by a linesman, and did not return for several minutes. Stark's nerves must have been kicking in. There was a portable bathroom nearby.

In Philadelphia and at Wimbledon I had tried to hide myself from

Stark's view, but this time I wanted to let him know I was there, and he saw me as he returned. I nodded and raised a hand in encouragement.

On the first point of the match, Stark hit an ace with a second serve, and it looked like a long day for Bjorkman. Stark's ball just exploded over Bjorkman's shoulder and ripped into the back fence, scattering the linespeople and ball boys. But there was an odd, stubborn pattern to Stark's serving, and Bjorkman knew how to read it. Stark *always* came in on a first or second serve, and he did not mix up the location of his serves as well as, say, Edberg did and Laver had. Stark had played Edberg in July in Washington, D.C., but lost to him 6–4, 6–4, and the lack of varied movement on his serve was part of the reason for that loss. It was almost as if Stark, about to hit his big serve, was telling his opponents, "Get ready. I am coming in on every single serve I hit. The first one will be up the middle to your backhand, and, if I need a second ball, I'll serve it to your backhand, too, and be running in behind it." The best big servers like Ivanisevic, Sampras, and Becker moved the ball around better. Stark dared opponents to return it. And Jonas Bjorkman did! The Swede hit a backhand return that flew up the middle so fast it nearly knocked the racket out of Stark's hand.

Stark held his serve, but Bjorkman bounced through his own service game in no time, winning it with a tomahawk overhead on a lob so high everyone thought Bjorkman was going to bounce it. At the last possible second, Bjorkman leaped up late and spiked the ball down onto the court, bouncing it over the fence, an incredible shot for its weird timing.

"I think this Swedish guy must ski a lot," said a New Yorker. "Will ya look at his thighs?"

I laughed. I like a New York battle.

Stark missed a serve off the top of the net, and the ball caromed seven feet back. Stark, like Becker, had the ability to pull himself out of the hole over and over again. Serving to Bjorkman into the ad-out court, Stark missed a first serve then hit an unreturnable second serve to win the game. A bit of bounce went out of Bjorkman's step. He fell behind in his service game, but he aced Stark back to tie the match at 2–all.

The linespeople were ducking at both sides of the court. They could hardly see the serves to call them in or out. Stark double-faulted to go down 0–15. Then Bjorkman dug a ball out of the back corner and floated the return back high, slow, and tricky. Stark almost let it float long, but instead, he crushed it away for a winning high backhand volley. Stark cut off another ball with a jackknife overhead. Both players were all pumped up. But at 30–all, Stark served his second double fault of the game. "God damn it! Come on!" Stark shouted at himself. Then came his third double fault of the game, and he flipped his racket in disgust at the changeover chair. Stark's inner electricity was bad. His hair was standing up in the middle of his head.

Bjorkman, up 3–2, was tough to dominate head-on, and that was the way Stark came at everybody. Jonas Bjorkman was a head-on kind of guy himself, and if there was going to be a collision here, it looked to me as if the Swede was riding in the Volvo. Bjorkman held his serve. Stark got down break point, saved it with a great low backhand volley, but then was passed twice in succession by Bjorkman returns of first serves in which the Swede actually stepped up on Stark's huge first serve, drilling incredible two-handed backhands past Stark before the ball could gather speed off the serve and shoot through to the backstop. Suddenly Stark was getting steamrolled. Bjorkman broke Stark again and held his own serve to take the first set 6–2.

I looked at Larry Stefanki's worried face across the court.

I was seated next to a balding British gentleman. He had a pair of opera glasses that appeared to be focused on Jonathan Stark in the changeover chair. He turned to me, sensing I knew something about Stark. "What *is* the matter?" he asked. "I thought Stark was top-twenty material. He is playing dreadfully now."

I smiled. I could not disagree, and I had no answer for Stark's present misery. I looked again across at Larry Stefanki, but Stefanki had adopted a coach's emotionless mask. In some situations, a coach can do no more, and this seemed to me to be one of them. Stark was on his own, and he was almost out of the running. Bjorkman was so fast he seemed able to soften the corners around each of his volleys. Stark remained so square and American into the ball, and he was late getting down to volley.

"I'm a lawyer from Wales," my newfound British companion advised me, "but this is my favorite tournament in the world. I come here every year on my vacation to watch. I prefer to watch the relative unknowns battle, don't you?"

I nodded silently, deep into it again. Suddenly Stark began to play well, as he had done late at Wimbledon against Karsten Braasch. The weather conditions were far better here. Stark broke Bjorkman's serve and went up 2–0 as the American crowd cheered him. Stark was not a quitter. But up 40–30 on serve, he double-faulted again. Then, finally, he played a great point. It seems strange to say, but it was actually the first really well contested point Stark had played the whole match. He and Bjorkman had a thirty-stroke rally from the baseline, full of the side-to-side movement in which Bjorkman excelled. But the best way to beat a player is to beat him convincingly at his own game, and then, once his heart is gone, to impose your own. The ground strokes from both players were sharp with willpower and bad intentions, and Stark won the battle. Then he hit an ace up the middle to go up 3–0 in the third set. This was the Stark that had nearly beaten Volkov.

"Come on, Jonathan!" roared a young American woman's voice.

On Bjorkman's first service point, Stark ran from one alley to the other and tossed a topspin lob winner over the acrobatic Bjorkman's head.

"He really is wonderful. His talent is absolutely boundless!" said the Welshman.

"Yeah," I said. "But he's got to win the damn thing."

Bjorkman held. Up 3–1 and only one service break to the good, Stark served a double fault long into the forehand alley. Again down 30–40, Stark served like a prince and went up 4–1. He was finally playing so hard he had managed to push himself beyond the edge of comfort to the near unconscious land where all the winning takes place. Between points I saw him reach over his shorts and push down as if, with nerves, his testes had shot up low into his stomach. I nodded in recognition. He had to fight like a coon cat now; he had to rip the other guy's toenails off, and then he might be right back in it.

Bjorkman just barely held his serve. Up 4–2, Stark fell behind 30–40 again but came in on his serve, brave but predictable. Stark's first volley was solid, but Bjorkman, fast as Michael Chang on an above-average night, raced across the court, tossed up a topspin lob like a cowboy drawing fast from his holster, and the ball slipped over Stark's head, spitting incredible juice until it bounced and danced away.

Bjorkman, having broken back to go down 3–4, was suddenly all bounce and congeniality again, and the Swede held serve at love. 4-all. Stark looked across the net and held his serve to go up 5–4. At 30–all on Jonas Bjorkman's serve, Stark ran across the court and ripped a winning two-handed backhand. Set point for Stark. Bjorkman hesitated, looked at Stark, then served hard and came in behind it, punching the high backhand volley and the set point away. Stark, upset, sailed two returns of serve long, just as he had the year before against Volkov, allowing Jonas Bjorkman to break back and win the third set 7–5, after trailing 4–1.

I looked a third time for Larry Stefanki, but this time he was gone. Stark had lost in straight sets. I was sorry. He was better than that, but Bjorkman was on the rise himself. Stark's ranking had fallen to forty-seven before the Open. After rising to number thirty-six in the world in Philadelphia in February, in August he was still higher than he had been the year before when I watched him against Volkov. But Stark had not reached his goal of cracking the top twenty.

"If I were Stark," said the Welsh lawyer pulling out his camera for one last picture, "I'd be worried. I bet he is."

A head taller than most of the crowd, Stark walked back to the changing room alone. A trio of nine-year-old girls asked him for his autograph. He signed and continued slowly on. He was numb. A solidly built woman in her sixties came up to Stark, got his autograph, and put a firm hand on his shoulder. This was not the way it was meant to be. It was the way it was. Stark continued on, looking straight ahead, his back disappearing toward the changing rooms. I saw him and he saw me, but I stayed away. He did not want to talk. What was there for him to say that his game had not already just said?

Tennis is not a string of victories, unless you're Pete Sampras or Steffi Graf. Tour life is not a highlight film shown in ten-second clips at night on the TV news. There is nothing quite like winning, but the tour for all but a handful of players is about dealing with losing and trying to make sure it happens less frequently. Still, Jonathan Stark had a better record than most players on the ATP Tour. Through August, his won-lost record was 57 percent, a winning percentage but not a champion's. Perhaps Stark's resilience was in his sheer ability to go on, as real pros do, to the next event. He seemed to still have that crucial professional ingredient—conceit, in the best sense of the word—that keeps the ego alive when it has just taken a pounding. Stark had the ability to regard victories and losses not as character judgments but as just one more step on the schedule.

Still, some losses are harder to ignore than others. The chink in his armor had been exposed. I had not given up on Stark. Stark did so many things so well. Truly. But he had not quite learned how to play at the next level up, at the level of his dreams.

As Stark showered and packed his wet clothes and rackets, coach Larry Stefanki said not a word to anyone but felt like saying plenty.

The junior tournament at the U.S. Open does not start until the second week of the grand slam event, when there are enough open courts to play it on. There is a certain nice, humbling sensation to its taking place on Courts 23, 24, 25, and 26, which are virtually impossible to find. In her first-round match, Ania Bleszynski was scheduled to play against the Hungarian Petra Mandula on Court 23, and I could not find the court. It was like looking for a different world. I walked around the back courts for about fifteen minutes like a driver who doesn't want to ask for directions. Finally, behind the shadow of the big stadium, at the rear of the "International Food Village," beside the road where the TV networks park their trailers, I found the four courts reserved for the juniors.

Anna Kournikova, whose mother had so gently and methodically braided her smooth blond hair in the wooden bleachers at the Orange Bowl, was making very short work of a girl six years her elder. The little Russian seemed to pout slightly between points as if she, a prima ballerina, was wondering why she had been scheduled on a court out in Siberia when, really, she was the new principal dancer with the

Bolshoi Ballet. When Kournikova won the match, she slapped the ball behind her with a disgust only a twelve-year-old would think appropriate after beating an eighteen-year-old hollow. Her mentor, Nick Bollettieri, was standing over by the low chain fence, where he had arrived in time for the last three points of the match. The little girl trotted across the courts, threw her arms around his neck, kissed Bollettieri once on each cheek, and listened as he gave her his blessing and admonishments in nearly the same short breath. Her braided pigtail bouncing happily again behind her back, Kournikova trotted back and completely ignored her older victim, wincing slightly as if there was an unpleasant, fishlike smell of defeat lingering in the air. Kournikova walked off the court like a champion and accepted a hug from her little blond bombshell of a mother, who was wearing Ray-Ban aviator sunglasses, black Nike tights, and a loose white T-shirt with a belt that sat low on her hips. Mother and daughter beamed and went off talking in animated Russian.

I walked back to the changing rooms to see if Ania Bleszynski was there and to talk to some of the other girls about her. Most of the girls I had spoken to down at the Orange Bowl were also competing here. Meilen Tu was the only girl to get a wild card into the women's open event. Tu, who had lost in the first round of the Orange Bowl only nine months before, had won the U.S. Nationals in the girl's eighteens, beating Bleszynski in the semifinals.

Meilen Tu had a young champion's aura about her. It reminded me of the way Jimmy Connors had been at the same age: beyond confident into cocky. When I was sixteen and saw Connors as a thirteen-year-old for the first time, I wanted to strangle the little pip. Anything *that* self-assured had to be good, and he was. I was all the more curious to hear how Meilen Tu and Ania Bleszynski played because the two California girls from different backgrounds had an affection for each other like that between Joan Crawford and Bette Davis in the film *What Ever Happened to Baby Jane?*

"I really didn't have much trouble with Ania," Meilen Tu confided to me with a merry smile. "I have been taking the ball so much earlier since I spoke to you at the Orange Bowl. I am trying to be really aggressive?" Tu had developed the modified valley-girl habit of inflecting her declarative statements into questions. She continued without prompting, "I'm hitting everything very hard now, and Ania just didn't react well enough?"

In a prior round, Ania Bleszynski had beaten Stephanie Nickitas, the talented U.S. National Team member who had smiled at courtside when Bleszynski went down to the little Brazilian at the Orange Bowl. Ania Bleszynski was now the third- or fourth-best junior player in the United States. Meilen Tu, who had quit school for "home study," was floating up to the next level more quickly. After overcoming Bleszynski in the semis, Tu beat Lilia Osterloh in the final. Tu was small and slender and so tough inside she looked as if she could crack an acorn with her smile. But the new American junior champion had not outshone Martina Hingis, the fourteen-year-old Czech star living in Switzerland who won three junior grand slams most recently at Wimbledon. Almost everyone was expecting Hingis to win again, but Meilen Tu had other ideas.

"At the Orange Bowl I was coming off an injury," Meilen Tu explained with great enthusiasm. "So afterwards I just worked on my all-court game, hitting the ball deeper, getting a different variety of spins on the ball, and attacking and coming to net a little bit more."

After the Open, Tu would surprise U.S. Coach Lynne Rolley by turning pro. Venus Williams, dying to play against the pros but unwilling to risk her future endorsements against other juniors, would also be allowed to turn pro at age fourteen by the new Women's Tennis Council rule, which took in three new young phenoms at the same time they set up a minimum age of sixteen for everyone who might come later. It was a step in the right direction, but it had a hitch in it. The women's professional game needed the young stars, because Navratilova was finished and the others were beginning to seem slightly stale and predictable. But even Tu, who was one of the few teenage girls who seemed ready mentally, had not yet met the real pro tour, which has an appetite all its own.

Meilen Tu, a year younger than Ania Bleszynski, had skipped school to focus on tennis. She had the right to do so, but I thought of other young girls and said to myself, "What is good for Tu is not necessarily good for you." Education makes more sense in 98 percent of the cases, and a parent who misjudges his or her child's talent is showing a dangerous type of false pride. Still, I admired Tu's spunk.

"Meilen," I asked, "did you play any pro tournaments before getting the wild card into the women's draw?" It was the wild card Bleszynski had hoped to get.

She grinned. "I played a twenty-five-thousand-dollar event in Coral Gables. I qualified, won a round, and lost second round to Audra Keller, the second seed." Tu paused with the drop-dead aplomb of a seasoned veteran. The giggly but incredibly focused little girl I had spoken to at the Orange Bowl nine months ago was gone. Meilen Tu could have lit up a cigar, and it would not have surprised me. She was interesting. "I think that loss to Audra Keller taught me a lot. I really learned what I had to do to get to the next level."

"What was the difference, Meilen, between the time you played Ania before and your match with Ania at the Nationals?"

"At Nationals, I was so much stronger physically. This time I just ripped balls by her." Tu turned her head away slightly and smiled her killer little smile, waiting for the next question.

Frank Brennan, the Stanford women's coach, had been there on the hill overlooking the hard courts at Ojai, California, to watch Bleszynski play Tu. "It was a typical big man–little man matchup," Brennan had told me. "The crowd is usually rooting for the shorter player. Meilen Tu was like a point guard in the NBA out there, running circles around Ania. Tu is a spindly little thing, very dedicated. She's just all over you. She calls balls on her side of the net. She calls balls on your side of the net. Tu's slapping her thigh and pumping her fist and saying, 'Yes!' every minute. She changes sides like she knows just where she's going. Right now, Ania is much more laid back. She's got a lot of power and talent. I think she should be able to overpower Tu. But I think there's something there when you are that tall and strong, the way Ania is. Everybody is motivated against you. Some girls look at Ania, and I can just see it in their eyes. They're saying to themselves, 'Oh, I would kill to be that tall and that beautiful. I'm going to beat the hell out of her today. That big goon, I just hate her.' "

Ania Bleszynski had been taking antibiotics for a bad summer cold. She did not use it as an excuse, but she wanted a chance to get back at Meilen Tu. At the U.S. Open, they met in doubles. Late in the week, Bleszynski would team with Amanda Basica, whose singles match I had watched at Wimbledon. Midway through the second set, Basica floated a service return and Tu, poaching, blasted Bleszynski with the volley and smiled. I thought the usually calm Ania was going to go ballistic. The two girls truly had it in for each other.

"What are the strengths and weaknesses of Ania's game, Meilen?"

"*Her* game?" Tu tittered nervously. "Her serve and being able to come in off it is her strength. Ania's weaknesses are her forehand, and she's too big, so she can't move very well on the baseline." Tu nodded, thought some more, and added apologetically, "Ania moves really well for a big person. I mean, compared to all other girls who are six foot one, her movement's *terrific*."

"Ania has to get to net to be effective?"

"Oh, I think so," said Meilen Tu, smiling again. "But she seems to have trouble getting up there. She's kind of a baseliner? If you leave the ball short, she can attack off it? But if you can return her serve, you're going to be OK?"

"What do you think about Ania's decision to go to college as opposed to going out fulltime on the tour as you have decided?"

"Oh, I don't think it hurts her. I think it's very wise for Ania to go to school," said Meilen Tu. "See, she is older. Also, Ania is very intelligent? She might want to do something else after tennis?"

I almost laughed. They were all so young, but Meilen Tu was sixteen going on ninety. "What was it like for you to play here in the first round of the main women's draw, Meilen?"

"I was excited, nervous, a little bit overwhelmed. Mainly overwhelmed." Tu spoke analytically, as if looking back on herself as on another person. "I didn't know if I could compete with the top pro girls. But I could. I had my chances in the match. The set I won was close, 7–6, 9–7 in the tiebreak. So I competed well. But I was so nervous in the first set when I was serving at 40–15 to go up 6–5. I started thinking, 'Oh my God, I can really start to go up in this match.' And that's when I lost my serve and the set. I wasn't used to her game. She kept pressing me. By the end of the match I realized that in the pros, every point I want to win, I have to earn."

Meilen Tu had just explained the difference between junior and professional tennis: every point you want to win, you have to earn. It was not unlike the work ethic of so many Chinese-Americans. Two days later, in her first-round junior match, Meilen Tu lost the first set 6–0. But she came back to win 0–6, 6–4, 6–4. Tu was a winner, but would she be strong enough physically at the pro level? The young girls and boys were all shooting for that next level, but as the U.S. coach, Lynne Rolley, had put it so aptly at the Orange Bowl, "Wanting it does not mean that you are going to get it."

Stephanie Nickitas, who at the U.S. Nationals had lost to Ania Bleszynski in the round of sixteen of the girls' eighteens and had won the Girls' junior doubles for the second year in a row with Cristina Moros, had a completely different perspective on how Ania Bleszynski was playing. Nickitas said in a friendly way of Bleszynski, who had not made the U.S. team, "I played pretty well, but Ania just played much better than me."

"She didn't let up?"

"No. Ania was unbelievable. She has a great serve, and it was really on. She's so tall. She was just serving and volleying on every first serve, and she was hitting some amazing drop volleys and stuff." This Ania Bleszynski sounded invincible, and Stephanie Nickitas was no slouch herself. "I mean, Ania and I play similar styles. I was trying to attack her, but Ania was just too solid."

"Was it hot out there in August?"

"Coming from Tampa in August, it almost felt cool for me in California," Nickitas said with a smile. "It was ninety or ninety-five degrees, I guess, but nice and dry."

"Meilen Tu was able to get into Ania pretty good in the semi? Did you see it?"

"No, but John Evert, Chrissie's brother who's with IMG, was out there with me," said Nickitas. "And John said how well Ania played against me. We both thought it was going to be a *much* closer match between Ania and Meilen."

"What do you think Ania's weakness is, if she has one?"

Nickitas paused. "Sometimes she gets a little discouraged."

Nickitas had the kind of touch in her hand that only the best players in the world have, a Rosie Casals kind of touch. I thought she was going to be a pro. She was still a kitten, but she was going to be a cat.

"You won the U.S. junior doubles with Cristina Moros?"

Nickitas nodded proudly. "Yeah. Now Cristina is going to go to college. She's already enrolled at Texas. I think I'm going to go to college, too."

I was pleased to hear it. "Do you think going to college is a good thing for young women who also might want to turn pro?"

"Well, it is for me," Nickitas said. "Some girls think they don't need college and can just go out and play pros. I don't know if I'll be there for all four years, but right now I know that I need it. College is the right thing for me to do." Stephanie Nickitas nodded for emphasis. Something about the pro world scared them. Most American juniors opted to ease into it, earning pro points while still in college, then eventually finding their abilities on the pro circuit. The problem was that there were two standards, one by which the young American women were judged, and another for the young Europeans, who were jumping into the water sooner and without a life preserver. Still, I agreed with Lynne Rolley that none of the young American women should turn pro, with the possible exception of Tu, who might be tough enough, and Venus Williams, who was naturally gifted beyond most of the girls her age. Stephanie Nickitas was not quite ready. The top American juniors played well enough to turn pro, but Stephanie Nickitas, for one, was bound to get hurt if she tried it right away.

"One day I want to play professionally," Nickitas said, brushing a lock of her thick brown hair off her eyes. "But for now I am looking at Berkeley, Stanford, Texas, Florida, and Arizona State." (Nickitas would eventually go to Florida.)

I went back to Court 23 with a charbroiled cheeseburger, medium-rare, and a Coke. I sat eating in the nearly empty stands where Ania Bleszynski and Petra Mandula were scheduled, thinking about Ania's future after her very good summer. She graduated from high school with honors, she won the California sectionals, won the Olympic Festival in St. Louis, and got to the semis of the U.S. Nationals. Robert Lansdorp had worked with her once a week on consistency and on trying to incorporate her size and power into an attacking game. Ania had a tendency to be modest as a person and to hang behind the baseline as a player. She had to let out a bit of the competitive arrogance I knew she had inside her. It was part of dominating. And yet, like most players, Ania Bleszynski had to be kinder with herself. After all, things were going her way. Kathy Bryan, the former tour player Kathy Blake, had coached Ania every other week, and Bryan, who had two sons of her own playing in the U.S. Open juniors, considered her big accomplishment as a coach getting Ania to ease up a little on herself and forget her world of physics Advanced Placement tests and world-class junior tennis long enough to go down to the California beach for a laugh and a swim without doing sets of wind sprints on the boardwalk.

In Canada, just the week before, Ania Bleszynski had her best win to date, beating the Dutch girl Kim de Weille, who was already ranked number two hundred in the world on the women's computer and soon was in the hundreds. I was dying to see her in action against Mandula.

Suddenly to my left, I saw Ania. She was wearing a bright lime green skirt and new white shirt, and her auburn hair was cut shorter than at the Orange Bowl and was held in place by a white Nike tennis visor she had tugged so low she seemed to want to hide her emotions under it. I had seen her triumph over Nicole London at the Orange Bowl and then lose to the Brazilian, D'Agostini, in a match that had left her in tears. Which Ania Bleszynski would show up today? She had confided in me all summer, and she was open again.

"Hi!" she said nervously, looking at the boys' match on court. "We start after this one."

The two tall boys were banging the ball a bit wildly, heading into their second set.

"How was Canada?" I asked.

"Great. I've got a family I always stay with up there, and I always play really well there. But it was really cold playing in the stadium at night. I beat Kim de Weille, the number one seed, in the third round, but then I lost to the other Dutch girl, Yvette Basting, in the quarters, and I should have beaten her. I won the hard one and lost the easier one."

I shrugged. In terms of pressure, the hard matches were sometimes easier to cope with. For many players it is easier to respond than to dominate. "Well, you're here now. How's it going?"

Ania blew air out through her mouth like Popeye. "They lost one of my bags the first day. I checked it in the players' trailer, but Vince Spadea and his mother insisted that it was his bag, and the woman in the bag trailer gave it to them without a ticket. So they took my tennis bag back with them to Florida after Vince lost. His mother called me last night to say they had it by mistake, and I guess the bag is on its way back to MacArthur Airport. Do you know where that is?"

I did, but I didn't want to upset her. It was halfway to Ronkonkoma out on Long Island.

Ania Bleszynski shook her head. "He didn't even look inside to be sure it was his. It had tennis dresses in it." She shrugged, watched a few more points, and smiled. "One good thing. I'm rooming with Nino Louarsabishvily. It's such a coincidence we are both reading the same book, *Anna Karenina*. But Nino is reading it in Russian. I wish I could, too."

It struck me that body types, not countries, really made people friends. I remembered having tried to spell the name of the tall Russian girl who had been seeded first at the Orange Bowl. Nino was about five foot ten. Ania was three inches taller. The two tallest girls in the juniors, a Russian and an American, were rooming together at the U.S. Open.

"Have you heard of the girl I play?" Ania asked me. "Her name is Petra Mandula. She's short, but they say she's very good."

"So are you," I said quickly. She smiled nervously in response to my gruff tone. I tried to change the subject. "How is your friend Nino playing? Did I hear she beat Jana Novotna a couple of weeks ago at Mahwah?"

"Yeah, she did," said Ania. "I asked Nino about Mandula." Ania raised her eyebrows warily. "She said Mandula can really play."

Gossip at tennis tournaments can be suicidal. Mandula was starting to sound like a cross between Chris Evert and Hana Mandlikova. "Psyche jobs" are a time-honored tennis tradition. As Muhammad Ali said before he fought Sonny Liston, "Everybody's got a mother, even Sonny." Connors and McEnroe used to talk about having "fun" playing at the Open, but everybody else sweated bullets.

I was about to tell Bleszynski she was a damn good player and to just knock off the nerves and believe in herself when, right in front of us, a tall, skinny, hairy-legged young guy named Gerargo Venegas from Mexico reached the end of his junior match with a talented young Swede named Magnus Norman and threw his racket down on the court in disgust. After shaking hands, the losing junior had a complete meltdown on court in the arms of his mother, his sister, and his girlfriend. Bleszynski excused herself, and I waited.

A few minutes later, the American linespeople arrived in their red shirts. The umpire carrying the nameplates of the two players appeared with Petra Mandula. Ania Bleszynski should have been there, if only to see how apprehensive her opponent was. Mandula shook out her legs, bounced up and down in place, and walked in nervous circles on her side of the net. She looked nearly sick with tension. The chair umpire used his walkie-talkie to call the women's locker room and say he was starting a five-minute countdown to a default of Bleszynski. Ania Bleszynski appeared two minutes later and hastily pulled out a spanking-new racket with bright green strings that matched her skirt.

The Hungarian Petra Mandula, wearing a black skirt and plain white shirt, tied her sleek black hair into a bouncy ponytail. Ania Bleszynski towered over her, and suddenly in her white tennis visor Ania looked more eastern European than American herself. The two girls gave each other a complete cold shoulder. Neither spoke at all as they met and spread out to opposite sides of the net. Mandula was so tense she hit the first three balls of the warm-up into the middle of the net. Bleszynski, a year older, began to take heart. She had long, strong, hard-court legs. Petra Mandula had short, clay-court legs, softer-looking but full of acceleration.

The first sign that little Mandula had any goods of her own came in a surprising way. Ania nailed a forehand drive in warm-up. Her ball struck another ball deep in the court, causing the bottom ball to ricochet to the fence and completely changing the direction of the ball she hit. Mandula, watching the two balls split like atoms, reacted from the forehand she was about to hit and took the ricocheting ball out of the air with a backhand volley. It all happened so fast, but that reflex volley seemed to send psychic messages back and forth across the net between the two girls. It was going to be not only a battle of a short girl and a tall girl but a battle between a Hungarian and a

Polish-American, a clay courter and a hard courter, a girl playing for her supper and a girl with a college degree as a potential option.

The other morning matches were finished. The two girls were out there alone on the hard green court in the one o'clock sun. Bleszynski's big serve came crashing down at Mandula, who netted it feebly. There was no question in my mind that Ania could overpower her opponent if she could get her first serve in consistently. She served and volleyed but dumped the volley into the bottom of the net. On the next point, Ania stayed back, perhaps feeling safer there, even though the baseline was Mandula's preferred, clay-court territory. Ania won the first baseline exchange, then followed another big first serve up to the net, ending the point with a great touch drop volley. Matches like this one swung back and forth on waves of confidence. The two girls did not talk as they changed sides. Petra Mandula slapped her thigh. Ania Bleszynski, waiting to return serve, strummed the green strings in her racket to hear the tension.

Mandula was a thinker. She went down 0–30 in her first service game, but she did not panic completely. Mandula's serve was an easy, clay-court serve, rarely hit as if Mandula expected it to do damage. Ania tried to climb all over it in Mandula's first service game. Seemingly weaponless, Mandula fought her way back to ad-in, and then she hit a drop shot. She wanted to see Ania run. The ball bounced up off the hard court and hung, and Ania starting late for it, slid a beautiful forehand winner cross-court. She huffed a bit and turned her back quickly as if insulted by Mandula's retrieving game, which included drop shots for tall girls on hard courts.

Petra Mandula smiled. She had lost the point but had discovered what Bleszynski did not like. Mandula had plenty more insults for Bleszynski to run for. At deuce, Mandula played another, even better drop shot, and Bleszynski could not quite get to this one. Drop shots are a strange hard-court tactic because the ball sits up, and I was not sure if Mandula was smart like a fox or just desperate enough to try them. She and Bleszynski traded five ad-deuce points. Suddenly Mandula double-faulted. Bleszynski finally had break point. The Hungarian had left the door wide-open.

With a disdain I always suspected she had, Bleszynski decided to attack Mandula's rocklike forehand. No sooner had Bleszynski left the ball short on her cross-court approach shot than she saw it whiz by her up the line for a winner. Mandula, down two break points in her first service game, held serve. The score was 1–all.

Now Ania Bleszynski had to serve into the sun. The glare poured directly into her eyes like liquid light. She threw the toss lower, but Mandula snuck in, chopping and driving her returns of serve into the corners, moving the larger Bleszynski brusquely from side to side, liquid light still in her eyes. Suddenly Bleszynski was down 2–1 instead of up 3–0.

The Californian started playing very well, but Mandula spread pressure across the court as if she were buttering toast. Ania Bleszynski responded well, with power. They both started playing great tennis, but it was Mandula who reached set point at 5–3, Bleszynski serving. When the young American's service toss was in the air, the two grown men in tennis shorts in the third row shouted out in unison, "Come Petra! Get her! Get her! Get her!"

Mandula's agent and coach were on the edge of their seats. They were behaving so badly, I felt like shouting back at them. I hadn't been as angry in a long time. Two grown men inserting themselves like that, midserve on ad-out, set point in a match between two girls, age seventeen and sixteen. They were desperate for a future dollar. I almost blew my cool. I wanted to balance the scale, to shout encouragement to Ania Bleszynski, but she lost that point and the first set so fast there was no chance to speak up. It was 6–3 Mandula.

"Get her! Get her!" again shouted the coach, a handsome man with a smooth black mustache. And the forty-year-old agent raised his fist as the young girls changed sides.

There was no one to shout encouragement in Ania Bleszynski's corner. I was not supposed to double as a parent or a cheerleader. For the first time I wondered if the decision of Marek and Elizabeth Bleszynski not to accompany their daughter on her tennis trips was as intelligent as I had initially thought it was. As mature as Ania Bleszynski was, the sound of that Hungarian coach calling out to his future meal ticket, Petra Mandula, stuck in my craw. The two strong male voices seemed to tilt the proceedings from a very competitive and interesting match between two girls of different sizes and temperaments into something far less appealing but more professional. I exhaled. The two girls had to suffer like pros before they could become pros. I suddenly heard the coach and agent laughing together, and it was then that I removed the press credential from around my neck and moved two rows in front of them, clapping for Ania Bleszynski as she went back to serve to start the second set. That shut them up.

The problem was that she was already upset. She felt as if she had caved in during the first set, and although she had been only one point away from breaking serve five times, she had not been able to do it a second time. Then a strange thing happened. The girl going to Stanford in the fall, the girl with the near 800 College Board scores, stopped thinking. Ania Bleszynski was running on pure emotion now. She served bigger, came in and crunched away a volley, making one wonder how the other girl could even be on the same court with her. But then Ania would stumble mentally on the very next point, choosing the wrong shot, the big cross-court forehand that sailed long, when she would have done better playing the same ball with three-quarter pace up the line to get back into the point. Suddenly Ania seemed to have no strategy, "no basis for the experiment," as her mother might have said. Bleszynski reminded me again of Christine Truman, the tall former British star I had met in the press lounge at Wimbledon. Mandula felt the other girl struggling, and she tried to let Bleszynski turn herself into a victim. Mandula suddenly seemed like the scholar of the tennis courts. She accepted as minor defeats three aces in a row by Ania Bleszynski and stared across the net blankly at Bleszynski as if nothing had actually happened. Mandula blew on her fingers as if she had dry ice inside her little Slavic soul.

In frustration, Ania flipped her racket end over end in the air and failed to catch the handle. Her racket rattled on the hard court. Mandula held serve to go up 5–2, and I kept thinking that the difference between the short Hungarian and the tall Polish-American was in part America itself. Ania Bleszynski was just that much softer.

As they changed sides again at 5–2, Mandula's coach and agent again yelled out for both players to hear, "Get it, Petra! Get it! Get it!"

I scowled and wanted to blast them back, but I just held a fist up for Bleszynski directly in front of them.

Like many top juniors, Ania Bleszynski was never better than when she was backed into a corner. Suddenly she started to play beautiful tennis. She finally got mad inside! I could see the anger blooming in her, and she seemed to need it. She served two aces and made an incredible get on another Mandula drop shot. Bleszynski was finally busting a gut, trying as if the match could still be had. She held her serve at love to trail 5–3. Petra Mandula looked nervously across the net, her mouth narrow and taut. Then without missing a beat, Mandula held her own serve at love and trotted to the net to shake hands with the taller girl, as the two men stood and cheered wildly.

I climbed over to them. "How old is your girl?" I asked them as if we were discussing one- and two-year-old horses preparing to become three-year-old Derby contenders.

"Just sixteen," said the handsome man with the mustache, smiling proudly.

"She's good," I said softly, and I meant it. Petra Mandula was a player. She could not help the adults hanging around her like horse-flies. Mandula had been just as nervous as Bleszynski, but Mandula had fought through her fears. She came not just from Hungary but from hunger. Ania Bleszynski, headed for Stanford with plenty of skills, played as if she came not from impoverished Poland but from middle-class America.

Ultimately, it made a big difference. You cannot perfect hunger or need as if they were backhands sliced or topped. It was no surprise to me that Sampras and Agassi were both sons of first-generation immigrants. With McEnroe, the desire to succeed had been more complicated. McEnroe, scrawny, freckled, not very good-looking as a child, created a myriad of imagined wrongs to overcome. He needed the fight. He imagined himself a deprived person, and in the intensity of his imagination, he was. It was the underlying irony of this supposedly once genteel sport that those who had always played tennis best in tournaments had played it the fiercest. From Tilden to Gonzales to McEnroe, not skipping Laver. Suzanne Lenglen to Helen Wills to Althea Gibson to Billie Jean King and Martina Navratilova. Everyone loves a loser who smiles and says the right thing. That is a learned art, like fox-trotting and salesmanship. The champions don't often smile when they lose. They learn to laugh and accept a loss, but inside where it counts they want to keep fighting again and again and again! I think of McEnroe, Connors, Riggs, and Gonzalez. They would beat a player till the wolves and the moon came out and would never get tired of doing it. Winning is a queer thing, addictive, appealing especially to the psychically needy. Why else must one keep proving one's own worth over and over again? Yet a champion must not weary of it. In Petra Mandula, I felt a basic need stronger than that in Ania Bleszynski. Bleszynski's need to prove herself made her a fierce competitor at times, but it seemed to me she was sometimes on the defensive and ultimately polite and well-mannered. Some champions show only a sugar-coated version of themselves, and many spectators love that candy. Some, like Rod Laver, Stefan Edberg, and Pete Sampras, are genuinely modest but unbending, though that is rare. Deprivation, unhappiness, even cruelty—not gentle love—are more often what bring results at the highest levels. A champion without something real or imagined to prove will not last as champion. Still, I wondered what the outcome would have been if Bleszynski had had the experience of competing at Junior Wimbledon the month before, as Mandula had.

The players' lounge was a wide-open expanse of green carpet where players ate badly, waited nervously, and draped their legs over the low-slung decorator-beige-and-brown couches inside the high-ceilinged, air-conditioned hall. After the Bleszynski match, I noticed Dick Savitt walk in. Although Savitt had won at Wimbledon in 1951, I think I was the only one that still turned to see the black-haired competitor's competitor. Savitt had put more splinters in the balls on the old Seventh Regiment Armory boards than even Barry McKay. Tall and square-shouldered, Savitt was walking now with an athlete's limp. He moved with an old sailor's roll, a hip probably about to go in for a plastic replacement. I smiled at the old competitor, so tough on grass or the fast wood indoor surfaces of the 1950s, and when I looked up, there was Ania Bleszynski. She was as tall as Dick Savitt, whom I used to think was a giant.

She had a hamburger on a paper plate, but chewing is not easy when you've had a cry. It had taken her an hour to shower and come down in a pair of clean jeans and a green Gap T-shirt, a kind of lanky James Taylor look, shy and disappointed with herself through the mouth.

"Hi," I said. "You weren't bad. She played a little better."

Ania Bleszynski nodded and straightened up as she recognized the mother of a California girl a couple of years younger than she was seated two tables over. She regained her composure.

Petra Mandula went on to beat the fourteenth seed, Anne Miller, before losing to Kim de Weille of Holland, whom Bleszynski had upset at the Canadian Open the week before. Bleszynski was feeling miserable about the loss, which I think is usually a lot better than feeling good about a loss because it means you still care. You can play so much tennis that eventually you lose all sensation of wins or losses and then it really is time to quit. But Ania Bleszynski was not faking her pain. She had gotten a very rough draw. Amanda Basica, whom she could beat, was seeded eleventh but lost to a girl Bleszynski could have beaten. But bad draws are part of the deal.

Ania bit into her overcooked burger and finally said of Petra Mandula, "She was too good. I couldn't do the things I wanted to do."

"Did you hear those two guys shouting in the stands?" I asked. "Was it distracting?"

Ania looked up, surprised. "No. I never heard anything."

I was stunned. "Good. You were inside the match. But sometimes it seemed as if you were on the outside of that match looking in."

"I know," said Ania, and she blew her lips out in discouragement like a horse. She shook her head. "I was so nervous."

I nodded. "I wanted to tell you how nervous *Mandula* was when she came out, but I didn't get the chance. Didn't you see how she hit the first three balls into the net."

Ania's eyes filled up again with tears. "I wanted to win just one first-round match at the U.S. Open." She was seventeen and would turn eighteen in October. It was her last chance in the juniors. "This is the third time I've lost here first round," said Ania Bleszynski.

Petra Mandula was a dangerous floater, a young woman with real pro potential because she played every point as if it was being pulled out of her soul. Ania Bleszynski liked to dominate play but had not yet mastered the technique of the dogfight. And yet, there was something in the Polish-American girl that could be a fighter: the girl left off the American team who had beaten Nicole London and Janet Lee at the Orange Bowl. Bleszynski's strength lay not in her good looks but in her current awkwardness, not in her successes but in the resentment the other girls felt toward her because she was tall, smart, and attractive. She was that strange combination of good looks and deep, self-critical shyness that after a loss would hang her own soul out to dry, punishing herself inwardly for what she had not done outwardly. In her deep disappointment with herself, I saw hope. Self-satisfaction in an athlete is fatal. Ania Bleszynski was not self-satisfied. She was emotionally spent, and the words poured out of her. She was feeling like an outsider.

"They can get so cliquey on the U.S. team," she said. "When you see them at tournaments, most of them don't talk to you. Especially Meilen Tu. She never talks to you except to ask how you did when she knows you just lost. Then she smiles when you tell her."

"So don't fall into her trap," I said. "Tell her it was just a good match, that the other girl played very well but that you're going to get her next time. Don't get down on yourself like a big bear, Ania. If they beat you on the court, don't let them beat you up off the court, too. Give Meilen hell next time. Did you ever consider that some of those girls may be shy and in awe of you because you are going to a college like Stanford? Tennis isn't everything, and I bet some of them know it, too."

Bleszynski had sounded pouty but accurate. The rivalries these young women had with each other were intense. After Bleszynski and Basica lost in three sets in doubles to Meilen Tu and Marissa Catlin, Ania called her mother and flew home that night on the red-eye to California. I sensed that she could still make a good pro if she learned to turn her self-disgust, which was still a kind of arrogance, into respect for her opponent. Ania was never rude on court, but she often ignored her opponent. I did not realize myself until it was almost too late that when you keep criticizing yourself for not playing better, you are missing the central fact that once in a while there *is* someone worthy on the other side of the net.

Ania Bleszynski nodded, somehow relieved and surprised.

"So what did you do when Vince Spadea and his mother walked off with your bag by mistake?"

"I tried to just forget it. I had to play anyway. Last night I just stayed in the hotel and talked with Nino."

Ania looked at me strangely. She was still upset about her loss in singles to Petra Mandula and the loss in doubles to her nemesis, Meilen Tu. It was easier for me to smile and take it in stride. Losing hurts. But Ania Bleszynski was already one of the top twenty-five junior girl players in the world. Very few American girls could say that.

There were three junior girls I felt sure would make it as pros: Anna Kournikova, Venus Williams, and Martina Hingis. Their personalities were already distinct, and there was a fine line between the amusing arrogance of young Anna Kournikova and the quiet self-confidence of Martina Hingis. Venus Williams was still in tissue paper, waiting to be unwrapped by her sponsors.

The best male players did not always reveal themselves in the juniors, but unfortunately for their educations, this was less true among the girls. Meilen Tu's game continued to improve, but my dark horse from among the crop of American juniors was Dawn Buth. Like Ania Bleszynski, Buth did not get taken to Wimbledon. I liked the fact that Buth would be going to the University of Florida, but I did not intend to ignore or completely put down the prodigies.

I was particularly partial to little Anna Kournikova, who at age twelve was impossibly pleased with herself. Kournikova played with all the savvy, guts, and hauteur of a Russian dancer who was already a thoroughly seasoned trouper. I saw Kournikova and her mother in the lobby of the Grand Hyatt on East Forty-second Street, and even though they were just waiting for the big bus like the rest of us, they held their heads up and backs straight as if waiting for an enormous pumpkin to roll down Forty-second Street and turn into Cinderella's coach. The Kournikova family was being housed at Bollettieri's camp in Bradenton, Florida. But when, as *Sports Illustrated* reported, Nick Bollettieri asked Kournikova to hit just a few balls with some of his better campers, Kournikova simply refused, implying she did not want to lose her rhythm on the ball for a minute with the plebeians who had to pay. That budding arrogance was part of what made a two-hour-ten-minute beauty out of the upcoming doubles match between Anna Kournikova and Nino Louarsabishvily, two Russians nearly a foot different in height, and the top American junior team of Cristina Moros and Stephanie Nickitas, both of whom had decided to go to college.

The girls' doubles match took place on Court 6. Kournikova's grunts were louder than Monica Seles's had been, and for whole games she was, incredibly at twelve years old, the best player on the court. It looked for a while as if Moros and Nickitas, the two-time American junior champions who had lost 6–3, 6–3 to Jana Novotna and Arantxa Sanchez-Vicario in the main U.S. Open draw, would lose to the Mutt-and-Jeff Russian girls. The match went deep into the third set, and at match point for the Americans there was a beautiful moment when Stephanie Nickitas, loser to Ania Bleszynski at the U.S. Nationals but still all bounce and hope for the future, had to return serve.

Louarsabishvily boomed a first serve into the far corner. Nickitas took her one-handed backhand back with a full swing and drove up and right through the heart of the ball with a light coating of topspin, splitting the middle on match point for a winner. After more than two hours of seesaw tennis, the four girls stopped moving and just smiled at the beauty of that shot. Nickitas grinned at the happy, swarthy Moros because, they both seemed to sense it, that one shot meant Stephanie Nickitas would have a pro career; it had been so consistent, so true and winning, and executed while Nickitas was under tremendous pressure.

There were so many levels of play visible in the U.S. Open girls junior play. That year Martina Hingis, who was fourteen, looked sixteen. She beat Kournikova in the second round 6–0, 6–0. Hingis had the best junior record since Jennifer Capriati, and although she struggled against Dawn Buth on a side court in the quarterfinals, she won the match at the very instant when Buth, who led 4–2 in the third set, had a moment's hesitation. Buth, who had beaten Bleszynski 7–6,

7–5 for third place at the National juniors, had been playing beautifully, but finally she did not seem to know how to calmly shut the
door in the Czech-Swiss girl's elegantly composed face.

Ania Bleszynski had played Dawn Buth dead even at the U.S.
Nationals, the talented Buth had been two points from beating
Martina Hingis; yet there was a critical difference between Bleszynski
and Hingis. Bleszynski's parents were intellectuals who had escaped
from Poland, taking with them what the Communists had always
feared losing more than cash: their brains. Hingis's mother, a former
top-ten Czech player who had competed against an up-and-coming
junior named Navratilova, had left her Czech husband and immi-
grated to Switzerland with a Swiss businessman who had been doing
business behind the Iron Curtain. Mrs. Hingis now stayed quietly but
firmly behind her daughter, Martina, and let Damir Keretic, a handsome former player and IMG agent, handle me and others seeking to
understand what made young Martina Hingis tick like a champion.

I watched Hingis beat Dawn Buth 4–6, 6–1, 6–4 by breaking her
at 5–4 after being down 4–1 in the third set. Hingis was confident
even when she struggled, but she did not know hard-court play as
well as she knew clay and grass, and she was having lots of problems
with the girl from Wichita, Kansas as I watched. Suddenly I felt
someone trying to get past me to sit down next to me in the second
row of the outside court. He was a large man in wide, classic-white
Fred Perry shorts and shirt. He came out early with his rackets to look
around. His classic English-style hair was gray, the belly so large it
seemed like an oak cask, but the shoulders and legs were still extremely powerful. It was Roy Emerson, and he sat down right next
to me.

When I was a boy watching Roy Emerson play tennis, my first love
was Chuck McKinley because he was American and had so much
bounce to the ounce. I loved McKinley's kick serves, his dramatic victories over Mike Sangster in the quarters at Forest Hills, and the joy
of the St. Louis star's first volleys and incredible touch. Chuck
McKinley could not quite beat Roy Emerson even on a good day, but

when McKinley, a little-big-man if there ever was one, died suddenly of a brain tumor at age forty-five, I cried as I read the obituary in the *New York Times*. Emerson was still going, though time had messed with him.

I didn't want to bug Emerson before his seniors' doubles match, but I did want to take advantage of the unexpected opportunity. I introduced myself and nodded to the court directly in front of us.

"Have you ever heard of this Martina Hingis?"

"I've heard of her, yeah," Emerson said in his still full Australian accent, nodding at the young girl. He watched a few points. "I'd say the other girl is giving her plenty, though."

The fourteen-year-old did not shake Dawn Buth until that very last moment of separation that comes in every match when, like stages of the same rocket, the two players separate forever.

Roy Emerson had a horselike element to him that the other players of his era rarely could match. He was a pure thoroughbred in his soul. In recent years, his body had tended to emphasize the Clydesdalelike aspects of his physique, and certain Rabelaisian proclivities for ale, wine, and other sources of expanded girth and nonlasting merriment. He was strong enough to carry the weight, but it seemed to have turned him gray and had broken blood vessels in his face to do so. The big Australian had been such a wonderful player that I sensed somehow that his girth now was in nearly direct proportion to his general disappointment with what had followed his active tennis career. Here we were, watching a fourteen-year-old millionaire, and Emerson had played in the era before the money arrived. You cannot choose when you play or live, and I am sure it was hard for many of the older players not to think about this. Fred Perry had reminded me that he and Emerson, who had won more grand-slam titles than any other man (twenty-seven), were the only players other than Budge and Laver to win four grand slams in a row, though Emerson's, like Perry's, had not occurred in the same year.

"How long was your active tennis-playing career, from after the juniors to the end?"

Emerson squinted, and I could see him envisioning himself as a young man just coming up into the world of Sedgman, Hoad, and

Rosewall in Australia. Tony Trabert, who would win three grand slams in 1955, and Vic Seixas were the tennis kings in the United States, reigning with Ham Richardson until Alex Olmedo took over in 1959. But in 1953, the Davis Cup Challenge Round was in Australia, and I recently saw a great picture of a very young Lew Hoad glaring at Tony Trabert's confident smile as if the bionic Hoad was going to wipe the smile away and retain the cup for Australia, which he did, beating Trabert 7–5 in the fifth set of the fifth match on a rainy Australian day long ago. Emerson was a grown boy then, dreaming the dream.

"Noindeen fifty-fawr," said Emerson. "There abouts." He paused. "To '71 or '72. About twenty years." His accent was broader than Jack Kennedy's.

"When did you play your best tennis?"

"The early and mid sixties," Emerson said without hesitating.

"I remember watching you at Forest Hills against Fred Stolle and Chuck McKinley. How long would you say you were at your absolute peak?"

"Two years," said Emerson, nodding, " '64 and '65."

"When you were coming up, was there one match you played when you said to yourself, 'I'm going to be in it now; I know I can play with all of these guys'?"

"In '59, I got through to the semis at Wimbledon," said Emerson. "I lost to Alex Olmedo, and he beat Laver in the final. From then on, though, I thought I had every chance of doing well," said the winner of twelve grand-slam singles events.

The modesty of the Australians, which runs as deep as their hard-earned talent, is still so lovely to see. We Americans—myself included—usually make a more strident, outwardly competitive sound if someone hits the competitive tuning fork inside us. Pete Sampras is the closest thing to Roy Emerson that this country has ever produced in terms of a splendid mixture of modesty and talent. No tennis player was ever stronger than Emerson—not Hoad, not Gonzalez. Emerson, a farm boy from Black Butt in Queensland, Australia, had wrists and forearms so powerful from milking cows and working the fields that when the ball met his backhand volley, it took off as if he had struck the tennis ball with an oar.

"On the other side of the coin, what was the match at the end of your career after which you said, 'Jesus Christ, this is it; I'm not going to be able to do this anymore.'?"

"Well, there's probably quite a few of them." Emerson turned to me with that broad Australian smile and started to chuckle.

"I want to ask you about Stefan Edberg," I said to Roy Emerson, as the girls battled.

"He was great," said Emerson. "Terrific. He did great things. Whenever he played a tournament, he always gave more than 100 percent. He had an attractive game to watch, and his court manner was impeccable."

The words we choose often reflect our own nature as much as the thing we are describing. The great Australian had described himself as well as the Swede whose game I found more magical to watch than either Borg's or Wilander's. "Do you rate Edberg up with yourself and the others in the top ten or fifteen of all time?"

"Yeah," said Emerson, "Stefan's right up there."

"Do you think he has reached that point in his career when he can't do quite the same things anymore?"

"Yeah, well, Stefan relies a lot on his moving and court coverage, and he must be slowing down a little in that department," said Emerson.

"What is it that makes the difference between the very few like yourself, Edberg, or Rosewall and someone who is a solid top-ten player?"

Roy Emerson thought for a moment. "I guess it might be that one is a little more dedicated and has the ability to play the big point better. There's not many points separating players once they get up in the top ten. It's the one who is in the better physical condition and the one who is able to play well on the bigger points. That's it."

"It seems to me that you have to have at least one big weapon, and you have to have a personality that is dominant in some way."

"Well," said the Australian champion with an indulgent, very practical smile, "I don't think you need a *personality*. I think you need a tennis game. The main thing is being able to move. Quickness around the court is the most important thing today with the way the balls are moving."

I nodded, thinking of large players from the past like Barry Mac-

Kay, Butch Buchholz, and Frank Froehling. Movement had always been important, the key to smaller men like Bitsy Grant, Segura, Rosewall, McEnroe, Agassi, and Laver beating bigger men.

"If you can't cover the court," continued Emerson, "boy, you better have a lot of other big weapons because you're starting each point a step behind."

"I guess what I meant by having the right personality is the ability to dig in and fight."

"Well, that's *character*," said the Australian, who had plenty of it, correcting me again.

I smiled. Emerson had put his finger on it exactly. There was a world of difference—maybe three or four decades—between what *character* and *personality* meant. Not that the present players lack character in the sense of inner fortitude and courage, Sampras, Courier, Muster, and Chang all had heaps of it. But the emphasis had somehow shifted through the marketing of sports from having "character" to having "personality," which, as Emerson suggested, was much closer to the surface. Beside "character" like Emerson's, "personality" was a bubble bath. Agassi had always had personality; he was just beginning to develop character.

"But you can have character and still not win," I countered. "What makes the big difference between the one or two best players in each generation and the ones who never quite make it to the very top?"

Emerson did not hesitate. "Making the right shot selection on big points. I find that's the big thing. There are always some top players who don't quite reach the very top because they never learn quite how to make the right choices on those big points."

"Was Chuck McKinley a bit like that against you and Stolle?"

"No," insisted Emerson, "McKinley was a very good competitor. He had good selection. I wouldn't really like to name anyone in particular. But there are guys like Edberg who consistently seem to make the right play under pressure. They're not hitting drop volleys down 30–40 on their serve."

Chuck McKinley, of course, had so much bounce to the ounce he was able to make drop volleys on big points against Tut Bartzen or even Dennis Ralston, but against Emerson or Stolle, McKinley would miss the same touch shot and then wince, smile, and swipe the top of the net with his racket as if trying to erase the shot. Tennis is all about pressure, and Emerson had been Chuck McKinley's insurmountable obstacle.

"Chuck was well up at the top," said Emerson, nodding respectfully.

Talking to Emerson, I felt Mike Sangster, Nicki Pietrangelli, Manuel Santana, and the era of wooden rackets all around him. The others could play with him but never really touch him. When I closed my eyes during a long Martina Hingis rally with Dawn Buth, in my mind's eye I could actually see Emerson against Chuck McKinley at Forest Hills, and I felt again McKinley's great athletic balance and muscle control as he raced and bounced bravely—damn the torpedoes—up to the net behind his kick serve or the flatter one. I saw McKinley's volleys played off the grass or on the fly into grassy openings now long forgotten. And Fred Stolle. Stolle had such a fast service motion that I used to try and imitate it as a boy. I could do famous serves the way Billy Crystal could do Jack Benny or Fernando Lamas. Stolle's service delivery was so fast it looked as if he was about to sneeze. And Stolle's serve had been almost as idiosyncratic as that of Emerson, who with his right elbow jutting out used to massage the top of the ball he was about to serve with a circular, sensual movement of his racket as if trying to feel the balls deeply before banging them into play.

"There. She broke back," Roy Emerson said, nodding at Martina Hingis, who had swept back and past Dawn Buth just when Buth had looked as if she was going to win.

"Thanks so much," I said to the craggy-faced Australian giant.

Emerson nodded easily. "All right, mate."

After the Hingis–Buth match, I waited for Martina Hingis as she came off the court. Up close, her forehead was round and incredibly smooth, like a piece of Dresden china. She wore pale red lipstick, and when she smiled, the rubber bands on her silver braces formed miniature London Bridges. She was a millionaire at fourteen. Arranging the interview required a bit of negotiation with her mother, Melanie Zogg-Hingis, and her agent, Damir Keretic.

On the way in from the court, a young reporter from a Chicago paper asked her guardian from IMG, "How does Martina feel about comparisons with Jennifer Capriati, who also seemed very happy about tennis when she was starting out. Is there a concern?"

The handsome Keretic, who had been one of the top hundred players in the world before becoming an IMG rep, shrugged. "Martina feels she is coming from a completely different background than Jennifer. She has a different country, family background, and personality."

It was true. To an extent. But Mrs. Hingis had given her daughter a tennis racket at age two and admitted that she had named her daughter for the other Martina, the legend who was retiring.

"She's a star," the young IMG man said, "but she lives in a little town in Switzerland. She goes to school. In America, if you're a tennis star, you are a *Star* with a capital *S*."

"How did she first come to you?"

"Well, she was already so good at age nine, age ten that most of the other agencies as well as us began talking to her then. About two and a half years ago when she started winning very big tournaments for sixteens when she was twelve, the family felt it was time to have someone on their side to advise them about . . ."

"Business," I said.

"Yes, business, but also because the mother is very idealistic in terms of tennis, to advise them in terms of tennis."

"What do you mean *idealistic*?"

"Idealistic," he repeated. "It means that for Mrs. Hingis, tennis is first and not the money or what comes after that."

"She wants her daughter to be the best player she can be."

"Exactly. That is her mother's main objective." He nodded. "We spend a lot of time together. So she trusts me," he continued mildly. "The mother is her coach also, so there is tennis in both of our backgrounds."

Back in the players' lounge, I sat with Keretic, his young American wife, who was nursing a two-week-old baby, and Mrs. Hingis, a thin, concerned-looking woman dressed in a pale-blue track suit. Not far from where we were sitting, racket stringers were busily weaving. Finally Martina Hingis returned from her shower and massage. She was not used to playing on hard courts. It affected her timing, as I had seen, and apparently she had taken a pounding in the legs and lower back as well. But now, with a cheeseburger and chips inside her, Martina Hingis, the "new" Martina, felt better and was ready to talk.

"*Wenn eine junge Damen spielt mit sie, denken sie das . . .*" I began.

They looked at me in horror, and I tried again in English, at least knowing enough German to recognize if Keretic was doing the translation right. I asked Martina Hingis, "Can you tell before you even hit a ball with the other person if you are going to win?"

Mother and daughter looked at each other strangely and smiled.

"I mean," I said, "that when you are walking with an opponent to the court and sensing her and feeling her with you, can you tell right away if you are going to be able to beat her—that she already feels defeated?" I asked this because I contend that most matches are over before they begin.

Hingis's light Swiss German seemed to go off at a sunny trot. "It is the constitution of the other player that gives the clue. When I played against Kournikova yesterday, for example, and I saw how she was built, I knew what Kournikova could and could not do."

"Aside from the size of the other person, can you tell very quickly in the first two or three games by the strokes and movement what the other person has or has not?"

"Ya." Hingis laughed gently and nodded. "I can tell by the way the other player is holding the racket—by the grips—where the strengths and weaknesses will be. At least with the women, the one-handed backhands are quite vulnerable."

"It's not so conscious," Keretic interrupted. "Martina just senses it."

I nodded, by way of asking him to be quiet. "Which do you think is more important for becoming a champion, a big talent or hard work?"

Martina Hingis laughed. "*Arbeit* is important. But you need the talent more."

"You have a talent, but what is it that you do better than the other girls?"

Again she laughed nervously and shrugged, then raced off with an answer the speed of which required Keretic's summary: "Martina says she has a very long experience on the court. And from that experience she has developed a great understanding of what to do in each situation. She thinks that is her main strength: she really knows what to do with each ball and in each situation."

"Say to Martina that I was sitting next to Roy Emerson watching her last match and I asked him what the difference was between somebody who was a champion and someone who almost made it to the very top, and Emerson said that he thought the most important thing was knowing when to play each shot."

Damir Keretic was excited that Emerson and Martina Hingis had both named the same tennis ability—shot selection—as the key to being a great player. He repeated what I had said. Martina Hingis looked at me oddly and said in German, *"Aber, wer ist die Roy Emerson?"*

I shook my head and laughed.

"She wasn't born," the IMG man said apologetically and explained to Martina Hingis that Roy Emerson had won more grand-slam singles' titles than any other man.

"Have you seen or played Venus Williams?" I asked Martina Hingis.

"No one has ever seen her," Mrs. Hingis suddenly interjected in German, speaking and competitive for the first time. "Nobody knows if this Venus Williams can play or not."

"Oh, she can play," I said. "One last question. Martina, is there anything about tennis at this point that you don't like?"

Young Martina Hingis looked down, then laughed as her agent answered that one for her. "She doesn't really enjoy practicing very much."

"Four hours a day?"

"Now only one and a half hours," Martina Hingis said in English, brushing her light brown hair to one side. But we all knew she had to have practiced six or seven hours a day when she was eight to twelve years old to get to that level.

"Good," I said to Martina Hingis. "Don't practice too much. Play."

"Martina does a lot of other things, too," added her agent, trying to help. "Basketball, soccer, swimming. Martina is very active. She does many, many things."

"Fun things?"

"Yes. Yes," her agent answered for her. "Many fun things."

"Vielen Dank," I said, thanking the agent, Damir Keretic, and smiling at Martina Hingis. She smiled back shyly and waved as she and her mother got up off the couch in their tennis warm-ups.

There was such a world of difference between Martina Hingis and even players as talented and coordinated as Dawn Buth and Ania Bleszynski, who was still upset about her loss to Petra Mandula. But it was Hingis, two days later, who was upset on the hard courts in straight sets by no-nonsense Meilen Tu. Still, Hingis, winner of three junior grand slams, had the presence and style of a long-term winner.

Andre Agassi was playing champion-like tennis. He was in shape, he was focused, he felt he was in love, and he played with flair and dedication. It was a tough combination to beat. Agassi fit the iconoclastic former Trinity College, Texas, tennis star Bill Harris's definition of a great player: "Many can serve, but few can return." Unseeded, ranked twentieth in the world in the aftermath of a slothful two-year period he was emerging from, Agassi beat Guy Forget in the second round, Wayne Ferreira, the twelfth seed, in the third round, and faced sixth-seed Michael Chang in the round of sixteen. Like McEnroe, Agassi always seemed to have Michael Chang's number in big events. Agassi could do to the amazing Chang what Chang did to others. Agassi returned serve even better than Chang and took the ball earlier. Agassi won their battle 6–1 in the fifth set, and the impetus from that victory set up his next win over the gritty Thomas Muster 7–6(5), 6–3, 6–0, a hard-court lesson for the clay-court specialist from Austria. In the semis, Agassi faced Todd Martin, who had taken him apart in the fifth set at Wimbledon. This time Agassi could cope. Martin's big serve was returnable on hard courts, and though the quiet, likable giant from Michigan fought hard, Agassi just had too much rhythm, flair and a champion's talent that, when Agassi scampered like a dog, was second only to Pete Sampras's in the world.

Agassi no longer regarded himself as a phenomenon but realized he had to be just a player, albeit it one with deeper reserves of talent than most of the others. Typical of the new Agassi, in the concrete press room at the U.S. Open, he confirmed the positive influence of his new coach, Brad Gilbert:

> This [a five-set win over Michael Chang] is a perfect example of a match I would not have gotten through even a year ago. I think now, thanks to Brad, I have been getting through situations like this. You don't get the results right away, but I have been staying at it. How has Brad helped me? Well, Brad spent his entire career winning matches he really should never have won. That's what most players feel about Brad. I hope he doesn't take that too personally. I have been kind of the opposite. I have lost a lot of matches in my career that I shouldn't have lost. I think the combination of the two of us has been really what I needed.

I was waiting on line for the media bus back to the city after Agassi's win over Michael Chang when I noticed a very tall black man—about six foot four—standing on line behind me talking to a lineswoman.

"Oh, Jesus," the man said to the woman honored as umpire of the year, "you probably called some of my damn matches, and I didn't even know it was you! I never listened to calls anyway, except when I played against McEnroe and had to listen to him get in and out of his goddamn diapers."

I turned, smiled, and introduced myself. It was Chip Hooper, the former top-thirty player who had been a blown knee away from the top twenty. I got on Hooper's hotel bus instead of mine, the better to hear him out. It had been a while since Hooper had played at the U.S. Open, and now, at age thirty-seven, he was coaching where the moonlight hits the road on its way through Kansas out on the tennis highway.

The big bus swung sideways as it left the National Tennis Center and lumbered out into Queens. There was a mixed air of power and vulnerability to Chip Hooper. Somewhere in the bending and movement of tennis, very big players have weak zones. They try to compensate with reach and power, but a player who can really control a ball when he or she hits it can break most big players down with movement. When Hooper played McEnroe or Gerulaitas, he used to give them plenty of problems until the swifter, more gifted players took his power away from him with their greater speed and accuracy. Still, I remembered Chip Hooper well. He had been tagged with that most disastrous of all tennis labels, "the next Arthur Ashe."

As a junior, I had played quite a lot with two excellent black players, Linwood Simpson from Virginia and Louis Glass from Jackson Heights, Queens, New York, and if anyone had seemed destined to become the next Arthur Ashe, it was Glass. Both Simpson and Glass had been pupils of the legendary black coach Dr. Walter Johnson, but while at UCLA Louis Glass's great talent was dissipated off the court, and he did not reach the level of his dreams. Chip Hooper had been a more powerful player than Louis Glass but not nearly as smooth around the court. However, God made only one Arthur Ashe.

Hooper experienced a short but solid career. He was ranked thirty-ninth in the world in 1982 before his knee blew out on him. He made $140,216 for that year, just ahead of Raul Ramirez's earnings for 1982. In 1983 Hooper was ranked forty-eighth in the world and won $94,027. In 1984, beginning to play hurt on the bad knee, he was ranked seventy-third and won $64,011. By 1985 he was largely out of the picture. Hooper could really play, but injuries had cut the big guy down. He looked back out the window at the vanishing tennis stadium where he had played in the stadium court just twelve years earlier. The bus lurched sideways again on the road as we hit the Grand Central Parkway and began to motor.

Chip Hooper reached down into a small bag and pulled out a brochure, "Flex Sports Presents Tennis 2000." On the cover was a picture of a tall black man in long white pants and long-sleeve white shirt rolled up as if playing circa 1910. He explained that it was himself. His brochure announced:

The tennis of the twenty-first century will be a striking sport rather than a traditional game of "strokes." The players will explode the ball off the racquet. The technique of the 21st Century will combine angular and circular movements when hitting

the tennis ball. Portions of the technique are evident in the arsenal of shots of today's top players. This explains how they can
generate such power and spin. The tennis racquet is built like a
weapon. Therefore it needs to be maneuvered like one.

"That sounds like Andre Agassi today," I said.

"He is the first but not the last," said Hooper enthusiastically. "See,
I am teaching a revolutionary new tennis technique based on martial
arts movement, greater flexibility, and striking the ball. Nine out of
ten tour players are so tight that as a result of their lack of flexibility
and inner tension, they hurt themselves. I believe in stretching, dance
techniques, and meditation. But the big change comes in the way
some of these guys are hitting the ball. Remember how they used to
teach stepping into the ball. Forget it. Agassi has. Look at him; he
hits the ball with a circular motion, like a boxer with a hook. The feet
don't have to face forward. Agassi's father was a boxer, that's where he
got it. Michael Chang. He had martial arts as a young boy. It's in his
culture. Chang doesn't strike the ball in the old way either.

"My point is that in any sport you cannot overcome lack of movement with strength. It doesn't work that way. Old Zivojinovic—
Slobodan—remember him? Big guy, strong as an ox. He could
bench-press three hundred pounds. Cracked the serve. But it didn't
matter . . ." Hooper smiled a bit crazily. "To be fast helps. It does. But
there's another thing about speed you *got* to know. Running is for
rabbits."

I looked at him and grinned. "And movement is for players."

"Exactly. Patterned movement. That's martial arts. Not racing
around aimlessly."

"McEnroe used to talk about taking tiny steps and then exploding.
Rosewall did the same thing for the first couple of steps, and
Rosewall moved like Fred Astaire."

Hooper shook his head. "Tiny steps are for tiny people. That's not
who is playing tennis today. Watch who is still in the tournament this
year. Michael Stich. He's a good mover and tall. He kind of slides
there like Edberg, but Stich could be much, much better. He's no way
complete. Movement is not just feet. It's angles; it's upper-body turn;
it's a whole thing. Most American athletes play baseball, football, golf,

and they don't get it at all. A guy like Jonathan Stark? Flexibility is a big problem for him. He's way too stiff. I could design stretches that would be great for him." Chip Hooper looked down. "But you can't be a zen master unless you get the zen student. It's a two-way thing."

"Is Stark a guy who could still get near the very top?"

"He could be top ten," said Chip Hooper. "Definitely top twenty. But consistency and patterns of movement are the results of dedicated practice. People are willing to practice strokes all day long. But if they were dancers—and I work with dancers as well as pro football players out in Kansas City—players would be working on their patterns of movement just as hard as on their strokes. That's what Chang has from kung fu. He's not just fast. He knows *how* to move in a certain way. Stark doesn't. I bet he doesn't practice his court movements either." Hooper frowned. "You watch a lot of students. They seem like they are running one way one time and another way the next. That's no good. And I'll tell you something else. Ninety percent of the players on tour are going to wind up in the hospital sooner or later because they don't listen when people talk to them about stretching or pure movement. They're all as tight as bankers."

Chip Hooper was intense and smiling. He gave me the feeling that one night he might drive up right behind you flashing his headlights, and the next time he might be driving the highway at night with his headlights off. But Hooper had "vision," which I always liked in tennis or in anything else, even if the big guy was not right all the time.

The bus plunged on over the bridge and into the city. "I'd love to teach a top tour player, but they haven't come to me yet," said Hooper softly. "I'm beginning to get some good young kids out in Kansas City, and it really is a dream job for me. I'm so happy with it. But yeah, I'd like to be back out here at the stadium with a kid I was coaching. I'd love to get ahold of one of these young guns like Stark and show him what he really could be."

I thought I understood Hooper. The best coaches tend to be those who have not quite fully realized their own athletic dreams.

Pete Sampras had been playing beautiful tennis through the early rounds. As the luck of the draw would have it, he again played big-serving Daniel Vacek, whom he had played at Wimbledon, and he beat Vacek again in New York with only a service break's difference in each set. It came as no surprise when Sampras beat Roger Smith, the Bahamian veteran, but Smith had taken a set from Sampras, and that was a clue that the best player of his generation was not feeling well. Still, I fully expected that Sampras would defeat Jamie Yzaga on the stadium court, so I opted to watch instead the girls' doubles match that was going on simultaneously on the outer courts, in which Stephanie Nickitas and Cristina Moros defeated Anna Kournikova and Nino Louarsabishvily. As it turned out, Sampras, run-down from all the year-round play, had caught a summer stomach virus. But he held on with all his mulelike stubbornness. The crowd at the big stadium let out thunderous cheers. There were only a dozen people watching the girls' doubles but by the sound of it, the stadium crowd was fiercely rooting for the underdog, Yzaga, until just the moment before Sampras lost, 3–6, 6–3, 4–6, 7–6(4), 7–5, when they urged Sampras on. When he lost, the roar of the crowd threatened to blow the sides off the stadium. The crowd was cheering the upset, the play, and themselves for being there.

Stefan Edberg was playing well, but his match was with Jonas Bjorkman, the player who had put out Jonathan Stark, and it was not easy.

"Do you think Edberg has lost a half step to a full step?" I asked Edberg's coach, Tony Pickard, before the match.

"Well," said the loyal, English former Davis Cup player with a smile, "Stefan Edberg a half step slower is still faster than 95 percent of the players out on tour."

Bill Tilden knew what it was to turn the corner on an athletic career, but Tilden's corner eventually became a never-ending circle: he could not quit. Stefan Edberg was back in New York for the U.S. Open he had won in 1991 and 1992. He was smiling cautiously, smart enough to sense that things were not quite the same, yet strong enough in his incredible legs to still play the game with all his heart to win.

The early spring doldrums that had hit Edberg in Florida when I saw Sergi Bruguera outplay him in that two-hour practice match in the deep Miami heat had led to a bad clay-court season. Tennis is called a game of inches not so much because the ball is often just in or just out but because if you are an inch or two late getting to each successive ball, you are going to lose by a mile.

It would be foolish to write off a player who has reached the age of twenty-eight or thirty. Such a player remains dangerous because he still has speed and has enough experience to invent seemingly routine answers to what may seem, in the eyes of the younger player, like difficult situations. The problem for Edberg was that despite all his answers, the scores of his matches kept getting closer anyway. Players that he used to dominate were going to three tiebreakers or taking sets. He had an absolutely beautiful moment in Washington, D.C. In the gauzy August Beltway heat, Edberg played flawlessly again for an entire week and beat Jason Stoltenberg 6–4, 6–2 in the final. At the end of the match, Stefan Edberg raised both his arms in triumph as he had when he beat Boris Becker at Wimbledon for the first time.

There is a physical and psychological difference, however, between a maximum three-set match and a five-set match. It's a different kind of drive. Five-set tournaments are the superhighways. Three-set tournaments can still be lovely country roads. No one in Washington could touch Edberg in three sets. But when one crosses the shadow line, as Edberg first had almost ten months earlier down in Australia, winning multiple matches in five sets becomes as difficult as the voyage became for the captain becalmed in Conrad's *The Shadow Line*.

The thing I always loved about Stefan Edberg was his bravery. I suppose he could have been Russian or American, but he seemed to me very Swedish in his bravery. He just went out and kept poling vigorously the way the competitors do in the great Nordic cross-country ski races. In the first round at the Open, Edberg beat a talented fellow Swede, Lars Jonsson. Jonsson played well enough to win the first set, but he got upset and lost it 7–5 and then showed he was too young to win and caved in on himself angrily, losing the next two sets to the very same Edberg, 6–1, 6–1.

The left-handed, unrhythmic Jeff Tarango was Edberg's second-round opponent. They played an eleven A.M. match I watched inside the big stadium in front of a sparse crowd. The day was white hot. Tarango won the points you thought he was going to lose and lost the points he needed to win. Edberg came sweeping into the net on his serve, which seemed quicker again and flatter than the serve Laver had described as fading. But it was one of those victories that is much closer than a 6–2, 6–3, 6–2 score.

Edberg's match against Jonas Bjorkman was another Swedish affair. The policeman's son from Västervik and the postman's son from neighboring Vaxjo, where Edberg's wife was born, knew each other's games inside out. In the early 1990s the older player had used the younger player as a practice partner, perhaps thinking they would never meet because of the age difference.

Players are like secrets that eventually become open books. Just as Sergi Bruguera had gotten to read Edberg in Florida, Bjorkman knew by heart all Edberg's subtle moves. Indeed, smart old players face a dilemma: they need to practice at a high speed which only young practice partners can generate; yet by doing so they run the risk of revealing themselves completely. Edberg had been Bjorkman's idol as a boy, but now Edberg looked a little tense as the two players walked out to play the last match of the night on an evening so cold and windy that the woman from England sitting in front of me in the press seats was wearing a hooded sweatshirt underneath her Burberry raincoat. Under the lights, even the green court looked hard and cool as a frozen lime pond. It was like tennis played on a cold fall morning on a hard court in Sweden.

"My son warmed Stefan up in Washington for his semifinal and final," said another female reporter and Edberg fan. "He was just so nice. He made it such fun for my boy."

I smiled. It was nice to be nice. But Bjorkman was hitting the ball a ton.

The public address announcer had introduced the two players at the night match like boxers on the main card. Edberg had been the first player ever to win the junior grand slam, in 1983, but at twenty-eight, he was playing in his twelfth U.S. Open. Bjorkman looked to me like the real deal. In a bad-looking green-and-white warm-up jacket and dark green shorts, Bjorkman did not look like a champion, but he looked like the kind of guy who could knock you out if you dropped your guard. Bjorkman's butterflies showed as he took his first steps around the court, but I thought the swirling wind might hurt Edberg's high service toss more than nerves would hurt the younger man.

Bjorkman almost lost the match in the first game. He hit two beautiful volleys, bending down to Edberg's returns like a hockey ref who glides in to drop the puck. But Edberg had decided to try to win in a hurry, and he fired backhand winners and reached break point in the first service game. The wind blew a paper cup into a cyclone behind the court, and a ball boy squashed it. Bjorkman, unflinching, stepped up and served an ace. It was a tough hold. Bjorkman seemed to know in his soul the difference between 1–0 and 0–1. So did Stefan Edberg.

Edberg leaped and smashed away Bjorkman's first return of serve, and the crowd roared, full of sentiment. But Bjorkman clearly had a plan. It was based on speed—an odd plan against the best-moving volleyer on court in the last ten years. Edberg was rushing the net, but Bjorkman kept giving him speed returns, less worried about where the ball was going than he was about how fast it flew back at Edberg. Bjorkman took half volleys instead of ground strokes, volleys instead of approach shots. Edberg, sensing the ploy, gave it back to Bjorkman like Marvin Hagler in his first fight with Tommy Hearns. It was an incredibly fast start. The players were trying to jump each other, *mano a mano*. Edberg double-faulted to go down an ad. He kicked in a wicked second serve and got back to deuce. Edberg then served a wind-propelled double fault to go down ad-out a second time. But the nervous Bjorkman tried a topspin lob that looked silly only because it was out, then overhit a setup into the net. With ad-in, Edberg raised his chin and served an ace. Holding serve was not easy. Stefan Edberg buttoned the top button on his shirt.

The next time Stefan Edberg came to net, Jonas Bjorkman drove a forehead right across Edberg's face, and it landed hard inside the opposite corner. Edberg serve and volleyed out of the ad-out hole again. Then at 3–all, Edberg held his serve at love. He was such a pro. But so was the bouncy-muscled Bjorkman, who held at love three games later to go up 5–4. It was then, at deuce, on a first serve, that Edberg fell. He literally took a fall. As he served on a court so cold that the edge of a sneaker could leave a streak on it like moisture, Edberg left a mark down the middle of the court like a car's skid mark. He went down over his ankle and rolled twice on the hard court and just lay there for a moment. Bjorkman came up to net to look. It was a wicked fall. It was as if Stefan Edberg had finally tripped over his own shadow line that once, in the loss to Todd Martin in Australia, had seemed barely visible. Yet here it was now, and he had fallen badly.

"He'll call for the trainer, surely," said one of the English reporters sitting near me.

But Edberg, like Rosewall and Laver, did not. He got up in sections, toweled off, and went back gingerly to serve at 4–5, ad-out. But it was not the same. He had averted landing on his head only by rolling on his shoulder. Edberg serve-volleyed but seemed to go in both directions at once as Bjorkman blasted his return with a run-around forehand. Stefan Edberg was frozen in that instant, stuck in the middle of his motion, split and immobile trying to pick up the ball in that flash moment between bright light and dark season, between now and then, and, still guessing its path from the blur of Bjorkman's black racket, Edberg felt the ball going down at his forehand, then by him. Only the remnants of superb reflexes allowed him to get his racket on the ball, but it was behind him and too heavy and the ball itself seemed to break him and he staggered again into the alley. The first set was Bjorkman's, 6–4.

Edberg's speed and footing improved in the second set. He was called for a foot fault after Bjorkman went up 4–3, but he held on to get to 4-all. Now he attacked Bjorkman's serve, chipping the ball low as Connors and McEnroe did on the return, rushing in to try to cut off a popped-up passing shot with a volley. But Bjorkman, with those hockey player's legs, bent low and played winning volleys where others would have played ground strokes. Bjorkman stopped on a dime when he held his serve, and marched to the changeover chair, up 5–4. Edberg sat in his chair with a towel around his neck, pensive. He was stuck in there with a little bull, and he knew it. It was tough serving second on cool nights. It was so cold even the press had to run to the bathroom twice a set.

Bjorkman seemed to like everything about the cold, black night. He played a great forehand return with no backswing up the line. Edberg raced over but netted it. He passed Edberg outright with the next return, a perfect doubles' return-of-serve from the backhand box, the kind that had handcuffed Stark. Undeterred, Stefan Edberg kept coming in. Bjorkman blasted another forehand return that delivered the ball at Edberg's feet. Edberg volleyed it like a matador letting the bull go by. The ball clipped the net cord, fell over, and Edberg raised his arms in triumph. He served a twisting kicker, punched the volley into the open court, and young Bjorkman raced over and volleyed Edberg's volley away for a winner. Speed kills on the tennis highway. Jonas Bjorkman turned away from Edberg and strummed his racket face like Chuck Berry's guitar.

Down 30–40 at set point, Edberg was full of tension. Bjorkman threw a low lob up into the maelstrom. Edberg leaped for the seemingly easy three-quarter-height overhead, but the shot went off the top of his racket head and flew ten feet wide and twenty feet out. The miss at the end of the second set was as dramatic as the fall had been at the end of the first set. Jonas Bjorkman took them both, 6–4.

"If his wrist is hurting from the fall, Edberg certainly is classy to finish," John McEnroe said in his commentary which I heard when I replayed the match at home.

Bjorkman was on fire. It was a kind of lust. He wanted the win so badly. He closed on the net the way Edberg used to. It was incredible. Edberg had the type of elastic, athletic body I thought would never lose its inner pop. But something had happened to the rubber band inside him. He had shot himself across the court too many times. It seemed unbelievable to me that Edberg, the man who had dismantled Jim Courier and Pete Sampras just two to three years before, was no longer young. It seemed impossible. Jonas Bjorkman went up 4–0 in the third set and did not lose another game, passing Edberg with a forehand on match point, 6–0.

They had both played so well in streaks, yet I felt more for Edberg because he was not the same, and when a player has been as great and as fast as he was, I felt as if I was in the process of losing a friend whose personal attributes might continue, but never with that same boundless heart, decency, and athletic grace.

Edberg came into the packed pressroom quickly, quietly. He raised his eyebrows. He smiled and answered questions as best he could.

"It can happen," said Stefan Edberg in his Swedish singsong voice, "I just wish that Jonas did not have his breakthrough against me. He really did play well."

I was crazy for Edberg. He could take it and dish it out. He had tried so hard and had come up so short. He had given his all. His eyes were bloodshot, his face was pale, and his narrow head looked like the head in Edvard Munch's painting *The Scream*. Still, he was outwardly calm, like a sea captain.

"Stefan," the *Sports Illustrated* reporter asked, "Pete Sampras was talking earlier today about a few bumps on the court. Have you noticed bumps on the court?"

"Oh, yes, I've noticed them, too. There are a few." Edberg smiled. "The bumps were not my problem." A champion knows when he is beaten, and Stefan Edberg took the loss like a champion. He seemed to sense that a phase of his life was over. He could still beat almost all of them in two of three sets. But he knew now what he had refused to allow himself to suspect when he was outplayed by Bruguera in practice at the Lipton. He would never win a five-set tournament again. Stefan Edberg answered questions in English, then in Swedish. I did not want to believe what I had seen because it was not only the passing of a champion, but the passing of time. He had been the greatest mover of his era, a fabulous athlete, a tennis player for all time. Stefan Edberg stood up with a shy smile and nodded.

A moment later, the younger player, Bjorkman, came in to be interviewed. He was all aglow. He had beaten his tennis hero.

There would be other losses and other wins for Edberg, including a two-set straight-set win over Goran Ivanisevic in the Grand Slam Cup. He would avenge his big losses that year by beating the big Dane, Kenneth Carlsen, in Davis Cup competition against Denmark with all of Sweden cheering him on. But Ivanisevic, like his native Croatia, was a time bomb, and Edberg's loss that night in New York was for me the final loss and the signal that Stefan Edberg, like Lendl and Brad Gilbert just before him, had not only crossed but had seen firsthand his shadow line. Coach Tony Pickard looked devastated, as if he, too, had lost the match.

Like his tennis soul mates Roy Emerson, Fred Perry, and John Newcombe, Stefan Edberg, though not quite a Laver, had been a champion's champion. In a certain sense his life was complete. In another sense, his life was just beginning. Younger hands were stretching forward to make that brave first volley.

AFTERWORD:

FARTHER DOWN
THE TENNIS HIGHWAY

When television commentator Mary Carillo said with wit at the start of the broadcast of the Stich–Agassi final, "Andre Agassi won the toss and has elected to break," Agassi *did* break Stich's serve—at love—in the opening game of the 1994 U.S. Open final, which Agassi dominated with his powerful return of serve and boxerlike ground strokes. Later, in 1995, Agassi began to beat Sampras and took over the number one ranking. But in the long run, I favored Pete Sampras in the great match-up.

Stark had not reached his personal goal of breaking into the top twenty. I thought I understood why, but I wanted Stefanki to sum up Stark's season. I was in for a surprise: Stark and Stefanki, like Edberg and Pickard, were no longer a team. (Edberg and Pickard would remain friends, but after eleven years with the same coach Edberg was struggling and wanted to try something new. Pickard sadly said goodbye, knowing his young friend would never be the same player.)

The first person I spoke to after the dust had settled on Andre Agassi's victory over Michael Stich at the U.S. Open was Larry Stefanki. Stark and Larry Stefanki had worked together for only one year. Like a couple getting a divorce, they had agreed to part ways just the day *before* Stark played Jonas Bjorkman at the U.S. Open. The rupture of their coaching relationship perhaps explained why Stefanki had avoided my gaze at the start of that match and disappeared so quickly afterward. In a sense he was already gone, and in fact Stark had played against Bjorkman as if he were missing his rudder. When the unshaven Stefanki had spoken to me in Florida at the old Spanish-style Biltmore Hotel, he had sounded tough but very hopeful about Stark's prospects—a perfect coaching outlook. But now when I reached him at home, things had changed.

"I'm just here baby-sitting my three kids, so I can't talk too much. Jonathan definitely made some improvement this year," Stefanki said carefully.

"In what areas?"

"Well, he's volleying better. And you may not consider improvement in doubles a big thing, but Jonathan improved in doubles."

"I'm aware of his doubles," I said. "He's been doing great in doubles. And he's made a ton of money. But . . ." I paused.

There was a long pause on Larry Stefanki's end of the line, and he asked his kids to leave the room. Then suddenly he let it all hang out; a season's worth of feelings just came bursting out. "You see," said Stefanki, "the problem with Jonathan Stark is that he just doesn't want it badly enough. I mean, fine, Jonathan has been making a load of money, but he really hasn't played that well. So now he thinks he knows how it's all done. He thinks he can do it his way."

"What is his way?"

"Jonathan's way is the easy way," shot back Stefanki. "He thinks he can go up and live in Seattle and train up there and see his friends and pal around and train a little and go out and then just play matches. *That's* what happened this year. In my opinion, he fooled himself. And the money fooled him, too."

"The money won't be there in two years if he does it that way again next year."

"No, it won't," said Stefanki.

"But he made almost seven hundred thousand dollars this year, didn't he? I'd like a couple of bad years like that." I laughed.

"He's made scads of it," said Stefanki, "but he still doesn't know how to play."

These words were such a reversal of the bright hopes both player and coach had expressed that spring in Florida. "What doesn't Stark know yet as a player?" I asked.

"A lot," said Stefanki. "He goes out on tour for ten weeks in a row and thinks he can improve just by playing matches. But you can't. I know; I've been around guys all my life who know what it is to train and to get ready to be a top professional player. I wanted to be of more help. But Jonathan thinks he's back in the fourteen-and-unders beating Jim Courier indoors. He's in a dream world. He doesn't have a clue as to what it takes. He says to me, 'Larry, I've got my serve.' Well, there are two hundred other guys out there who have their serves, too. Granted, Jonathan has a good one. But if he thinks he can take the easy way out and just serve people off the court like he did when he was in the juniors, he's dead wrong. Jonathan does not want to do what the really top people do for training. I mean, his return of serve didn't improve at all." Stefanki took a breath.

"He kept swinging at it," I said softly, "but he's got to put the ball on the court more, doesn't he? I remember seeing him miss that one return against Volkov that probably cost him that match, and then against Karsten Braasch at Wimbledon this year he missed two or three crucial returns of serve by going for too much at the wrong time."

"That's right," said Stefanki. "I was with him up in the locker room after that fourth set at Wimbledon, during the rain delay. And I told him, 'All right, bud, this is a one-set match. Tomorrow is another day, but if you don't go after this set with your teeth bared, there will be no tomorrow for you.' I mean, hell! [Henri] Leconte came up to the locker room at the same time and told me it was so windy out there that he hadn't hit a ball with his strings for three sets."

"But Leconte won."

"Leconte *won* because he played like he would die rather than lose!" said Larry Stefanki. "The conditions were *lousy*. Graf and Stich went down the same day. But in a goddamn windstorm, you got to bring the ship into port anyway. I told him he just *had to* win that fifth set against Braasch."

I wasn't sure about that "had to" as a coaching technique. But Stefanki was like Berlitz—he liked the direct method. "And what did Stark say?"

"He just looked at me like I was talking another language. See, we knew from the beginning in this coaching relationship that we were very different people. I'm the kind of guy who says exactly what I see all the time. And Jonathan doesn't like that. Jonathan doesn't like to hear that he needs to take two or three weeks off from the tour and work seven hours a day at the parts of his game that need it. Jonathan doesn't want to play two hundred low volleys in a row. He'll play five in a row, smile, and tell me that's enough. That's not enough! You have to do it until you are doing it in your sleep. You can't win up here with just one big weapon. These guys have a serve *and* a solid fundamental game. Jonathan doesn't want to hear that, and he doesn't want to hurt. He doesn't like the pain that is involved with this game. Tennis hurts!" said Larry Stefanki with passion. "It hurts when you lose, and it especially hurts when you've trained really hard."

"I was a little surprised in Philadelphia when he got bombed so badly by Michael Chang." I paused, remembering. "I went into the locker room and Stark looked pretty trim, but I asked him why he hadn't done a hundred or two hundred sit-ups after he lost. To punish himself a bit, to make himself stronger."

"It doesn't have to go that far," said Stefanki. "But the best Jonathan played this year was when he took off a couple of weeks and trained with me down . . ."

"Down at Palm Desert," I recalled. "When he beat Pioline and Chesnokov and then lost to Muster four-and-four."

"Exactly," said Stefanki. "See, I believe that when something is your profession, you have to be around it all the time. You can't live in Montana and be a professional golfer. And you can't live in Seattle and be a world-class tennis player, practicing your big serve indoors against guys who can't even get it back. You have to live near tennis players, and when you get up in the morning, you have to be able to have a glass of orange juice and step outside and *smile* because there's a tennis court right there for you to practice on all day. That's the way Borg was with Vitas. That's the way McEnroe was."

"That's what Becker used to do, and Agassi, too."

"You have to think about your game constantly," said Larry Stefanki. "You have to want to know how to improve it and experiment with it and work and work on it. Jonathan did not do that this past year. He does not like to work. It's that simple. He's a nice guy.

He's got a pretty major talent, but that doesn't mean anything either. At least not outside the fourteen-and-unders."

I took part of what Stefanki said with a large grain of salt. Getting fired from a tennis job was no more fun than getting fired from any other job. But Stefanki spoke with such conviction and feeling, I was fascinated. "The thing I want to know is what happened? Did he play too much doubles because the money was surer in the doubles?"

"He could be falling into the doubles trap," said Stefanki. "I know about it myself, because I eventually went that way, too."

"But it's lousy for your singles' ranking."

"It can be. The money is so good that even though you don't admit it, unconsciously you know that if you're out of the singles you can still make money by doing well in the doubles. But Jonathan's trouble this year in singles went beyond playing good doubles."

"He seemed so hot a year ago. He lost that tight one to Volkov. He had gone 6–4 in the third set to Sampras at Indianapolis—"

"I was with him in Indianapolis, too. He was playing great. It was 4–all in the third set against Pete, and then Pete just took it. But hell, Jonathan beat Jim Courier 6–4, 6–2 out in Japan, and Courier was ranked one in the world at the time."

"So what happened?"

"Simple, really. He did not want to do what it takes to get to that next step up. There is a very fine line in this game between one level and the next. And I think Jonathan could have gotten there if he had taken all the right steps."

"Todd Martin takes all the necessary steps."

"That's right. Todd is a worker. Todd moves as badly as Jonathan does, maybe worse, but his game is so fundamentally sound and he's *worked* to make himself a very efficient mover. *That's* why Todd is in the top ten and Jonathan has gone from thirty-seven to sixty-seven."

"Is there anything he can do about it now?"

"Yes," said Stefanki. "But I don't think he's going to. He's got his schedule set up for next year to play a lot of singles and put his doubles second, but I'm not sure he can resist the doubles temptation and really take the time off to work on his game instead of taking time off to vacation."

"I remember seeing a picture of Jonathan in *Tennis* magazine last summer, and he was playing soccer with his shirt off. I looked at his stomach, and said, 'Whoa, he's got a little jelly roll down there'; I thought he looked awfully soft for a twenty-three-year-old star athlete. Was that beer in that jelly roll?"

"No," said Stefanki. "But I know what you mean. Jonathan eats about six meals a day. His parents called him up and said he was looking too thin. His diet is all wrong. He thinks it's great, but on top of the salads he's eating Big Macs and all this other fast-food junk."

I shook my head. "I like him. He's very likable."

"He's *too* likable," said Stefanki. "Too nice to be a top-ten player. I won't be working with him next year. He wants to make Seattle his home base because he built a house up there and has all his buddies up there. Basically, he likes to be around people who like him and say nice things to him. I pick another way, a harder way, and I swear by it. I want Jonathan Stark to be down in southern California someplace, maybe out in the desert with me, working just on his game. But he thinks he knows better. We'll see."

"How did you two decide you wouldn't be working together anymore?"

"He told me what his game plan was," said Stefanki, "and I told him I didn't buy it at all, and we didn't have to say much else."

"He looked just awful against Bjorkman at the Open. I can honestly say I have never seen him play worse. He won two service games a set almost at love and did nothing else."

"Jonathan thinks he can pull that with these guys," Stefanki said incredulously. "I'd tell him he needs to work on his movement—his feet and knees are no longer bothering him—or his return of serve. But he'd just smile and say, 'I'll get him with the serve.' I mean, Bjorkman just kicked his butt."

I nodded. It was a fair assessment. The fact that Bjorkman went on in the draw to do the same thing to Stefan Edberg was not entirely a mitigating circumstance. You can't play a tennis draw backward, by comparing scores. Stark had played so badly I had not even tried to ask him for an explanation. I worried that he was satisfied.

"See, Jonathan likes to enjoy his tennis," said Stefanki. "But he's got this professional thing backward. He thinks the tour is a place that hurts you, but he doesn't get ready for the hurt. He goes out there for ten weeks in a row and starts to get depressed, and then he wants to get as far away from it as he can. He takes a vacation. Then he goes back and it starts to hurt again, and he wants to go back to Seattle or off to Mexico. But the place that it should hurt is back where you are living and training. You want to make it hurt so much back there and prepare so well before you go out on tour that, hell, the tour will be *fun* by comparison. That's what Lendl did, and Borg did, and McEnroe did. That's what Vitas did. Because if you want to win in tennis or in *anything*, it has to be fun to do. But it also has to hurt a little first. Tennis is not fun right now for Jonathan Stark. Not anymore. He says it still is, but he's trying to fool himself. He wishes the tour was easier, and while he's out there he's smiling and trying to finesse it. But you can't finesse the tour. Now even Andre seems to have woken up. Maybe Jonathan will one day, too. But not with me."

"Do you think this was a critical year for Stark as a singles player? Is it the type of thing that he can recover from, or is he going to fall out of the top hundred in a flash?"

"I think it was a very important year for Starky," said Larry Stefanki more softly. "But if he wants to be a player, he will have to get mad with himself. The problem is that the money is so good for playing so badly that he may never hear the message."

"But the money doesn't last," I insisted. "Especially if you don't maintain your ranking. The computer is cold. The computer doesn't care."

"That's going to be Jonathan's own problem, not mine," said Larry Stefanki. "As a coach I only go out on the tour with a player I think has a real chance to crack the top twenty. I took that chance with Jonathan. He may go back to the USTA for coaching now. They tend to be more positive than a guy like me who tells it like I see it. Gully [Tom Gullikson] and the rest. They know tennis, but they will be more supportive than I would be or than I think anyone should be with Jonathan right now. He thinks everything is great, but it's not, and he better find that out soon and start to work till it hurts in practice and take time off to peak for events, or he is going to continue to backslide. Having a good talent and a nice smile don't mean jack at 4–all in the fifth set."

• • •

When I contacted Stark at his brand-new house in Seattle, a water pipe had burst overnight, flooding out the basement and first floor. His older brother, Eric, the public defender from Oregon, had come up to help him take care of things after the flood. The two brothers seemed to have the situation under control, although the first-floor living room was still under a couple of feet of water.

Jonathan Stark was older in many ways than most twenty-three-year-olds. His voice, like his serve, had the authority to speak and to be heard. He had the tact yet sharpness to speak to the workmen about his house, a kind of verbal presence that most men of that age lack, possibly because most of them can't even think about buying a home. Stark had made more money in one year on tour than Larry Stefanki had made in his entire career, but then again, Rod Laver's lifetime earnings on the tour had been only $1,564,000. I could not help thinking that Stark had been in water damage situations before—Wimbledon came to mind—so I thought I would give him one last call. Stark did not get upset easily.

"I don't want to say anything negative about Larry Stefanki," said Stark. "But I'm thinking of going back to my old coach here in Medford, Oregon. Tennis aside, we had a real special relationship growing up here, and I feel comfortable with him."

"Kind of the way Stefan Edberg felt comfortable with Tony Pickard?"

"Yeah. We had a great friendship. For me, that's real important. Between you and me, Larry and I didn't have that. Larry's the type of personality that's going to blow off a lot of people. I'm just not that way. Our personalities just didn't click. Let's just leave it like that. I didn't really trust him too much when I wanted to. He gets real aggressive when things get tight or when things are going wrong. I'm pretty much the opposite. I'm trying hard, but I don't make a big deal of showing aggression. I get aggressive, but not like that. It's impor-tant to have someone with me who is just a friend. There's enough tension out there without trying to create more of it."

Stark paused, looking back at his season. "I was the player. Whatever I did was mine. But the thing with Larry got to a point where it just had to stop. I have a lot of respect for him as a coach. Sometimes it works well for a player to have a coach with a different personality. But mostly, I don't think that it does. He was good for McEnroe, but I'm not McEnroe. I'm Jonathan Stark. I actually did better this year when I just had a friend from home travel with me. It kept me loose. I played well in Indianapolis. I got to the quarters. I beat Wilander there, and I beat Volkov."

"Ah, you beat Volkov. Was Yaroslava there?"

"Yeah, she was there, too," said Stark with an easy laugh.

"Was it sweet revenge to beat Volkov?"

"Yeah, it was. He was pissed, too." Stark laughed again, then paused. "But I lost in the quarters in Indianapolis to Delaitre, and that was a disappointment because I had been playing so well. I was just flat against Bjorkman. I didn't have anything for some reason. I won't tell you that I was happy with my season. Because I wasn't. I started at like seventy-six; I got up to thirty-six. I thought I was going top twenty. I really did. But I slid back to sixty-seven. I probably tried to play too many tournaments. But the money is awfully good. Next year I'm not going to play as much doubles. There were a lot of times when Byron [Black] and I were in the final of the doubles and had to travel on a Sunday night or Monday morning and start the singles on a Tuesday and start playing doubles, too. The scheduling was my own fault, but I'll know better next year. Will I ever make it into the top ten or top twenty? I don't know. Maybe not top ten. Do I think I can still do it? Yes. It's definitely worth the gamble."

"Have any of the top players you've practiced with all year said anything to you about your game in an instructive or friendly manner?"

"No. Not really. They kind of keep to themselves. But I know what they think."

"What do they think of you?"

"They think that if they just get the ball back a little bit, I'm going to make an error, miss a volley, something like that. They don't say it ever, but that's what they think of me." Stark paused. He knew himself a bit now. "At the end of the year I was not as fit as I had been at the beginning. I could see that. I had a groin pull that just wouldn't go away. I know that sounds like pissing and moaning, but it just would not go. The humidity down in Jakarta for the World Doubles helped loosen me up. It was better there."

"That's another thing Stefanki said. He felt you should live in warm tennis weather."

"Well, listen, I'm not up here in Seattle that often. But I'm from the Pacific Northwest. I like it," said Stark. "I *need* it every once in a while. It's home. It brings me back. I need to unwind. For me, it's important." He paused. "Listen, Eliot, if I'm number sixty in the world for the rest of my career, that's not too bad. If I'm top three in the world in doubles, that's not too bad either. I've won a grand-slam title in doubles, and hopefully I'm going to win more. I know I can still improve. I know I can get in better shape. But I'm going to try to just play like I used to play when I was real raw and just out of college. I needed some help then, but I was doing a lot of things well, right out of Stanford. People can overcriticize. I just want to go out and serve and volley again. Darn it, I've won a lot of matches, and I've done well. So obviously I know something about the game. If I get too technical, if I think too much about it—that's just not in my personality, not in my game. I've got to fire away. You have to kind of know what you can and can't do, and I think that is what I learned this year."

I nodded in assent. It had not been an easy year, and I confess that part of me thought Stark had missed the boat with Larry Stefanki. I would probably have responded better to a coach like Stefanki than he had. But Stark was different. I did think that at the very least Stark needed to put himself now in the hands of someone who would push him into incredible physical shape because Stark was a more physical than cerebral player, a potential dominator with his serve and volley. If physical he was going to be, a player like Stark had to be three-quarters horse, one-quarter mule. People forget that in all Sampras's beauty, there is a healthy streak of mulishness. Stark had some mule in him, too. But his obstinacy would continue to get him into trouble unless he became much fitter. Up in the big leagues they find a sliver of weakness, isolate it, talk about it, tease it, and stick forks in it just to see if it will heal or continue to bleed.

"Let me read you something," I said to Stark over the phone, "to kind of sum it all up for us. This is a quote from Bill Tilden's great little book, *On Tennis*: 'Before you can really dish it out in tennis, you have to learn to take it. Only by going through the mill of many defeats can a player gain the experience needed to show him what shot to play and when and where to play it. Champions are born in the labor of defeat.' What do you think of that?"

"Gosh," said Stark. "I hope it's 100 percent true. You do learn way more in defeat than you do in winning."

I wished him well. In the background I heard his brother helping him.

Stark set off for Australia a few days later without Larry Stefanki. He lost in the first round of the Australian Open and appeared to tank his doubles, which he and Byron Black, the third seeds, lost 6–4, 6–0 to two lower-ranked Germans. Stark packed his bags and flew back to California, saying that his new year was going to have to start in February because he was 0–for–Australia in January. His ranking fell back to seventy-three, which was almost exactly where it was when I first saw him play against Alexander Volkov on the grandstand court at the U.S. Open.

Back in the United States, Stark headed into the indoor season, which the previous year had included that rough loss to Michael Chang late at night in Philadelphia, a loss that had stopped his upward rise in its tracks. But in 1995 at the St. Jude Classic in Memphis, Stark began to turn it on again. He reached the quarterfinals and encountered his old nemesis, Michael Chang, again. Chip Hooper was right about this: no two forces ever stay exactly the same. Something happened. Though it had not shown down in Australia, Stark had worked like a dog in the winter. His legs showed new strength. He was moving better. Stark played a great sunrise of a match, and he beat Michael Chang 4–6, 6–3, 6–4. Stark could really play. He reached the semifinals in Memphis, and in one week his ranking rose back up to number sixty. His spirits rose, too. He was back in the fast lane on his own, doing what he thought himself capable of doing. That was freedom, if it did not slip into self-delusion.

A few weeks later, he had a blowout. Stark lost to Mexico's Luis Herrera, who was ranked out of the top hundred. After beating Chang in Memphis, the loss to Herrera seemed inexplicable—except when you consider that the left-handed Mexican was being mentored by Marcelo Rios's new coach, Larry Stefanki.

In 1995 Stark did win another grand slam—the Wimbledon mixed doubles with Martina Navratilova. The best women's doubles player who ever existed, Navratilova had slowed down quite a bit, as was evident in her post-Wimbledon exhibition match against Monica Seles in Atlantic City. But Navratilova always knew how to pick a partner. She needed one with a big weapon, and Stark with his serve fit the bill. Playing in front of a Wimbledon TV audience across the world, Stark had to hold serve to win the match. On match point, Stark served an ace up the middle, and Navratilova, who always loved a winner, leaped up into his arms and gave him a big kiss on the mouth. Stark had won the doubles at the French Open and the mixed doubles at Wimbledon, and later, in August of 1995 in Indianapolis, he again extended Pete Sampras to 6–4 in the third set. Almost there.

There would be many ups and downs for players like Jonathan Stark out on the tennis highway. The top twenty now seemed a remote goal, but Stark made his living playing others for money. He was a pro, and he headed back out on the road again with determination tempered by reality and eight new rackets in his travel bag.

The amazing Gardnar Mulloy sent in his entry to get into the senior's draw, and at eighty-one he won the U.S. National Championships in the eighty-and-under singles and doubles events. Mulloy and Dodo Cheney, his remarkable counterpart in the women's over-eighty national tour, had kept playing in part because winning feels good at any age, in part because in their on-court movement, a mere shadow of their 1930s and 1940s excellence, they still felt so alive. They liked that powerful feeling of the pulsing heart, the aching legs, and that burst of sweat that opens your mind and lets it fill back up with laughter as you run and hit the ball. Tennis, much more than golf, gives you such a feeling of movement, of exhilaration, of being young at any age.

■   ■   ■

Ania Bleszynski's tennis continued to improve in 1995. She could become either a fine pro tennis player or an outstanding scientist, and I felt that she was going to try tennis first. If you have the tennis gift, it is so natural to want to use it. Still, from my vantage point, I preferred the range of her educational options. They still existed because she had not packed in her studies at age sixteen.

Frank Brennan, the Stanford women's tennis coach, is only somewhat less of a coaching legend than the men's coach, Dick Gould, whose 1995 team went undefeated with Scott Humphries and Paul Goldstein playing numbers two and three. Prior to the season, I finally talked to Brennan about Ania Bleszynski, junior girls' tennis, and the efficacy of college tennis. I started out with what may have struck the Stanford coach as a strange question, but he seemed to catch my drift.

"Ania is very bright," I said. "Is that a plus for her?"

"As far as being a tennis player?" Frank Brennan chuckled, then hesitated. "You know, I tell you. I sort of believe that the best ones, the ones who are going to be in the top ten, maybe even top twenty, are the girls who are not ever going to see the inside of a college. Those girls are going to get very good at a very young age and go play pro tennis. That is one kind of player. Fortunately, there is another kind of player, somebody who maybe isn't top ten when they are fifteen or sixteen, somebody who goes to college and gets four free years of an education and then goes out and plays her years on the pro circuit. And we at Stanford have had women who do quite well out there. Do I think Ania is going to be top ten? I don't think she's going to be top ten, but she may be good enough to be top twenty or top thirty."

"You think there's a possibility of that?"

"Yeah, I do. I don't really know her that well. When you are recruiting somebody, you are very limited in your contacts. Once I get her here at school, I'll find out a lot more about what makes her tick. You can see a lot on the tennis court, but that isn't everything that's inside them."

"There is the notion that so many of these young kids are abandoning the idea of college for the possibility of being one of those mythic 'top ten.' Do they seem to have jumped the gun? Or is that the only way to approach it if you really want to become a top-ten player?"

"I think it's starting to swing back again. Ever since the Capriati thing, I think kids, at least American kids, are starting to slow up. Even the parents are starting to take a second look at what they are attempting. It's really a logic question," said the Stanford coach. "If all top-ten players turn pro at the age of sixteen, does it mean that all people who turn pro at age sixteen are going to be top-ten players? You see what I mean? A lot of the girls who didn't make it are bag girls at the Shop-Rite right now. . . . I sometimes think we should have a record book and just start printing in it all the names of the kids who passed up college and passed up having a life, names nobody ever heard of. We know about Gabriela Sabatini and Michael Chang. But for every Michael Chang and Jennifer Capriati who actually make it for a while, there are fifty kids out there who pursued that dream and gave up everything else and came up *way* short." Brennan paused. "Jennifer Capriati is by no means the only girl who had trouble with this. In fact, she did great for quite a while, but everyone including Jennifer, kept expecting more from her than she could actually do.

"Right now we've been dealing with a young lady out here in California named Maggie Cole. She turned pro when she was fourteen because her father was a guy just this side of Mary Pierce's father, Jim. Anyway, Maggie's father ended up divorcing her mother, and now he's out of the picture totally. But now Maggie's getting ready to go off to college. She applied to get her amateur status back from the USTA, and she received it so she could play junior tournaments. She then applied for her amateur status to play college tennis so she could get a college scholarship, which she needs. But now the NCAA says no. I'm very curious to see how that plays out. You can see both sides of it. It wasn't her fault she was fourteen and had a father pushing her. But Maggie did turn pro."

"Did she make any money?"

"No. She didn't make any money at all. The reason she's considered a pro is because the family took backing from a financial guy who said, 'I believe in your daughter and here's eighty thousand dollars; go hit some balls.' "

"This financial sponsorship is more and more prevalent now. I'm hearing about it a lot among the very young players."

"There are definitely 'backers' out there," said the Stanford coach disparagingly. "Not even regular pro agents but, basically, 'investors in children.' They've got more money than brains. And probably more money than scruples. Heck, it's one thing to back a twenty-two-year-old going out on the golf tour. It's another for a grown man to get involved with a thirteen- or fourteen-year-old girl. I mean, why would anyone encourage a young girl to give up her life to pursue this tennis dream, when I could grab any ten coaches at the U.S. Open and have her work out with them, and they could tell her in *ten* minutes, 'I'm very sorry, but there's just *no way.*' I hate to see these kids wasting their lives."

"You use the phrase *wasting their lives.* That's pretty strong. Do you really feel it's that serious?'

The Stanford women's coach nodded. "I do. The old saw is that you can always go to college later, that college is always going to be there. But check on how many players ever go back. Did McEnroe? Did Chris Evert? Did Borg or Gerulaitas? The feeling these kids get is that they might be the next McEnroe or Evert. They think, 'I'm fifteen. I'm really hot right now. I can make my mark out on the pro tour.' I believe just the opposite is true. I believe college is the experience you have from age seventeen to twenty-one or eighteen to twenty-two. *That's* when it's going to be fun. You grow up at a normal pace. To go back to college when you're twenty-seven or twenty-eight?" Brennan sighed. "First of all, I don't see anyone doing it. Second of all, dorm life at twenty-eight just isn't going to be much fun. So most of the ones who skip college knock around, try to give a few lessons, try to make a comeback, and by the time they realize it they're thirty-five and stuck. Then they have to start competing for club jobs with younger players." Frank Brennan paused. "It really pays to know yourself."

That was what I liked about Ania Bleszynski. She kept trying on more than one front. She loved sports *and* learning. Perhaps for a tennis prodigy she was not sufficiently committed, but I was sure that her future and the futures of many girls like her lay in maintaining a balance and continuing their education. My own rule of thumb is that if a girl is the least bit undecided about whether to go to college or turn pro, she should not turn pro. Otherwise, she is asking for mis-

ery on the pro tour. Some girls can handle the tour at a younger age.
Meilen Tu, for one, was a sixteen-year-old who seemed emotionally to
be at least thirty-five. But Ania Bleszynski was an eighteen-year-old
who was eighteen.

"Do you think Ania will stay all four years at Stanford?"

"I don't know for sure. She could turn pro next year. She'll play
some pro events. But Ania is by *far* the most academically qualified
student I have ever had on a team at Stanford. Her recruiting trip had
nothing to do with the parties or tennis. Ania wanted to meet the
head of the Biology Department. She went to the Physics Department
to find out about their courses. She wanted to meet an athlete who
was majoring in molecular biology. She asked questions about courses
I couldn't even pronounce. I've never had a student like that at
Stanford, and we have great students. Ania is focused, no matter what
she does. When Ania came to visit, she already knew we were in California and had tennis. See, Ania wanted to know what she *didn't*
already know."

I liked hearing that. Still, I thought she had pro potential. I tried
to do what Ania Bleszynski had so far been unable to do herself—pin
down her future plans. "Will she play some pro tournaments? It's
good experience for the college players to get some taste of them. It
definitely can raise their tennis a couple of levels."

"Aaah, I'm not sure it's really good for them," said the college
coach protectively. "Number one, it's hard to work pro tennis into
their schedule. Number two, if they go off, they aren't totally motivated because they are afraid of missing class time or a test, and they
don't perform very well. Or the worst thing is that . . . [a college
player] could catch some thirty-three-year-old pro on the way down
who is ranked number forty in the world and beat her. And then come
back to Stanford and say, 'Hey, I should be out on tour.' Expectation
levels start to rise. A girl gets a couple of good results, and people get
all bent out of shape talking about pro tennis for her." Brennan
paused. "Two wins are nothing."

"I have been following Jonathan Stark. And I guess he just felt it
was time to go."

"It's not all that illogical for the guys," said Brennan. "At seventeen
or eighteen the guys aren't physically ready the way the girls generally

are. But we've had girls go out on the tour, and it hasn't mattered at all if they left early. They say to themselves, 'Hey, I'm number forty-two in the world; imagine how good I'll be if I don't have to study and play college doubles.' Then the player tells me she has to go do her thing, and of course I let her."

"There's so much more pressure when you play tennis full-time," I said softly.

"Absolutely. You burn all your bridges behind you. You go out and play somebody from Hungary in Minneapolis at twelve midnight. You lose to a baseliner who can't even speak English, but you know she can't stand you. She'd just as soon kill you. You go back to the locker room, and suddenly you say to yourself, 'I gave up Stanford for this?' "

We both laughed. Coach Brennan continued, "The ranking starts to plummet. You go to eighty-five, then a hundred and twelve. You start to have to qualify again. And you begin to say, 'Hey. What happened to forty-two?' " He paused. "You see, it doesn't always work that you get better every year. It doesn't necessarily work either that the harder you try, the better you get."

I smiled. Brennan, like many others who taught the college game, was really a fine coach. The better coaches all teach "life" as well as tennis. College is that quieter part of the tennis highway where coaching and educating still occasionally come together. Frank Brennan concluded, "If getting better was that easy, we'd just start the clock and say this twelve-year-old will get better every year until she is eighteen and then she will be incredible. It doesn't always work that way. In fact, it rarely does."

I called Ania Bleszynski only twice during her freshman year. That fall when I called, her roommate told me she was out watching the Stanford baseball team practice. I decided to call back in the spring and I did, after the tennis season was over. I wanted to hear how she had done in tennis and in life.

We talked tennis first. As a freshman playing at the NCAA Division I Women's Championships held at Pepperdine College's Ralph-Strauss Tennis Center in Malibu, California, Ania Bleszynski reached the quarterfinals, just as she had at the Orange Bowl. She was the only freshman player in the country to get that far. She was named an All-American in singles and in doubles, playing with Stanford's number one player, Katie Schlukebir. Only Bleszynski's friendly rival from junior days, tenacious Dawn Buth of Florida, got ranked ahead of her among freshman in the NCAA rankings. Yet when I finally spoke to Bleszynski, I sensed that something was changing. After all, she was now nineteen.

"Hi," I said. "How are you doing?"

"School's almost over," she said cheerfully. "I've got my last final tomorrow."

"Was it tough doing both things at Stanford: studying hard *and* playing all those matches?"

Ania Bleszynski, her 1550+ College Board scores behind her, paused. "It was really hard. Much tougher than I had ever imagined."

"I see you got to the quarterfinals at the NCAA's. That's great."

"I haven't seen the rankings yet. Have you?"

"As a matter of fact, I have. You got ranked seventeenth."

There was quite a pause. Ania Bleszynski had played behind the sophomore Katie Schlukebir, and playing at number two, Bleszynski had twelve wins and three losses during the Stanford women's regular season matches. Still, I was a bit surprised by the ranking because in the big year-end NCAA tournament Bleszynski had gotten to the quarterfinals, what the English call "the last eight."

"Did Katie Schlukebir get ranked ahead of me?" she finally asked.

"Yeah. She was ranked fourteenth."

Ania did not say anything, but I could hear her competitive wheels turning.

"Ranking committees don't always get it right," I said. "Just go out next year and show them all over again that you can play." I paused. "By the way, what are your plans for the summer? Are you going to be playing some pro challenges or some satellite events? Are you going to work on your pro ranking over the summer?"

There was another long pause. Ania Bleszynski hesitated. "Well, no."

"You aren't going to play this summer?" I asked.

"Well"—she laughed nervously—"I will play, but mostly in California. My father has kind of stepped in. I missed two courses at Stanford during the school year, and my dad doesn't want me to fall behind any more. He says I can continue my tennis at college, but as far as playing pro events this summer, that's out. I'm going to take two physics courses at UCLA in summer school instead." Ania Bleszynski with the help of her father and mother had made a big choice. It did not seem to upset her once it had been made. "So that," continued Ania Bleszynski with the same quiet determination she had brought to her tennis, "is what I am going to do with my summer this year."

Fred Perry died. He was a rebel-gentleman in an era when he was considered an outlaw for wanting to be paid for what he loved to do. Perry and Tilden, before Bobby Riggs, Jack Kramer, and Pancho Gonzalez, were the real starters of what has become the ATP Tour. Perry died in January, 1995, in Australia, where he was doing BBC radio broadcasts at the Australian Open (won by Andre Agassi). Early in the tournament, Perry fell and broke four ribs. He got himself released from the hospital. A day or so later he fell again and was taken back to the hospital, where he died of heart failure. His death came only six months after he had climbed so nimbly up and down those steep metal stairs at Wimbledon before our talk. Champions are rarely great organization people. It is just not part of their soul. But Fred Perry had a confidence as clear as a shot of Vodka. Like Pancho Gonzalez, he had a champion's fire his entire life. As related in one obituary, when asked if he used to get nervous in the locker room before he had to go out and play a big match, Fred Perry chuckled and said, "No. When I was waiting, I always thought *my opponent* was nervous. I knew he had to go out and play Fred Perry."

Bobby Riggs, who had been battling prostate cancer, died at the end of October 1995 at age seventy-seven. He was a master of the drop-shot game, the soft angle followed up to net with a put-away volley. And his lob was as difficult to see coming as the topspin surprises launched by Agassi and Chang. Riggs was a great showman, a precursor of Jimmy Connors. He loved the gamble of life and pursued it with the manic delight and laughter of those who find the action more fun than the event of life itself. He experienced both the highs (winning all three titles at Wimbledon in 1939 and beating Don Budge 23–21 in their 1946 tour) and the lows (losing the tour to Jack Kramer after winning their first match at the old Madison Square Garden before a crowd of more than 15,000 who came to see their first 1947 battle despite a twenty-five-inch blizzard in New York). Riggs and Pancho Segura remain the two least heralded of great players, perhaps in part because they were small and cunning not tall and hard serving.

In 1973, away from top flight competition for more than twenty years, Riggs beat a nervous Margaret Court in one Battle of the Sexes but then lost to Billie Jean King, who kept her cool under fire. If Riggs bet on King, as many (mostly male) players have suggested, it would not be a surprise at all. Yet if he did so, I suspect he was hedging his bet in case he did not win the larger prize money for first place, which I think Riggs fully expected to win, having beaten Court so decisively. But King played great tennis under pressure that night, and, in my mind, she actually beat him. Still, in the Bobby Riggs tradition, he would bet that you could never figure out which way his bet was laid.

Stefan Edberg continued to play. He always performed well in Davis Cup matches for Sweden. He struggled at the French Open in 1995 and again at Wimbledon in June. Stefan Edberg could no longer win consistently in a five-set context. Over the course of two weeks, he just could not win six or seven matches in a row. In my mind, though, this did not diminish at all but rather put into perspective what he had accomplished in those prior years when, moving on seemingly sculpted legs, he had swept in above the net, defeating Wilander, Cash, Becker, Courier, and Sampras in grand slam finals dramatic and one-sided.

I had not wanted to let Stefan Edberg know how closely I was watching him, but now I was interested in comparing notes. I called him.

"Did your match against Todd Martin down in Australia seem like a turning point in your career?" I asked, thinking of that distant shadow line and how Edberg had crossed it.

"It was a match I should have won," said Edberg from a tournament he was playing in Hong Kong in the fall of 1995. "It is hard to say that was the turning point. It was a missed opportunity. I was playing very well at the time."

"The loss against Kenneth Carlsen at Wimbledon was another," I said. "You had never lost to him before that. You played well but lost a great match. Did it hurt?"

"Yes," said Stefan Edberg. "It stayed in my belly for quite a while. A couple of weeks."

"How did you stay at or very near the top for so long? They talk of you now as the 'Iron Man,' like Cal Ripken or Lou Gehrig, because you are the only player ever to play in fifty Grand Slam events in a row."

"A bit of luck and staying healthy," said Edberg. "Mentally, you have to keep setting goals to keep yourself motivated. I haven't been telling anybody, but you need to have something that you want to achieve each year."

"And were your goals always beyond what you were able to reach?"

"Well," said Stefan Edberg, "sometimes it has been better than I thought. Sometimes it has been worse. It works both ways. It doesn't always work out the way you want it to. Obviously I have talent. But you have to work very hard to make talent work, to produce the results you would like. I have been a pretty hard worker."

Now the decline that had been nearly imperceptible at first was hard to miss. Edberg slipped out of the top ten, then out of the top sixteen. The ranking system eventually becomes the enemy of the older players, for though it supports them for a while by letting them discard their worst losses, the IBM computer's Catch-22 is that each player must compete against his or her own record from the previous year as well as against opponents in order to maintain or improve upon his or her ranking. At only twenty-nine, with thirteen years out on the pro tour, Stefan Edberg had taken himself to the limit again and again, only to find he no longer had as much speed or consistency when he tried to press the accelerator to the floor. But before he was through, he did make one magnificent stand.

Pancho Gonzalez, who had died just a couple of weeks before Stefan Edberg's heroics in July 1995 at the Legg Mason tournament in Washington, D.C., would have approved of Edberg's tenacity. Gonzalez, who died with his ex-wife Ruta Agassi, Andre's older sister at his side, had fought for everything he ever accomplished. Stefan Edberg showed he had that kind of stubborness and drive, too.

The end of a career is an odd time. The body is slightly thicker. The good looks are often still there. As Goran Ivanisevic's coach, Bob Brett, had pointed out, first the concentration goes, followed shortly by the legs. Stefan Edberg was a leg man, the most fluid mover to the net since John McEnroe and John Newcombe. But now he knew that the "upsets," which started two years before when Edberg had been "upset" in Australia by Todd Martin, had continued, and now they were called "upsets" less frequently.

There was a month-long stretch in the summer of 1995 that must have been as hot as any stretch of summer on record across the United States. In the midst of this heat wave, the tour pulled into Washington, D.C., which has the earliest springs and most disastrously humid summers of any East Coast city. It was late July. More than two hundred people died from the heat that weekend in Chicago. At the Legg Mason tournament in Washington, Edberg struggled every time he played but reached the semifinals against Australia's quick, sharp-volleying Patrick Rafter. The temperature on the sunken stadium court was 102 degrees. It was so hot the hard court felt soft. Edberg's shoulder was hurting him.

Before the match Edberg had made an uncharacteristic admission, "Well, I can't hit my serve. So now I must go more for placement." He sounded like a fastball pitcher trying desperately to develop an off-speed pitch.

Against Rafter, Edberg was incredibly tenacious and brave. He decided that he could no longer rush the net on every serve because the ball was shooting back past him faster than he could get up there. So instead of coming in against the talented young Australian, Edberg decided to stay back on numerous first serves. This was both an admission that time had diminished his speed and a blunt message to Patrick Rafter: "Fundamentally, I am still sounder than you. I was a champion. I will beat you from the baseline." Rafter got the message right away, and Edberg struggled to prove what his baseline play was saying.

Edberg won the first set in a sweat, 7–5, and he had three break points in the first game of the second set, but Rafter made great volleys and gamely held his serve. The sun started to poison Stefan Edberg. He was continually called for foot faults, one of which became a double fault and contributed directly to his losing the hard-fought second set by an identical 7–5 score. Rafter and Edberg each changed shirts twice. It was the kind of match in which the players were so deeply involved with the crystallike idea of victory that they had absolutely no dislike for each other. It was a pure battle of wills between an older player on the decline and a younger player whose talent was never quite as refined. In fairness, Edberg looked exhausted. Rafter looked keen and decidedly younger. There simply comes a time when youth, if it is going to become great, must leap past the aging opponent in full assertion of its own powers. Edberg seemed to sense all of this, and he was totally unwilling to let it happen. The third set was that struggle.

I was so sure Rafter was going to put him away in time. Pale, his face twisted with effort, his walk slowing between points to a side-to-side shoulder roll reminiscent of Borg, Edberg fought Rafter from the baseline, and he managed to break Rafter's serve in the first and third games of the third set. But then Edberg faltered. It was almost inevitable. He held five match points on Rafter. He double-faulted on two of them, one of which was the result of a second-serve foot fault. They could barely stand in the heat between points. Finally Edberg attacked, and after Rafter searched for time by sending up a high, defensive lob, Stefan Edberg, whose overhead was as automatic as one of his failing body parts, snapped an overhead winner into the open court.

Edberg fell almost immediately. He started to raise his arms above his head in triumph, but instead, he just collapsed as if his left leg had been hit by a bullet or a cramp. It was an incredible win for a star on the decline. For a moment, Edberg rolled on his back and from that position, smiling in painful relief, raised his arms in triumph two or three times.

The next day, playing Andre Agassi in the final, Edberg was

counted out by Agassi, by Agassi's girlfriend, Brooke Shields, by the fans, in short, by everybody but Edberg. In reaching the final in the Washington tournament, which had a two-of-three-sets format, Agassi had spent an average of one hour and fifteen minutes playing each match. It had taken Stefan Edberg an average of one hour and fifty-seven minutes to win his four prior matches, and two hours a day in that heat was a bit like the tin prison cell in the film *Bridge on the River Kwai*.

In the early going, Agassi seemed to have a limitless inner acceleration. His ground strokes flew at Edberg as if released by a slingshot, gathering pace as they landed on the lines. Stefan Edberg's face kept contorting as he looked for air, squinting, wincing, trying to stay with the Agassi phenomenon in full stride. But Edberg, dressed in white, was used to the sun, having been nearly killed by it over the course of the week in Washington, and Agassi, who had played primarily at night, was wearing black shorts, black sneakers, and a baggy black-and-white shirt in the 105 degree sun.

A few weeks before, the short-cropped Agassi had taken to wearing a white Nike bandanna tight to his head until *Sports Illustrated*'s Sally Jenkins pointed out that it made Andre look like a cleaning woman. Agassi, wearing nothing on his head and all-black below, suddenly cracked in the sun. As if hit by sunstroke, Agassi moved listlessly, barely running for the balls, and Edberg, after leading 5–1, took the second set from Agassi 6–2.

Brooke Shields was biting her nails. Andre looked legless, all calf muscle, no thighs under the baggy black shorts. Agassi was learning that people had worn white in the old days not just to conform but because white did not absorb heat. He looked ready to pass out. After sending an approach shot an inch long, Agassi blasted a volley high into the stands in frustration. No code violation was given, but Agassi gave himself a rebuke—something he was incapable of when younger—and he reached match point with Edberg serving down 2–5, 15–40 in the third set.

The older player was not done. Edberg serve and volleyed, and played an Agassi return off his shoe tops for a winner to hold serve. When Edberg broke Agassi's serve after Agassi went up 30–0 on it, it was apparent what had made Edberg great through all his championship years. He played as if he could hold on for an hour by his finger-tips to the side of a building. Agassi, sun-softened, flung his racket into the backstop and was given a code violation. I felt for both of them. The sun was glazing the court.

Stefan Edberg's long, sweeping topspin backhands, generated by full shoulder turns, kept flying straight and hard over the net, pene-trating the way they used to. He swung harder than usual, giving Agassi no time to step in and take the ball on the rise, because the ball was not rising but was skidding through. Edberg held serve. It was 5–all, but Agassi, not Edberg, was completely exhausted.

It was almost as if Edberg's career had been allowed one last great performance. It was Agassi who slipped out the back of the court and took a two-minute-ten-second break in the air-conditioning at 5–all in the third set. Edberg stayed on the court, covered his head in a towel he had poured water on, and sat down to wait in the sun. Consider-ably refreshed, when he came back, Agassi almost immediately broke Edberg's serve to take the last set 7–5.

Stefan Edberg moved up to the net as the crowd, understanding that he was near the end, stood and cheered. Agassi would have many other, greater days. But Edberg, from where I watched, had created for himself a kind of requiem. He had been a star in the beginning, winning the junior grand slam. He had had his time in the sun, those days when nothing can go wrong. He had trounced Jim Courier and Pete Sampras in back-to-back U.S. Open finals. He had beaten Becker at Wimbledon in 1990 and they had aged together. Stefan Edberg nodded quickly at Agassi, as if to remind Andre that the time of champions is brief. And when they presented the older player with his runner's-up award, Stefan Edberg smiled with a hint of irony and waved up to the crowd.

INDEX